ASIAN DEFENCE REVIEW 2007

ASIAN DEFENCE REVIEW 2007

Air Commodore

Jasjit Singh

AVSM VrC VM IAF (Retd)

Editor

in association with

KNOWLEDGE WORLD

KW PUBLISHERS PVT LTD

CENTRE FOR AIR POWER STUDIES

The **Centre for Air Power Studies** is an independent, non-profit, academic research institution established in 2002 under a registered Trust to undertake and promote policy-related research, study and discussion on the trends and developments in defence and military issues, especially air power and the aerospace arena, for civil and military purposes. Its publications seek to expand and deepen the understanding of defence, military power, air power and aerospace issues without necessarily reflecting the views of any institution or individuals except those of the authors.

Jasjit Singh
Director
Centre for Air Power Studies
Subroto Park
New Delhi 110010

Tele: (91-11) 25699131
E-mail: office@aerospaceindia.org

KNOWLEDGE WORLD
KW Publishers Pvt Ltd
5A/4A Ansari Road, Daryaganj, New Delhi 110002

Published in India by KW Publishers Pvt Ltd

ISBN: 978-81-87966-56-2
Printed by Chaman Offset Printers, New Delhi. Published by Kalpana Shukla, KW Publishers Pvt Ltd, 5A/4A Ansari Road, Daryaganj, New Delhi 110002
email: knowledgeworld@vsnl.net, website: www.kwpublishers.com

Typeset by Black Innovation, New Delhi

Contents

Contributors

Brigadier **Gurmeet Kanwal** (Retd) is a Senior Fellow at the Centre for Air Power Studies, New Delhi.

Ms. **Shalini Chawla** is a Research Fellow at the Centre for Air Power Studies, New Delhi.

Dr. (Ms.) **Manpreet Sethi** is a Senior Fellow at the Centre for Air Power Studies, New Delhi.

Ms. **Monika Chansoria** is a Research Associate at the Centre for Air Power Studies, New Delhi.

Mr. **Amiya Kumar Ghosh** is a Distinguished Fellow at the Centre for Air Power Studies, New Delhi.

Wing Commander **V.N. Srinivas** is a Research Fellow at the Centre for Air Power Studies, New Delhi.

Wing Commander **Sanjay Poduval** is a Research Fellow at the Centre for Air Power Studies, New Delhi.

Group Captain **Arjun Subramaniam** is on the faculty of Defence Services Staff College, Wellington. Others who contributed include Wing Commander **R. Bhasin**, Major **Alex Merz**, USAF, Wing Commander **S.K. Nair**, Wing Commander **P. Navad**, Wing Commander **S.K. Paul**, Wing Commander **Sarabjit Singh** and Squadron Leader **K. Sundarmani**, all student officers at the College.

Wing Commander **K.K. Nair** is a Research Fellow at the Centre for Air Power Studies, New Delhi.

Introduction

Jasjit Singh

The rise of Asia, forecast by many nearly two decades ago, now has sufficient empirical indicators to confirm that the process is well on its way, and is unlikely to be derailed in spite of the widespread violence on the continent. There is a clear global power shift from the West to the East, from a Euro-Atlantic-centred world to an Asia-centred future. The issue that needs to be noted is that historical power shifts have inevitably been accompanied by wars and armed conflict. Asia is already the cockpit of global *jihadi* terrorism as well as the global war against terrorism waged by the United States and other countries. The problem is that *jihadi* terrorism, centred in the Pakistan-Afghanistan region, not only shows no signs of withdrawal, but indicates a step forward toward increasing radical ideological violence.

Israel and Palestine continue to be engulfed in continuing terrorism, and resurgence of Kurdish violence in Turkey appears imminent. The United States, in spite of its enormous power and resources, has not been able to establish even a semblance of peace and stability in Iraq. It may not be entirely correct to term the source of violence as being driven by the Islamic *jihad*, at least not of the type being witnessed in other parts of the world. But it would be equally mistaken to put a cloak of ethnic divisions over what is fundamentally anti-Americanism (and opposition to the Iraqi regime installed through American initiatives and support) on one side, and the ruthless and raw domestic struggle for power, often transcending tribal and ethnic loyalties, on the other. At stake is the future control over Iraq and its oil resources. The levels of violence have grown dramatically since it became clear that the United States would pull out the bulk of its military forces from Iraq in the coming months, leaving behind a political presence in the shape of a garrison force, enough to protect itself and launch some punitive attacks, mostly from the air.

As if this was not enough to disturb peace and stability in West Asia, the US-North Atlantic Treaty Organisation (NATO) forces in Afghanistan appear poised for diminishing successes for a variety of reasons that we may not go into here. There are strong indicators of the resurgence of the Taliban who receive enormous support from Pakistan and its agencies, many among which tend to believe it to be Pakistan's "trump card" in dealing with the US and the world to national advantage. Iran, the country between Iraq and Afghanistan, continues to be in a state of fluctuating confrontation with the US, where even the lowest level of confrontation has serious consequences for peace and stability in the region. Pakistan itself, in spite of army rule for eight years, is on the threshold of greater instability which is bound to have a serious fallout beyond the immediate region. The people, who have generally been permissive of military rule, appear to be getting restive.

In the past, the Pakistan Army sought to install a civil political face to its rule and tolerated it as long the political regime did not encroach on its dominance over the power structure at the national as well as organisational levels. This was the cardinal principle established over the previous decades that Nawaz Sharif tried to change, rather rapidly, to retrieve power back to the elected leadership, with predictable results, especially after the Kargil misadventure launched by the army led by Gen. Pervez Musharraf. For nearly a year now, the army leadership has been negotiating and crafting the reestablishment of the old preferred pattern of a civilian façade to an essentially military managed rule. This was the process that judicial actions threatened to stymie, leading to the removal of the chief justice of the country, adding to the internal tensions and increasing Benazir Bhutto's apparent negotiating leverages for her return to power. All charges against her which had necessitated her exile for nearly a decade, already lie in the dustbin of history, encouraging Nawaz Sharif to threaten to return to his home country.

While the return of a civilian elected democratic government in Islamabad is to be welcomed, its likely consequences leave disturbing thoughts. With the spread of Islamic *jihadi* radicalism in the country, from the centre of Islamabad to the periphery of Waziristan and Baluchistan, the resurgence of the Taliban and its expanding influence in the badlands of Afghanistan and Pakistan, the risks of further expansion of religious terrorism are high. If the 1990s comprise any precedent, the United States and the international community would have to address their concerns on terrorism to the elected government facing the internal pulls and pressures of religious groups and political parties, with little power to control policy and events. On the other hand, the army and Inter-Services Intelligence (ISI) in Pakistan would have greater scope to promote the Taliban and Islamic *jihad* without being accountable.

When this is seen in the context of the historical belief that the "Mujahideen" had defeated the superpower Soviet Union two decades ago, leading to its collapse, and to the eruption of Islamic terrorism from the Balkans through Kashmir all the way to the Philippines and Indonesia, the picture of the future is anything but promising. The sole superpower and its allies are not succeeding in Iraq and Afghanistan. This translates into the perception that that they are losing. What would be consequences of this perception spreading across the world?

It is also in this context that we need to view the nuclear issues which have dominated world (especially Asian) events during the recent years. North Korea is a *de-facto* nuclear weapon state, making it the ninth country in the world — and eighth in Asia (with the US a *de-facto* Asian power and France an Indian Ocean power, and Russia, China, Israel, India and Pakistan being the others) — possessing nuclear weapons. Many uncertainties remain about the future of Iran's nuclear power programme and its consequences. What is clear is that the global nuclear non-proliferation had reached its plateau by 1995 when the nuclear Non-Proliferation Treaty (NPT) was permanently extended and nuclear disarmament banished from public policy. The only option left was to deal with residual issues in country-specific approaches. Classifying them in terms of "axis of evil" was no doubt unproductive to say the least, leading as it did to a costly war in Iraq, and continuing insecurity all around, an unending confrontation with Iran, and North Korea crossing the nuclear Rubicon, with the international community unable to do anything about it, not even bargaining to stop North Korean ballistic missile proliferation across the world in general and Asia in particular. No wonder that Russia, flush with petro-dollars, has decided to refurbish its nuclear arsenal and take it forward, as the US and China are doing.

On the other hand, significant changes are affecting conventional military power, leading to a paradoxical development which is making military power far more effective than ever before in history and yet making it less usable. At a fundamental level, territory as a viable objective of war was no longer a viable option even toward the end of the last century for a variety of reasons, as Saddam Hussein found to his detriment in 1990. Prime Minister Manmohan Singh has stated a number of times that boundaries cannot be redrawn, at least not by force. This, in turn, implies that the traditional role of land forces has been undergoing a seminal change; and with the passage of time, they may no longer remain the primary expression of a nation's military power. Traditional belief in the possibility of "victory" leave alone a "decisive military victory" in warfare had been seriously undermined long ago by the existence of nuclear weapons` in the control of more than one power. Such weapons circumscribe the role of conventional military power in general and land forces in particular, especially if the war takes place closer to national borders.

However, this does not imply that land power is becoming obsolete. The role of land forces as the final guarantor of national security and stability would remain paramount. They would continue to play a crucial role in conventional wars as well as the back-up contingency force in sub-conventional wars. The military's role in conquering territory has no doubt been circumscribed. But many of the factors responsible for this have also raised the premium of pockets of territory being occupied to serve as negotiating chips for political goals. Employment of land forces in an offensive as well as defensive role would need to factor in these trends. This raises the basic question: if land forces are going to be constrained from exploiting their full potential, especially in a nuclear weapon environment, how does a country impose its will, for good reasons or bad, on its adversary through military power? And how would we define victory and defeat in the future?

The answer clearly rests with air power becoming the instrument of choice for this purpose since it can destroy targets on the ground without encountering the complexities of defeating the opposing force and/or capturing and holding territory, like land forces have to do. The most effective role of military power in the future would be a synergy that is based on the land forces strategically on the defensive and air forces strategically on the offensive to create strategic effect. Naval forces would continue to play the crucial roles of defence and security of national interests, besides defence diplomacy, not conceptually far removed from the gunboat diplomacy of an earlier era. China perhaps has been the most perceptive in this regard. It had concluded by the mid-1980s that a general war was no longer a viable probability. It, accordingly, altered its military doctrine and policy by 1987 to prepare for "local border wars" in the future. As it started to modernise its military and acquire high technology weapons and systems, it started bringing in greater clarity to its military doctrine and strategy. By the end of 2004, it had officially declared publicly in its White Paper on National Defence that it plans to achieve military victory in local border wars through "command of the air" and "command of the seas," while reducing the size of the army. For a country with little transparency in even less sensitive issues, this was indeed remarkable, though understandable as a signal to its neighbours.

It is in the context of some of these thoughts and the broader trends in Asia that we offer the second volume of our annual publication from the Centre for Air Power Studies covering a range of issues of importance. The views expressed in the essays are those of the contributing authors and do not necessarily reflect the views and policies of any institution or organisation. The responsibility for the volume as such remains that of the editor.

1

China's Defence Strategy and Military Posture

Gurmeet Kanwal

Introduction

Though it is still a developing country when evaluated against most socio-economic parameters, it is clear in the first decade of the 21st century that China has already emerged as an economic giant and is well on its way to becoming a major world power. With its near double-digit growth rate, it is poised to overtake the United States (US) economy between 2030 and 2040 and become the *numero uno* in the world's economy. China's military power is also increasing steadily and keeping pace with the rapid rise in its economic power. Whether China's rise will be entirely peaceful, as its leaders have repeatedly professed, or one that may be marked by turbulence and chaos, as some analysts fear, is a vexing issue. History is witness to the fact that major power shifts have never occurred without large-scale upheavals. Managing the rise of China successfully is the most important fundamental challenge confronting the international community in the 21st century. Writing about China's rise, Michael D. Swaine and Ashley J. Tellis have said:[1] "This process is significant not only because it promises the internal transformation of one of the world's oldest civilisations, but also because *if concluded successfully* it could result in a dramatic power transition within the international system."

China's historical approach to security, driven by its ruling elite's perception of cultural superiority, has been to attach equal importance to diplomacy and the use of force as instruments to further the interests of the state. However, no Chinese ruler ever hesitated to use force when it was considered necessary. In the modern era, the Chinese government has preferred the use of force to the soft power of diplomacy whenever it thought it could get away with using force. This is reflected in its proclivity to teach lessons to states that refuse to do its bidding. This approach is at variance with Confucian ideology and is driven by China's subsequent exposure to the totalitarian and coercive facets of the practices followed by nomadic invaders. In the modern era, post-1911, China's political leadership has followed a personalised style of governance. As a result of this, internal jockeying for political power often influences the formulation of major national policies.

Chinese analysts often write that in modern history, China has been compelled to take part in war and even then has sought to restrict it to within certain limits. The Chinese call their military intervention in the Korean War (1950-53) a "war to resist US aggression and aid Korea." They term the border wars fought by China against several land neighbours – India (1962), the Soviet Union (1969), and Vietnam (1979) – as "counter-attacks in self-defence" and maintain that the guiding principle was always to be on "just ground, to our advantage and with restraint... In terms of employment of fighting means China showed great sobriety, caution and restraint. This is a fundamental character of China's tradition of strategic culture."[2] This appears to be the party line that is taught in China's military academies and, quite obviously, it is far from the truth. The border war with India in 1962 and that with Vietnam in 1979 were far from "counter-attacks in self-defence."

Alastair Iain Johnston is of the view that China follows a *realpolitik*-based strategic culture that "in essence argues that the best way to deal with security threats is to eliminate them through the use of force. This preference is tempered by the explicit sensitivity to one's relative capacity to do this. At the simplest, the operational strategic culture predisposes those socialised in it to act more creatively against the enemy as relative capabilities become more favourable." In a similar vein, Christine A. Cleary has written:[3] "Historically, the PRC has demonstrated its inclination to use force in situations perceived as threatening to its national goals or its credibility to defend vital interests. For example, analyses of China's conventional wars, such as the Korean War and the Sino-Indian border war, showed China willing to back up threats with force in order for its pronouncements to be taken seriously." The carefully constructed government policy is to publicly state that lofty principles (*Panchsheel* or non-intervention in the internal affairs of other countries, war only in self-defence and "no first use" nuclear doctrine) guide China's international interactions. In reality, China follows pragmatic hard-nosed security policies. It would be fair to conclude that in recent times, certainly since it has been ruled by a Communist oligarchy in the second half of the 20th century, China's strategic culture has become more robust and less tolerant of perceptions that are different from its own.

Grand Strategy

China, without doubt, a revisionist power, is moving steadily forward on its long march to acquire world power status and has formulated a meticulously crafted, though not formally stated, grand strategy to chart its course towards that goal. China's aim is clearly to become the dominant economic and military power in the Asia-Pacific region by 2010-15 and a major power internationally by about 2030-40. Its strategy of "four modernisations", formally adopted in 1978, is bearing fruit and is leading to fairly rapid, though regionally skewed, development and modernisation, including modernisation of the armed forces. China's grand strategy is aimed at "firmly preserving China's core interests, strengthening its relations with neighbouring countries, consolidating friendships with the broad majority of developing countries and improving relations with developed countries."[4] In order to emphasise the benign nature of its grand strategy, China points out that its major themes are "peace and development," the non-use of force in settling international disputes, non-intervention in the internal affairs of other transfer to before zones countries, the defensive nature of China's military strategy, its "no first use of nuclear weapons" declaration and its support for nuclear weapon-free zones. China claims that it will never deploy its military forces on foreign soil. However, Deng Xiaoping's 24-character strategy "keep cool-headed to observe, be composed to make reactions, stand firmly, hide our capabilities and bide our time, never try to take the lead, and be able to accomplish something" suggests a desire to downplay China's ambitions.

Development of Comprehensive National Power

China's grand strategy seeks to preserve national independence and increase national power through the balancing of two competing objectives: the development of comprehensive national power (CNP – *zonghe guoli*) and the exploitation of existing "strategic configuration of power" or "*shi*".[5] China's grand strategy affirms that national unity, sovereignty and stability guarantee the survival of the state, and the development of a national strategy with China at the centre of Asia. Incorporated in this strategy is Chinese patience or willingness to live with ambiguity before considering the employment of force such that advantage is obtained, moral high ground is occupied and supporters or non-supporters are identified. China's national security policy objectives, "dynamic stability" and "economic growth," are directly linked to the maintenance of unity through preservation of the regime, domestic order and territorial integrity. In a RAND study, Swaine and Tellis have written that China's grand strategy seeks to achieve the following three interrelated objectives:[6]

- The preservation of domestic order and well-being in the face of different forms of social strife.
- Defence against persistent external threats to national sovereignty and territory.
- The attainment and maintenance of geo-political influence as a major and, perhaps, primary state.

China's grand strategy, as China defines it, is one of: maintaining balance among competing priorities for sustaining momentum in national economic development; and, maintaining favourable trends in the security environment within which such economic development can occur.[7] Khadong Oh Hassig of the Institute of Defence Analyses has described China's primary strategic objectives as the protection of China's soveriegnty, maintaining China's security and preventing Taiwan's independence.[8] Michael Swaine and Ashley Tellis are of the view that China's strategic objectives inlcude "assuring domestic order and social well-being, maintaining an adequate defence against threats to the heartland, increasing the level of influence and control over the periphery with an eye to warding off threats that may eventually menace the political regime and, restoring China to regional pre-eminence…"[9]

China's strategic planners evaluate and measure China's national standing in relation to other nations through CNP. The yardsticks for CNP include qualitative and quantitative measures of territorial size, economic capability, military power, natural resources, diplomatic influence, quality of domestic governance and the extent of China's cultural influence. Of all the yardsticks, China's strategy to build its CNP lays maximum emphasis on economic development. "China's 11th Five-Year Plan (2006-2010), ratified during the March 2006 session of the National People's Congress, calls for a 20 percent reduction in per capita energy consumption by 2010, a doubling of China's 2000 Gross Domestic Product (GDP) by 2010, and an overall GDP of $4 trillion by 2020. The plan stresses coordinated, sustainable development and greater investment and urbanisation in the rural interior to address widening income disparities and resultant social unrest."[10] However, as China's economy expands, its interests will also expand and China will perceive a need to upgrade its military capability to protect those interests.

China's attempts to advance its concept of a "peaceful rise," also called "peaceful ascendancy," are consistent with its belief that it was historically a great empire (the Middle Kingdom) and deserves to be a major world power in the modern era. The Chinese are constantly looking for ways in which they can ensure that China's rise and integration with the world order is orderly and peaceful. Japanese columnist Y. Funabashi quotes a member of the Chinese People's Political Consultative Conference as having asked him: "How did historic empires and major powers rise and what reactions do they trigger? What should we do so as not to cause excessive wariness? This is what we are currently studying internally."[11]

In 1997, Foreign Minister Qian Qichen and Defence Minister Chi Haotian enunciated China's "New Security Concept". The major elements of this concept include several well-known Chinese beliefs like the primacy of the five principles of peaceful coexistence and faith in the emergence of a multipolar world order as well as some new foreign policy themes like the embrace of multilateral security mechanisms and strategic partnerships with other countries.[12] The Chinese now also emphasise efforts towards strengthening international trade and economic cooperation and appear to be genuinely eager to integrate China's economy with that of the rest of the world. While China's political leadership is of the view that China has never had such a secure and stable periphery and regional environment as has obtained in the first decade of the 21st century, many People's Liberation Army (PLA) analysts see greater sources of instability, particularly at the global level. Senior Colonel Li Qinggong, director of the General Staff Department's First Bureau, had identified the following set of factors as causing global instability soon after the Kosovo conflict:[13]

- American hegemony and the attempt to conquer the world by force.
- Western "humanitarian intervention" and the "Clinton Doctrine."
- The increasing intensification of local ethnic conflicts, as in Chechnya, Eritrea, Indonesia and Yugoslavia.
- The decline of arms control efforts and the build-up of regional military forces.
- The rise of ethno-religious separatism and increase in terrorist acts.

Other destabilising factors noted by PLA analysts include the power imbalance caused by the collapse of the bipolar system, contest and conflict between the global hegemon (US) and "regional hegemons," a surge in "national extremism," the damage done to international arms control efforts by the South Asian nuclear tests, transnational crime and drug trafficking, disputes over economic resources and environmental issues. China is also acutely conscious of the world's dwindling fossil fuel resources in the light of its own unavoidable dependency on them.

It has been moving aggressively to acquire controlling interest in oil and gas fields where it can, for example, in several countries in Africa, Central Asia and Myanmar, and sign long-term supply contracts where it cannot. It is likely to take even more vigorous steps in the future to safeguard its energy security.

Defence Strategy

China's Defence Policy

China's National Defence in 2006, the White Paper issued by the Government of China in December 2006, expresses satisfaction with the overall security environment and lists it as "sound". It describes China's defence policy in these words:[14] "China will not engage in any arms race or pose a military threat to any other country. At the new stage in the new century, we will take the scientific development outlook as an important guiding principle for the building of national defense and military affairs, vigorously advance the revolution in military affairs with Chinese features, and strive to realize an all-round, coordinated and sustainable development in our country's national defense and military capabilities." According to the 2006 Defence White Paper, "China's national defense policy for the new stage in the new century is defined as follows":[15]

- *Upholding national security and unity and ensuring the interests of national development*: This includes guarding against and resisting aggression, defending against violation of China's territorial sea and air space, and borders; opposing and containing the separatist forces for "Taiwan independence" and their activities, taking precautions against and cracking down on terrorism, separatism and extremism in all forms…
- *Achieving the all-round, coordinated and sustainable development of China's national defense and armed forces*: China pursues a policy of coordinated development of national defense and economy… so as to ensure that the modernization of its national defense and armed forces advances in step with the national modernization drive. China works in a comprehensive way to ensure that its armed forces are revolutionary

in nature, modernized and regularized. It strives to ensure coordination between the revolution in military affairs with Chinese features and preparations for military struggle, mechanization and informationization...

- *Enhancing the performance of the armed forces with informationization as the major measuring criterion*: The PLA, taking mechanization as the foundation and informationization as the driving force, promotes the composite development of informationization and mechanization to achieve overall capability improvement in the fields of firepower, assault, mobility, protection and information... It is stepping up its efforts to build a joint operational command system, training system and support system for fighting informationized wars and enhance the building of systems integration of services and arms...
- *Implementing the military strategy of active defence*: The PLA will... upgrade and develop the strategic concept of people's war, and work for close coordination between military struggle and political, economic, diplomatic, cultural and legal endeavors, uses strategies and tactics in a comprehensive way, and takes the initiative to prevent and defuse crises and deter conflicts and wars. The PLA will establish step by step a modern national defence mobilization system that is centralized and unified, well structured, rapid in reaction, and authoritative and efficient. Taking joint operations as the basic form, the PLA aims to bring the operational strengths of different services and arms into full play...
- *Pursuing a self-defensive nuclear strategy*: (China's) fundamental goal is to deter other countries from using or threatening to use nuclear weapons against China. China remains firmly committed to the policy of no first use of nuclear weapons at any time and under any circumstances... China upholds the principles of counterattack in self-defense and limited development of nuclear weapons, and aims at building a lean and effective nuclear force capable of meeting national security needs...
- *Fostering a security environment conducive to China's peaceful development*: China maintains military contacts with other countries on the basis of the Five Principles of Peaceful Coexistence, and develops cooperative military relations that are non-aligned, non-

confrontational and not directed against any third party. China takes part in international security cooperation… It plays an active part in maintaining global and regional peace and stability…

National Security Goals

From China's stated defence policy, its national security goals may be assessed to be the following:

- To prevent separatist tendencies and promote reunification, guard against, and resist, aggression and defend national sovereignty, territorial integrity and maritime rights and interests.
- To promote economic and social development in a coordinated and sustainable manner and steadily increase comprehensive national strength.
- To pursue an independent foreign policy with a view to securing a favourable international and regional environment.
- To modernise China's armed forces in line with the trend in international military developments, particularly technological developments.
- To improve operational capabilities for active defence under informationised conditions.
- To safeguard the political, economic and cultural rights and interests of the Chinese people and maintain public order and social stability.

National Security Strategy

For meeting its national security goals, China's national security strategy may be assessed to be the following:

- The primary objective is to create a security environment favourable to the country's economic development.
- Peaceful reunification of the Motherland is one of the strategic objectives set by the Chinese government.
- Safeguarding the country's territorial integrity is the foremost responsibility entrusted to the PLA.
- China will continue to claim that it will persist in the principle of non-use of force in settling boundary differences. However, it may be

expected to follow a more robust policy with preemptive strategies, particularly in relation to Taiwan.

- Towards its regional neighbours, China will continue to follow a stick and carrot policy of enhancing friendly relations through bilateral security cooperation, military sales and aid and bilateral trade, while remaining intolerant of major dissent and alliances.
- Actively aid international efforts to prevent nuclear proliferation, particularly in respect of North Korea.
- The government guideline for the PLA's transformation in the next 15 to 20 years is to build a smaller but more modern army, navy and air force to be able to face the revolution in military affairs (RMA)-ready Western forces.
- China's earlier people's war military strategy of "luring the enemy in deep" will be gradually replaced completely by the present strategy of "active defence under hi-tech conditions."
- While China will endeavour to prevent conflict, if conflict breaks out, its military strategy is likely to be proactive and will be designed to take the fight into enemy territory.

China has always placed immense emphasis on diplomacy as a tool to balance out security threats and challenges through intricate alliances and strategic partnerships. In Brig Arun Sahgal's view:[16] "China's growing military capabilities, backed by strategic arms sales programmes, enable it to create a series of special strategic relations with friendly states (potentially with Myanmar, Bangladesh, Thailand, South Korea, Cambodia, Malaysia and Iran), quasi-alliances (Pakistan, North Korea) and external military assets (Gwadar, Maldives, Chittagong). This will increasingly allow China to manipulate the regional balance of power in a manner that enhances its political economic and security interests and allows it to engage in coercive diplomacy against any state in the neighbourhood that is seen to be acting against its interests. This Chinese strategy of growth of military capability and creeping influence is in no way in contradiction with stress on partnership, economic interdependence and promoting relations with neighbours and major powers. In fact, it complements regional and global engagement strategy at a period when China is preoccupied with domestic economic reforms and is still attempting to establish political structures in tune with its modernisation drive and relatively weak power base in comparison to its principal rivals."

Military Strategy

China's military strategy is still guided by the PLA's historical experience of "people's war." Though in its overall approach the people's war strategy is predicated on "strategic defensive," within that rubric, it is a fairly balanced blend of defensive and offensive action. "The basic military strategy Mao formulated, known as 'active defense,' was one of a protracted, defensive war… The concept of active defense means taking tactically offensive action within a basically defensive strategy… The active defense strategy consists of three phases: strategic defense, strategic stalemate and strategic counter-attack."[17] Deng Xiaoping was of the view, "Active defense itself is not necessarily limited to a defensive concept… Active defense also contains an offensive element. If we are attacked, we will certainly counterattack… anyone who wants to destroy us will be subject to retaliation."[18]

Strategic defence is considered important at the beginning of the conflict as China views its forces as weaker than those of its potential adversaries. The aim in this phase is to defeat the enemy's offensive action and, in fact, ideally to preempt him and disrupt his preparations. The strategic stalemate phase is designed to weaken the enemy by forcing him to fight on lines of communication that have been stretched. The aim is to stabilise the situation and enable Chinese forces to begin turning the tide from defensive to offensive operations. In the strategic counter-attack phase, the aim is to defeat the weakened enemy through a counter-offensive or riposte.

Since China's ignominious incursion into Vietnam in 1979, the PLA doctrine evolved from Mao's "people's war," characterised by protracted, large-scale land warfare, through a "limited/local war" phase, to "people's war under modern conditions" introduced in 1993. Subsequently, after the Cold War ended and following the Gulf War in

1991, the Chinese leadership concluded that the "big peace" at the geo-strategic level cannot prevent local or small wars at the regional level. The PLA then graduated to thinking about fighting local or limited wars and sought to focus on the following:[19]

- Small-scale conflicts restricted to contested border territory.
- Conflict over territorial seas and islands.
- Surprise air attacks.
- Defence against deliberately limited attacks into Chinese territory.
- Punitive counter-attacks launched by China into enemy territory to "oppose invasion, protect sovereignty, or to uphold justice and dispel threats."

Underpinning the new professionalism of the PLA is the new doctrine of "active defence" (*jiji fangyu*) that seeks to conduct "people's war under modern conditions" but is better understood as "local wars under hi-tech conditions" (*gaojishu tiaojian xia de jubu zhanzheng*). The "active defence" doctrine calls for integrated, deep strikes – a concentration of superior firepower that is to be utilised to destroy the opponent's retaliatory capabilities through preemptive strikes employing long-range artillery, short-range ballistic missiles (SRBMs) and precision-guided munitions (PGMs). David Shambaugh has written:[20] "Rather than conducting a 'people's war' (a strategy to 'lure the enemy in deep' into one's own territory), the PLA doctrine of 'active defense' calls for forward positioning, frontier defense, engagement of the enemy at or over the border and potential engagement in conflict beyond China's immediate periphery. Compared with China's historically reactive stance of luring the adversary deep inside and destroying him through strategic defense, this doctrine is essentially proactive and seeks to take the battle into enemy territory." The doctrine emphasises the effective use of advanced equipment wielded by elite units, with a focus on joint operations. The overall aim in this "limited war under hi-tech conditions" doctrine is to disrupt the enemy's combat forces and logistics but not annihilate him so as to bring about a negotiated end to the conflict or dictate terms if possible. Beijing has defined the following five likely limited war scenarios:

- Military conflict with neighbouring countries in a limited region.
- Military conflict on territorial waters.
- Undeclared air attack by enemy countries.
- Territorial defence in a limited military operation.
- Punitive offensive with a minor incursion into a neighbouring country.

The new doctrine and the strategy and tactics associated with it have been influenced by the lessons of the Gulf War in 1991 and the Iraq War of 2003. Both these wars have been extensively studied by Chinese scholars and military analysts. The doctrine demands the creation of a capability to project force across China's borders through rapid deployment, conventional SRBMs and cruise missiles, information warfare, electronic warfare, precision-guided munitions, night fighting capabilities and other advanced military technologies. The building of these capabilities, in turn, drives procurement and defence production policies, command and control structures, and training. The present doctrine represents a Chinese adaptation of the United States' RMA concepts to achieve victory by reorganising the military to exploit rapid advances in technology. The PLA has appreciated that modern hi-tech war, whether defensive or offensive, generally has limited political goals and it is necessary to achieve political objectives as quickly as possible and with the minimum possible casualties. This is to be achieved by:[21]

- Gaining the initiative by striking first.
- Achieving victory with one strike.
- Concentrating China's strength to attack the core of enemy defence.

The new doctrine is also more assertive than previously and is not bound by any restrictions to confine and limit future conflict to within China's national boundaries. China claims that it has only peaceful intentions and does not believe in launching aggression and that it fights wars only to defend its sovereignty and territorial integrity. According to China's White Papers on national defence, active defence is a defensive military strategy. However, it is clear from Chinese writings that the major characteristics of active defence are distinctly offensive in nature. The PLA publication *The Study of Campaigns*

(*Zhanyi Xue*) published in 2000, highlights this offensive approach:[22] "While strategically the guideline is active defense, in military campaigns, though, the emphasis is placed on taking the initiative in 'active offence.' Only in this way the strategic objectives of 'active defensc' can be realized."

Informationisation as a Tool in Military Strategy

Subsequently, early in the 21st century, based on recent conflicts, the Central Military Commission (CMC) called for a detailed study of the concept of "people's war under informationization conditions." Ka Po Ng, an associate professor at Aichi Bunkyo University, Japan, sums up the new concept in these words:[23] "...What the PLA is prepared to fight is a people's war in the form of a 'local war under high-tech conditions' with increasing attention to the application of information technology." It emerges clearly that China is engaged in assessing the implications of information technology and knowledge-based warfare on the modern battlefield.

The PLA expects to fight the next war under conditions of what it calls "informationization" or "informationalization."[24] In the White Paper on national defence issued in 2004, informationisation has been explained only in general terms:[25]

- To adapt itself to the changes both in the international strategic situation and the national security environment and rise to the challenges presented by the RMA worldwide, China adheres to the military strategy of active defense and works to speed up the RMA with Chinese characteristics.
- To take the road of composite and leapfrog development. Going with the tide of the world's military development and moving along the direction of informationalization in the process of modernization, the People's Liberation Army (PLA) shall gradually achieve the transition from mechanization and semi-mechanization to informationalization. Based on China's national conditions and the PLA's own conditions, the PLA persists in taking mechanization as the foundation to promote informationalization, and informationalization as the driving force to

bring forward mechanization. The PLA will promote coordinated development of firepower, mobility and information capability, enhance the development of its operational strength with priority given to the Navy, Air Force and Second Artillery Force, and strengthen its comprehensive deterrence and warfighting capabilities.

- To build a strong military by means of science and technology. The PLA works to improve its combat capabilities by taking advantage of scientific and technological advances and aims at building qualitative efficiency instead of a mere quantitative scale, and transforming the military from a manpower-intensive one to a technology-intensive one. Implementing the Strategic Project for Talented People, the PLA focuses on training a new type of high-caliber military personnel. It works to build up a complete system of weaponry and equipment by stepping up development of new and high-tech weaponry and equipment while upgrading those in active service. In an innovative spirit, the PLA endeavors to improve its training system as well as the means and methods of training so as to raise its military training to a higher level. Relying on national economic, scientific and technological development, the PLA is devoted to improving the level of scientific management and achieving a higher overall cost-effectiveness in military expenditure so as to modernize the armed forces with less inputs and better results.
- To deepen the reform of the armed forces. Based on the transformation of modern warfare and the requirements of the socialist market economy, the PLA seeks to achieve development and breakthroughs in the process of reform and innovation. The PLA develops its military theories in an innovative spirit, and explores the laws of building the Army and conducting operations under the condition of informationalization. In accordance with the principle of making the troops smaller and better, as well as more integrated and efficient, and with emphasis on adjusting the organizational structure and reforming the command system, the PLA works to build and further improve the military structure and organization to make them appropriate in size, optimal in structure, streamlined in institutional set-up and flexible and swift in command. The PLA also works to readjust and regulate the relationship within the military as well

as that with the government and society so as to put in place policies and mechanisms, which will help motivate officers and soldiers.

- To step up preparations for military struggle. The PLA takes as its objective to win local wars under the conditions of informationalization and gives priority to developing weaponry and equipment, to building joint operational capabilities, and to making full preparations in the battlefields. Meanwhile, it adheres to the people's war concept and develops the strategies and tactics of the people's war. To meet the requirements of integrated and joint operations, the PLA endeavors to establish a modern operational system capable of giving full play to the overall efficiency of the armed forces as well as the national war potentials. The PLA conducts more training and exercises with specific objectives in order to raise its capabilities in coping with various crises and contingencies.
- To carry out military exchanges and cooperation. In line with the national foreign policy, the PLA conducts military cooperation that is non-aligned, non-confrontational and not directed against any third party. The PLA takes part in the UN peacekeeping operations and international counter-terrorism cooperation. While promoting military exchanges in various forms, the PLA works to establish security dialogue mechanisms in order to create a military security environment featuring mutual trust and mutual benefit. It takes part in bilateral or multilateral joint military exercises in non-traditional security fields so as to enhance the joint capabilities to cope with threats in those fields. The PLA learns from, and draws on, the valuable experience of foreign armed forces, and introduces, on a selective basis, technologically advanced equipment and better management expertise from abroad to advance the modernization of the Chinese armed forces.

PLA analysts have called the ongoing RMA an "informationized military revolution."[26] It emerges that informationisation "clearly relates to the PLA's ability to adopt information technologies to command, intelligence, training and weapon systems. This would include broad investment in new automatic command systems linked by fibre-optic Internet, satellite and new high-frequency digital radio systems… The

PLA can also contest the information battle space with its new space-based, airborne, naval and ground-based surveillance and intelligence gathering systems and its new anti-satellite, anti-radar, electronic warfare and information warfare systems... there is increasing 'information content' for new PLA weapons as it moves to link new space, airborne and ELINT sensors to missile, air, naval and ground-based 'shooters' to enable all its services to better use new precision-strike weapons."[27] According to the 2004 White Paper, "In its modernization drive, the PLA takes informationalization as its orientation and strategic focus." The PLA has adopted what it calls a "double historical mission" and a "leapfrog development strategy" – accelerating military informationisation while undergoing mechanisation.[28]

The denial of information, strategic deception and the achievement of psychological surprise have for long been an integral part of Chinese military doctrine. The Chinese find information warfare (IW) extremely attractive as they view it as an asymmetric tool that will enable them to overcome their relative backwardness in military hardware. The Chinese are devoting considerable time and energy to perfecting the techniques of IW to target the rapidly modernising Western armed forces that are becoming increasingly more dependent on the software that runs computer networks and modern communications. In Chinese thinking, IW presents a level playing field for projecting power and prevailing upon the adversary in future wars. However, it has not been possible to ascertain from open public sources whether IW is fully integrated with the doctrine of people's war under modern conditions or if it is still treated as a separate but complementary pattern of war (*zhanzheng xingtai*). There is also some confusion created by the use of the term informationised warfare (*xinxihua zhanzheng*) instead of IW (*xinxi zhanzheng*).[29] However, there is no ambiguity in the manner in which the Chinese view information operations:[30]

- Intelligence operations, which include intelligence reconnaissance and protection.
- Command and control (C2) operations to disrupt enemy information flow and weaken his C2 capability while protecting one's own.

- Electronic warfare by seizing the electromagnetic initiative through electronic attack, electronic protection and electronic warfare support.
- Targeting enemy computer systems and networks to damage and destroy critical machines and networks and the data stored on them.
- Physical destruction of enemy sources like information infrastructure such as command, control, communications, computers, intelligence, surveillance, reconnaissance (C4ISR) through the application of firepower.

The Chinese call their pursuit of information warfare and other hi-tech means to counter Washington's overwhelmingly superior conventional military capabilities "acupuncture warfare," a term that first surfaced in a 1997 PLA National Defence University publication entitled "On Commanding Warfighting Under High-Tech Conditions."[31] Acupuncture warfare (also called "paralysis warfare"[32] or "unrestricted warfare") is described as, "Paralyzing the enemy by attacking the weak link of his command, control, communications and information as if hitting his acupuncture point in *kung fu* combat." Acupuncture warfare is a form of asymmetrical warfare that takes its bearings from the teachings of Sun Tzu, China's preeminent military strategist from the 5th century BC. For quite some time now, the PLA has been simulating computer virus attacks in its military exercises.

According to a US Congressional Research Service report entitled "Cyberwarfare," authored by Steve Hildreth, China is developing a strategic information warfare unit called "Net Force" to neutralise the military capabilities of technologically superior adversaries.[33] This new information warfare unit will "wage combat through computer networks to manipulate enemy information systems spanning spare parts deliveries to fire control and guidance systems." Though the PLA's research into the theoretical aspects of information warfare is fairly advanced, it does not appear to have developed a coordinated and integrated information warfare doctrine as yet.

Chong-Pin Lee, vice chairman of Taiwan's Mainland Affairs Council, says Beijing is redirecting its emphasis away from nuclear deterrence to this new asymmetrical strategy and its "overarching purpose is to deter the United States from intervening around China's peripheries and to seize Taiwan with minimum bloodshed and destruction."[34] In another five to ten years, China will develop depth and sophistication in its understanding and handling of information warfare techniques and information operations. With Indian society becoming increasingly dependent on automated data processing and vast computer networks, India will also become extremely vulnerable to such information warfare techniques. The fact that it can be practised from virtually any place on the earth even during peace-time makes acupuncture warfare even more diabolical. India can ill-afford to ignore this new challenge to its security.

Defence analysts Timperlake and Triplett have written that economic, political and social systems are essentially unprotected against Chinese information warfare attacks. In their view, China has adopted a comprehensive strategy to further its information warfare plans:[35]

- Information warfare has the support of the top PLA brass.
- The PLA's best strategists and defence scientists have had extensive open discussions about information warfare.
- The PLA is conducting military exercises in information warfare.
- It is expanding its already strong signals intelligence (SIGINT) capability in Cuba.
- The PLA is buying the hardware necessary. (As supercomputers require huge capital investments, a strong political and financial commitment is implied.)
- The Chinese are recruiting scientists and technicians.
- The PLA is building related weapons (high-powered microwave weapons).

To prepare itself for a conflict with an RMA-ready opponent, China's military thinkers recommend that China must:[36]

- Close the information gap.
- Network all forces.
- Attack the enemy's C3I (command, control, communication, intelligence) to paralyse it.
- Use directed energy weapons.
- Use computer viruses.

- Use submarine-launched munitions.
- Use anti-satellite weapons.
- Use forces to prevent a logistics build-up.
- Use special operations raids.

Compared with China's historically reactive stance of luring the enemy in deep and destroying him through strategic defence, the present doctrine is essentially proactive and seeks to take the battle into enemy territory. It also strives to achieve surprise in a proactive manner that is demonstrated by new "quick-strike" tactics. The aim is to catch the enemy unprepared in order to inflict substantial damage on strategic targets and disrupt logistics to gain psychological ascendancy. While the land frontier is expected to continue to generate some local tensions, the Central Military Commission (CMC) has identified space and the oceans as the new areas where future conflict might take place.

The Chinese have rejected the doctrine of deterrence as, in their view, it is associated with imperialism, amounts to military blackmail, glorifies the use of force and would be an empty threat if not substantiated by tangible power.[37] The "active defence" doctrine also calls for integrated, deep strikes – a concentration of superior firepower that is to be utilised to destroy the opponent's retaliatory capabilities by employing long-range artillery, SRBMs and precision-guided munitions. The doctrine emphasises the effective use of advanced equipment wielded by elite units, with a focus on joint operations. The overall aim in this "limited war under hi-tech conditions" doctrine is to disrupt the enemy's combat forces and logistics but not annihilate him so as to bring about a negotiated end to the conflict or dictate terms, if possible.

Military Posture

Military postures the world over are evolving in line with emerging threats and challenges and the changing nature of warfare. With the probability of large-scale conventional conflict receding rapidly, contemporary conflict is becoming increasingly asymmetric. The asymmetric character of contemporary conflict is challenging conventional thinking and demanding fresh responses. Gen Rupert Smith has identified six key trends that define modern warfare:[38] The growing role of non-state actors as well as multinational forces as combatants; looking for creative new uses for old weapons; emphasis on force protection rather than using force at any cost; the prolonged nature of modern wars; a new focus on winning the hearts and minds of people; and, a shift from absolute objectives to more flexible ones. He writes that in the Clausewitzian trinity (army, state and people), the balance among the three has changed. "There was a time when armies dominated — as they still do in the country of warlords; later, states were able to command the complete obedience of their people. Now it is the people who are in charge and the strategic objective is their hearts and minds."[39] China is no exception to the rule except that its government is relatively less concerned about the people's thinking on military issues.

For almost two decades now, the PLA has been pursuing a systematic plan to downsize its regular army and transfer some of the personnel to reserves and paramilitary forces. In December 2005, the PLA completed another round of downsizing, reducing personnel by some 200,000. This brought the size of the PLA to about 2.3 million, according to official statistics. The inclusion of the paramilitary People's Armed Police (PAP — which has upwards of 1.5 million personnel) and reserves (800,000) increases the total figure for active, reserve, and paramilitary units to over 4.6 million. The 2004 Defence White Paper also declares that China can draw upon more than 10 million organised militia members.

The People's Liberation Army's 2.25-million-strong force makes it the largest in the world, in terms of number of troops (3.25 million if active paramilitary personnel are included).[40] The ground forces comprising 1.6 million personnel (about 70 per cent of the total force) are divided into 7 military regions. The regular forces of the ground forces consist of 18 group group armies, which are corps-size combined arms units each with 35,000-65,000 personnel. The group armies contain nine armoured divisions, three mechanised infantry divisions, 24 motorised infantry divisions, 15 infantry divisions, two amphibious assault divisions, one mechanised infantry brigade, 12 armoured brigades, seven artillery divisions, 14 artillery brigades, 19 anti-aircraft artillery missile brigades, and 10 army aviation (helicopter) regiments. In addition, three air-borne divisions are manned by the PLAAF. The PLAN has two multi-arm marine brigades.[41] The PAP is organised into 14 mobile divisions, 31 provisional/municipal internal security general corps, and 23 provisional/municipal border defence general corps.[42]

Srikanth Kondapalli cites Ku Guisheng, deputy director of education at the National Defence University, Beijing, as having said that the PLA should undertake reforms in four fields:[43]

- Downsizing and rationalising structure.
- Integrating and 'modularising' troop composition.
- Making the command system network-based and real-time.
- Integrating and 'informationising' support systems.

The PLAN's aspirations to acquire blue water capability and to eventually reach out to the Indian Ocean are well known. It is engaged in transformation aimed at information-based platforms with "stealth, 'modularization' and intelligence-based capabilities." "The concept of a navy is no longer the traditional one of seaborne fighting strength but rather one of a comprehensive military service with high concentrations of technology and knowledge and possessing air, surface, sub-surface and amphibious strengths."[44] Recent Chinese naval operations included an "intrusion" of a Han-class nuclear submarine into Japanese territorial waters. Amphibious landings are being increasingly practised by the marine corps, as witnessed during exercise "Peace Mission 2005" with Russia held in the last week of August 2005.[45]

The PLAAF is gradually moving away from quantity to quality. It has already acquired and is now manufacturing SU-27 (J-11) fighter aircraft and has begun the process of obtaining SU-30MKK multi-role fighters from Russia as well as air-to-air refuelling capabilities. At the same time, it has been upgrading its electronic support measures (ESM) capabilities and acquiring beyond visual range air-to-air missiles. Plans are also afoot to acquire AWACS capability in the near future. The PLAAF has also increased its aerial footprint and Chinese fighters have been flying farther into the South China Sea.[46] However, the PLAAF still suffers from obsolescence, lack of adequate command and control capability and poor training standards and has a long way to go before it can be called a truly modern air force with RMA capabilities.

The PLA Army has been actively engaged in downsizing its regular and paramilitary forces, increasing the number of rapid deployment units and improving mobility and logistics support capability, while simultaneously upgrading the ability to undertake all-weather operations, improve air defence capability and institute modern command and control systems. The PLA Army is in the process of upgrading one division in each military region to the status of a rapid deployment division. China's simultaneous efforts to gradually upgrade the PLAN to "blue water" status and to acquire mid-air refuelling capability, deep penetration strike and strategic lift transport aircraft for the PLAAF are also significant. All these endeavours aim to create a modern fighting force capable of undertaking swift offensive operations in areas away from China's borders. According to a US Department of Defence report, the ultimate goal of the Communist giant is "parity in economic, political and military strength with the world's leading powers by the middle of the next (21st) century."[47]

Recent developments in the field of modernisation of China's strategic forces hinge around the miniaturisation of warheads, progress towards developing multiple independent reentry vehicle (MIRV) capabilities and further improvement in the design of ballistic missiles using solid-fuel propellants. The development of the DF-31A ICBM that can target any city in the US from the Chinese mainland is reported to have been completed. China has also stepped up its plans for the development of a ballistic missile system and is in the process of improving the accuracy of its land attack cruise missiles to about 5-10 metres.[48]

Some military activities during 2006 and early 2007 are noteworthy. A Chinese Song class submarine that had obviously been tailing a US carrier battle group chose to make its presence known by surfacing close to the USS *Kitty Hawk* off Okinawa in November 2006.[49] The Chinese are also developing modern ground-to-ground and ground-to-air missiles to give shape to a new "anti-access" strategy aimed at

Doctrinal Evolution: Local Wars Under the Conditions of Informationization*

Despite advances in technology, Mao Zedong's concept of People's War remains a dominant theme in Chinese military thinking on a par with Soviet national military doctrine. For Chinese leaders, People's War serves as the underlying principle for, and provides a scientific assessment of, how wars must be fought. It envisions defense of the Chinese mainland against a more advanced adversary by capitalizing on China's inherent strengths (large population and depth of land-mass), employing civil-military integration and mobilization, and applying traditional warfighting skills of speed, surprise, deception, and stratagem. For Chinese military planners, the most likely type of future combat they will face — local wars on China's periphery — will be fought with the principles of People's War in mind.

In response to China's evolving security environment and threat perceptions, however, China's military planners understand that the types of wars they must prepare to fight have undergone a series of transformations. During the Maoist era, China focused on preparing to fight an early war, a major war, and a nuclear war, prescribing army building based on mass, depth, and preparation for protracted wars.

In the post-Mao era, this focus shifted as PLA strategists began to conceive of future wars as being short, intense, and of limited geographic scope. External factors, such as US-Soviet detente and US-China cooperation, also diminished the perceived threat of China's involvement in a nuclear conflict. A concept of local war under modern conditions emerged during the 1980s to guide army building through the major round of military-wide reforms launched in 1985, during which the PLA cut one million personnel, reduced the number of military regions from 11 to 7, and restructured the PLA's 36 army corps into combined-arms group armies. Ground forces received less emphasis in favor of navy and air force programs, responding to new requirements for greater speed, mobility, and multi-service operations.

Following the 1991 Persian Gulf War, which brought home to China's leaders how the advance of technology threatened to leave them behind, PLA planners began preparing for local wars under high tech conditions. This shift reflected lessons learned from that conflict with an emphasis on C4ISR, information warfare, precision strike, and advanced air defense and logistics. The 1995-1996 Taiwan Strait crisis served as a catalyst to focus China's efforts and mobilize resources for military modernization and expansion. The crisis also provided China's military planners with a specific scenario to guide force planning — a war over Taiwan that featured US military intervention. This view was reinforced by the 1999 NATO Operation ALLIED FORCE over Kosovo. In its December 2004 Defense White Paper, China replaced local wars under high tech conditions with local wars under the conditions of informationalization. This new concept summarizes China's experiences and assessments of the implications of the revolution in military affairs — primarily the impact of information technology and knowledge-based warfare.

* *Military Power of the People's Republic of China* (Office of the Secretary of Defence, United States Department of Defence: Annual Report to Congress, 2006).

countering the US ability to operate near their borders. China's new S-300PMU2, a surface-to-air missile with a 150-km range, will allow it to engage aircraft flying over Taiwan. This will enable China to shore up its air defences against US aircraft aiding Taiwan in a future confrontation. All of these apparently belligerent activities are indicative of an emerging China that is becoming increasingly more comfortable with flaunting its military power.

Nuclear Posture

As per current indicators, China's "fourth generation" leadership, with President Hu Jintao and Prime Minister Wen Jiabao at the helm, is likely to continue to maintain a defensive orientation in China's nuclear strategy while simultaneously pursuing a well-charted course towards the modernisation of the Second Artillery. Given China's traditional opacity, it could take up to a decade before more is known about the fourth generation leadership's thinking on China's nuclear strategy. Meanwhile, China's nuclear posture remains reactive and there is no evidence that China may change its stated "no first use" policy or that it is even reconsidering it. However, a debate has been on in academic circles about the efficacy of this policy. Among others, Shen Dingli of Fudan University in Shanghai has written:[50] "If China's conventional forces are devastated, and if Taiwan takes the opportunity to declare *de jure* independence, it is inconceivable that China would allow its nuclear weapons to be destroyed by a precision attack with conventional munitions, rather than use them as a true means of deterrence." The credibility of this debate assumes greater significance in the light of what Maj Gen Zhu Chenghu said while speaking about China's response to a US attack on Chinese territory. He expressed the view that China would respond with nuclear weapons. While the Chinese government clarified that Zhu's views were just his personal opinions, most analysts believe that what he said was with tacit approval from China's leaders. "They think it's good to have a mad dog in your closet who might scare your potential adversaries," said retired Admiral Dennis Blair, former commander-in-chief of the US Pacific Command, who had heard Zhu make similar comments earlier too. "It always helps your leverage if your adversaries think you might do something stupid."[51]

Nuclear Force Modernisation

Despite the lack of solid, publicly available evidence, it is well accepted by almost all the China watchers among Western analysts that the Chinese government is modernising and expanding its nuclear arsenal. It is systematically fielding more sophisticated ballistic missiles capable of striking India, Russia and almost the entire continental US. According to the Department of Defence's (DoD's) 2006 annual report to the US Congress, in 2004-05, China increased the number of mobile CSS-6 and CSS-7 SRBMs deployed on the coast opposite Taiwan from 500 to between 600 and 700. The Chinese are now producing and deploying about 100 SRBMs per year. They are also concentrating on further improving the range and accuracy of the missiles. With the induction of advanced Russian Su-30 and Su-27 fighter jets and the new indigenous fighter, the F-10, China now has more than 700 aircraft that can fly to Taiwan without refuelling. According to US military analysts, the mobile DF-31 and DF-31A ICBMs, both of which are expected to become operational by 2007-08, are of even greater concern. As these ICBMs are mobile, they are not as vulnerable to destruction by a first strike as older ones that are silo-based. The new missiles will give China a genuine second-strike capability against the US and other nuclear powers. Also, China is likely to respond to the US decision to deploy a limited ballistic missile defence (BMD) by increasing both the number of missiles and launchers and the number of nuclear warheads on missiles able to reach the US by means of MIRVs so as to saturate the BMD system with multiple simultaneous attacks. The Central Intelligence Agency (CIA) has assessed that China could enhance the number of warheads designed to deter the US from about 20 at present to between 75 and 100 in the next decade.[52] It is also likely to enhance research into decoys, chaff and manoeuvrable warheads. Whether China will itself develop a BMD system in the future is a possibility that is difficult to predict with any degree of certainty at present.

Expeditionary Ambitions

The PLA's expeditionary forces include three airborne divisions, two amphibious infantry divisions, two marine brigades, about seven special operations groups, and one regimental-size reconnaissance element in the Second Artillery. Besides training for an invasion of Taiwan, these forces are being prepared for employment to seize or regain the Spratly and Paracel Islands in the South China Sea and, in future, to guarantee China's uniterupted access to the sea lanes through the Malacca Strait for oil and gas supplies and maritime trade. At present, Chinese access to the Malacca Strait depends on US acquiescence as the US Navy dominates and controls the oceans outside China's territorial waters. As freedom of the seas has become a fundamental national interest for China, it would prefer to safeguard vitally important sea lanes on its own rather than be dependent on the goodwill of another major power, which it sees as inimcal to its interests. It can be said with a fair degree of certainty that China's military build-up is broadening the reach of its forces in Asia and poses a long-term challenge not only to Taiwan but also to other military forces operating in the Pacific and to regional powers such as India and Japan.

Domination of Space

On January 11, 2007, China launched an anti-satellite rocket that intercepted and physically destroyed an ageing Feng Yun 1C weather satellite belonging to China in low earth orbit in outer space.[53]It appeared to have been a kinetic strike that physically hit the satellite and shattered it into thousands of pieces, spraying the space around with a huge cloud of debris. Though this spectacular event cannot be classified as a statement of intent, it was certainly a statement of capability. It sends out a clear signal that China will thwart the growing US desire to deploy ballistic missile defences by asymmetric means. Chinese anti-satellite capabilities have been suspected for many years. It has now emerged quite clearly that China is engaged in developing space warfare capabilities and has acquired the expertise necessary to destroy satellites in low earth orbit where most military reconnaissance satellites are normally deployed. It would be reasonable to deduce that China will use this capability to offset its conventional asymmetry with the US and its allies that are so heavily dependent on space-based C4ISR for their military operations.

Participation in UN Peace-Keeping

Over the last 10 years, China has steadily increased its contribution to United Nations peace-keeping operations. China now has some 1,000 civilian police and support personnel serving as peace-keepers abroad, including 595 attached to the UN Observer Mission in Liberia (UNMIL), 230 with the UN Observer Mission in the Democratic Republic of the Congo (MONUC), and 127 as part of the UN Mission for Stabilisation in Haiti (MINUSTAH). China is said to be considering committing troops to peace-keeping operations in Sudan, provided this meets with approval from the African Union and the Government of Sudan.

Conclusion

China is already a major Asian power and is on the fast track to achieving world power status in the 21st century. Not much has changed since Ngok Lee wrote over a decade and a half ago:[54] "As a nuclear power with limited second-strike capability, China has reinforced its position as a force to be reckoned with by the superpowers." As most of China's development has led to the rise of important political and economic centres in the coastal regions, "China's military strategy has shifted from defending the continent to defending areas on China's periphery and maritime force projection… PLA strategists expect such conflicts to be characterized by limited political objectives and the use of information technology and by being highly mobile, lethal, and resource intensive."[55]

In cases where Chinese use of force involves core interests, such as sovereignty or territorial claims (including Taiwan), Beijing could claim military preemption as a strategically defensive option. However, China is simultaneously concentrating on giving greater play to softer diplomatic options so as to allay fears that its rise may be accompanied by violence and instability. Chinese operational-level military doctrine defines such options as "non-war" use of force – an extension of political coercion and not an act of war. Examples of such non-war use of force can be seen in the 1995 and 1996 amphibious exercises and missile firings in the Taiwan Strait. Chinese doctrinal materials suggest this concept of non-war use of force goes beyond missile firings to include air and missile strikes, assassinations and sabotage.

While the Chinese continue to claim that their intentions are peaceful, that they continue to believe in peaceful coexistence and that they wish to integrate their economy with the international economy to lift their people out of poverty, their burgeoning military capability and muscular military posture has given the world cause for concern. China's past track record has not been such that it inspires visions of a peaceful Chinese rise to world power status. A pragmatic conclusion would be that as China's capabilities grow, its leaders could consider using force or threats to use force to achieve their strategic objectives.

Notes

1. Michael D. Swaine and Ashley J. Tellis, *Interpreting China's Grand Strategy: Past, Present and Future* (RAND: Santa Monica, CA, 2000), p. 1. (Emphasis in the original.)
2. Peng Guangqian and Yao Youzhi, eds., *The Science of Military Strategy* (Beijing: Military Science Publishing House, 2005), p. 77.
3. Christine A. Cleary, "Culture, Strategy and Security," in Paul J. Bolt and Albert S. Wiiner, eds., *China's Nuclear Future* (Boulder, Colorado: Lynne Rienner Publishers, Inc., 2006), p. 16.
4. Yang Jiemian, "International Environment and Sino-US Interaction: Strategic Thinking and Policy Planning," *China International Studies*, Winter 2005, p. 61.
5. *Military Power of the People's Republic of China* (Office of the Secretary of Defence, United States Department of Defence: Annual Report to Congress, 2002). The report explains "*shi*" as the "alignment of forces," the "propensity of things," or the "potential born of disposition," that only a skilled strategist can exploit to ensure victory over a superior force. Similarly, only a sophisticated assessment by an adversary can recognise the potential exploitation of "*shi*."
6. Swaine and Tellis, n. 1, p. x.
7. n. 5.
8. Khadang Oh Hassig, "Northeast Asian Security Environment," Defence Threat Reduction Agency Study, August 22, 2001, www.dtra.mi/about/organization/asian.pdf.

9. Swaine and Tellis, n. 1, p. 112.

10. Swaine and Tellis, Ibid.

11. Yoichi Funabashi, "China is Preparing for Peaceful Ascendancy," *International Herald Tribune*, December 30, 2003. Also see Swaine and Tellis, Ibid.

12. David Shambaugh, *Modernising China's Military: Progress, Problems and Prospects* (New Delhi: Bookmart Publishers, 2004), p. 292.

13. Li Qinggong, "A Review of and Prospects for the World Military Situation," I*nternational Strategic Studies*, January 2000, pp. 29-33, cited by Shambaugh, Ibid., p. 295. For other PLA views, see Shambaugh, Ibid., pp. 295-297.

14. *China's National Defence in 2006*, White Paper on National Defence published by the Government of the People's Republic of China on December 30, 2006.

15. Ibid.

16. Personal interview with the author on April 30, 2007.

17. Kenneth W. Allen, Glenn Krumel and Jonathan D. Pollack, *China's Air Force Enters the 21st Century* (Santa Monica, CA: RAND, 1995), p. 24.

18. John Wilson Lewis and Xue Litai, "China's Search for a Modern Air Force", *International Security*, vol. 24, no. 1, Summer 1999, p. 78.

19. Lewis and Litai, Ibid., p. 29.

20. David Shambaugh, "China's Security and Military Policy and Potential for CBMs in the Region," *Asian Security Series* (Washington D.C.: Henry L. Stimson Centre), December 1996.

21. US DoD report to Congress Pursuant to the FY2000 National Defence Authorisation Act, http://www.defenselink.mil/news/Jun2000/china06222000.htm

22. United States Department of Defence, *Annual Report to Congress: The Military Power of the People's Republic of China 2004*, Section II: Trends in Military Strategy, Doctrine and Training – China's Military Strategy.

23. Ka Po Ng, *Interpreting China's Military Power: Doctrine Makes Readiness* (Abingdon, Oxon: Frank Cass, 2005), p. 21.

24. Western governments and analysts are using both the terms "informationisation" and "informationalisation" interchangeably. It has not been possible to get an exact equivalent to the corresponding Chinese phrase from an authoritative source. From the point of view of language aesthetics and phonetics, the term informationisation is preferred here.

25. n. 5, p. 5.

26. Zhou Fangyin, "The Impact of Information Revolution Upon Military Affairs and Security," *Contemporary International Relations*, July 7, 2001, p. 28.

27. "China's Military Power: An Assessment From Open Sources," Testimony of

Richard D. Fisher, Jr., International Assessment and Strategy Centre, before the Armed Services Committee of the US House of Representatives, July 27, 2005; www.strategycenter.net.

28. Ng, n. 23, p. 109.

29. Ng, Ibid., p. 110.

30. Ng, Ibid., p. 111.

31. Barbara Opall-Rome, "PLA Pursues Acupuncture Warfare," *Defense News* (Springfield, Virginia USA), March 1, 1999.

32. "According to the Taiwanese Ministry of National Defence, China is shifting from deterrence-based strategy to preemptive strike strategy… Paralysis warfare features web-based information warfare, saturation ballistic missile attacks, joint precision strikes and seizure of the enemy's capital city by special operation units… Such tactics will become major options for the Chinese military in its choice of modes of modes of attack…" Srikanth Kondapalli, *A Great Leap Forward Modernization: China's Armed Forces in 2003* (Taiwan: Centre for China Studies, National Chengchi University, 2005), p. 27, cited from Brian Hsu, "China Developing 'Paralysis Warfare,'" *Taipei Times*, October 8, 2003, FBIS-CHI-2003-1008, October 10, 2003.

33. Jason Sherman, "Report: China Developing Force to Tackle Information Warfare," *Defense News*, November 27, 2000.

34. Robert Karniol, "Power to the People," *Jane's Defence Weekly* (Surrey, UK), July 12, 2000.

35. Edward Timperlake and William C. Triplett III, *Red Dragon Rising: Communist China's Military Threat to America* (Washington D.C.: Regnery Publishing Inc., 1999).

36. J.S. Bajwa, *Modernisation of the PLA: Gauging its Latent Future Potential* (New Delhi: Lancer Publishers, 2002), p. 216. (Cited from Michael Pillsbury, "PLA Capabilities in the 21st Century: How Does China Assess its Future Security Needs?" article in Larry M. Wortzel, ed., *The Chinese Armed Forces in the 21st Century,* pp. 113-114).

37. Narendra Singh, "Chinese Armed Forces," *USI Journal* (New Delhi), October-December 1998, pp. 587-608.

38. Rupert Smith, *The Utility of Force: The Art of War in the Modern World* (London: Allen Lane, 2005), reviewed by C. Raja Mohan, "Ways to War," *Indian Express*, June 18, 2006.

39. Robert Cooper, "The Utility of Force by General Rupert Smith," *The Sunday Times*, September 18, 2005, http://www.timesonline.co.uk/article/0,,23112-1779750,00.html

40. http://en.wikipedia.org/wiki/People's_Liberation_Army

41. Ibid.

42. Ibid.

43. Kondapalli, n.32, p. 27, cited from Ku Guisheng, "The New Change in MI Affairs Calls for the Renewal of the Organizational Set-up of China's Military," *Liaowang*, July 28, 2003, FBIS-CHI-2003-0805, August 15, 2003.

44. Kondapalli, Ibid., cited from Zhong Hailin, "Naval Development Trends of the New Century," *Liaowang*, July 21, 2003, FBIS-CHI-2003-0730, October 6, 2003.

45. "Russia-China Joint Military Exercises," Worldpress.org, http://www.worldpress. org/Asia/2138.cfm, accessed October 30, 2005.

46. Ann Scott Tyson, "Chinese Build-up Seen as Threat to Region," *Washington Post*, July 20, 2005.

47. Anil K. Joseph, "PLA to Project Chinese Power in Asia: Pentagon," *The Times of India*, December 8, 1998.

48. Kondapalli, n. 43, p. 45.

49. "China Sub Stalked US Fleet," *The Washington Times*, November 13, 2006.http:// www.washtimes.com/national/20061113-121539-3317r.htm

50. Shen Dingli, "Nuclear Deterrence in the 21st Century," *China Security*, Autumn 2005

51. Tyson, n.46.

52. Brad Roberts, "Alternative Futures", in Paul J. Bolt and Albert S. Wiiner, eds., *China's Nuclear Future* (Boulder, Colorado: Lynne Rienner Publishers, Inc., 2006), p. 173-174.

53. For an analysis from an Indian point of view, see "ASAT Test and China's Strategic Ambitions," *Strategic Comments* (New Delhi: Institute for Defence Studies and Analyses), February 13, 2007, http://www.idsa.in/publications/stratcomments/JagannathPanda120207.htm

54. Ngok Lee, *China's Defence Modernization and Military Leadership* (Rushcutters Bay, NSW: Pergamon Press, Australia, Pty Ltd, 1989), p. 260.

55. Roger Cliff, Mark Burles, Michael S. Chase, Derek Eaton and Kevin L. Pollpeter, *The Dragon's Lair: Chinese Anti-Access Strategies and Their Implications for the United States* (Santa Monica: RAND, 2007), pp. 16-17.

2
Defence Production in Pakistan

Shalini Chawla

After being established as a sovereign state in August 1947, Pakistan inherited a small portion of an otherwise miniscule defence industry in India. The perceived security threats and security concerns, along with the desire to be self-sufficient, became the main reasons for the build-up of indigenous capability in Pakistan. According to the former Army Chief Gen Abdul Waheed, "It is a time-tested fact that no country can maintain her armed forces on borrowed weapons. To be self-confident in the community of nations Pakistan must become self-sufficient in defence production."[1] This paper aims to study the evolution and development of Pakistan's indigenous defence capability with regard to conventional weapons.

Early efforts in the direction can be traced to the tenure of the first Prime Minister of Pakistan, Liaquat Ali Khan, who issued a directive to establish an ordnance factory to manufacture .303 calibre rifles and their ammunition in Rawalpindi. After Khan's assassination, the second Prime Minister of Pakistan, Khawaja Nizam-ud-Din proceeded with the plans, and in 1951, the foundation stone of four industries at Wah Cantonment was laid and four workshops were opened. Presently, Pakistan has 14 large factories and subsidiaries fulfilling the defence needs of its armed forces.

Eventually, the industrial complex at Wah was started, and by 1954, a few other facilities were completed. The production of various stores such as 25 Pdr and 40 mm anti-aircraft guns, ammunition, 2" and 3" mortar bombs, etc was started. In the early 1960s, the explosive factory, which included the manufacture of nitric acid, sulphuric acid recycling plants for recovery of waste acids, plants for production of intermediates such as acetone, ether, and plants for production of propellants and explosives were set up with foreign assistance.[2] However, the decades of the 1950s and 1960s did not witness much growth of defence production facilities. Pakistan remained dependent on external powers even for very basic and simple arms and ammunition. In this period, the nation's defence needs were met mostly by the United States. The suspension of military aid and the arms embargoes during and after the 1965 War comprised a major driving factor for the nation to go in for self-reliance in military production and also for the diversification of the sources of arms procurement. While Pakistan was receiving support from the United Sates, the domestic industry was given less importance, but after the US assistance was cut off, defence production was accorded priority, and insistence on self-sufficiency increased. President Zulfiquar Ali Bhutto pursued a conscious policy towards domestic arms production. Bhutto was motivated towards indigenous production because, firstly, he realised that being constantly hostage to external powers meant that war-fighting potential was severely restricted (as happened in 1965 and 1971). Secondly, he wanted to control the Bonapartist tendencies in the Pakistan Army. Thirdly, he thought the defence infrastructure development would have a positive effect on the overall economic development of the country. And, fourthly, he viewed Pakistan as an influential actor in the Islamic world in the future, and modern weaponry, he believed, would enable Pakistan to successfully play the role of the *praetorian guard of the Islamic bloc*.[3] Thus, a Defence Production Division in the Ministry of Defence was created in 1972 (see Fig 1). Bhutto also established joint defence industries in other Muslim countries like Iran and Turkey in 1975.[4]

Gen Zia-ul-Haq accorded high priority to building defence capability. Defence expenditure increased substantially during his tenure. He believed in building up the self-reliance of the nation and, thus, several indigenisation projects were promoted. Domestic capability build-up was boosted but this was not at the cost of equipment technology acquisition arrangements with the USA and the People's Republic of China (PRC), but complementary to them. The nation's defence industry increasingly became the "training post" for technology.[5] The 1980s and 1990s saw a wide expansion of defence production activities and a large number of varied projects were undertaken in this period.

Fig 1: Defence Production Division

Federal Minister for Defence		
Federal Secretary (Defence Production Division)		
Additional Secretary (1&2)	Director-General (Defence Procurement)	Director General (Munitions Production)
Pakistan Ordnance Factories	Director Procurement (Army)	Director Munitions Production (Army)
Heavy Industries, Taxila	Director Procurement (Navy)	Director Munitions Production (Navy)
Pakistan Aeronautical Complex	Director Procurement (Air Force)	Director Munitions Production (Air Force)
Margalla Electronics	Procurement Field Office	
Institute of Optronics	Director General Procurement (Army)	
Armament Research and Development Establishment	Director Procurement (Navy)	
Military Vehicles Research and Development Establishment	Director Procurement (Air Force)	
Defence Science & Technology Organisation		

Source: Ayesha Siddiqa-Agha, *Pakistan's Arms Procurement and Military Buildup, 1979-99; In Search of a Policy* (New York: Palgrave, 2001), p. 44.

Ministry of Defence Production

The birth of the Ministry of Defence Production can be traced to1972 with the creation of the Defence Production Division. The division was given the mandate to lay down policy, formulate plans, and coordinate between procurement and development and also to accelerate technical development in order to build up indigenous capability. Later, the Ministry of Defence Production was formally established with the Defence Production Division as its main establishment.

The primary roles of the ministry are:

- To provide the base for maximum self-reliance and production of defence material.
- To accelerate the pace of technological development to contemporary levels.
- To identify, integrate and utilise the industrial potential available in the public and private sectors for production and procurement of defence stores and equipment.
- To attain economy of scales through optimum production.[6]

Facilities

Starting with an establishment at Wah, in cooperation with British Royal Ordnance, a number of defence production facilities were developed in Pakistan. Today, there are over 20 public sector units and over 100 private sector units engaged in the production of defence related products. The major public sector units which have expanded significantly and contributed towards self-reliance of the defence industry are briefly outlined in the succeeding paragraphs.

Pakistan Ordnance Factories

The Pakistan Ordnance Factories (POF), comprising 14 factories, is the oldest and the largest complex of defence production units in the country. Progressively set up after 1950 on the model of the Indian Ordnance Factories, meeting almost the total ordnance needs of the Pakistani armed forces, it is considered as the mother industry for the entire defence production spectrum. The POF completed its fifty years in 2001. The POF complex is spread over a radius of 100 km and employs more than 40,000 personnel. This complex has helped to establish and develop a number of sister defence production facilities. All the factories are controlled by the Pakistan Ordnance Factories Board comprising a chairman, a financial advisor and two career technical members. The POF Board lays down the basic guidelines to be followed in the functioning of the factories.

The 14 factories in the complex of POF which are ISO 9001 certified, consist of the following facilities:[7]

1. Weapons Factory.
2. Machine Gun Factory.
3. Small Arms Ammunition Factory.
4. Tank and Anti-Tank Ammunition Factory.
5. Medium Artillery Ammunition Factory.
6. Heavy Artillery Ammunition Factory.
7. Brass Mill.
8. Steel Foundry.
9. Tungsten Carbide Factory.
10. Tungsten Alloy Factory.
11. Explosives Factory.
12. Propellants Factory.
13. Filling Factory.
14. Clothing Factory for Uniforms.

The two main subsidiaries of the POF established to utilise the spare capacities of ordnance factories for commercial applications were Wah Industries Ltd, and Wah Nobel Ltd. Eventually, other subsidiaries came up to fulfil the requirements of the civil markets. The POF has eight subsidiaries for cartridges, detonators, explosives, chemicals, etc. They produce around 70 major items and millions of components for supply to the Pakistan Army, Navy and Air Force. Apart from the raw material, every other input like steel products, carbide, fuses, rocket and artillery propellants, all kinds of explosives, required for the manufacture of the arms and ammunition are produced by this facility.[8]

Initially, POF products were mostly of British origin, produced under licence. With the infusion of massive arms aid from the US since the mid-1950s, Pakistan's military switched over almost entirely to American weapons and equipment. Consequently, the POF also changed over to US standards, military specifications and products. Within a decade, it was forced to diversify to Chinese and European products after the US embargo consequent to Pakistan's military aggression in 1965. The calibres of most of the Chinese weapons and ordnance (which followed the Soviet system) were different from the North Atlantic Treaty Organisation (NATO)/US calibres. The POF inevitably had to sustain multiple production facilities to cater to a large variety of weapons, calibres and standards. This was obviously economically inefficient in view of the small production runs for different munitions. In turn, this provided the incentive for exports to enlarge production runs and compensate costs. At present, POF products follow both NATO and other international standards.[9]

The POF product range includes:

- Weapons, which include submachine guns MP5A2 to MP5P5, machine gun MG3, SMG-PK, automatic rifle G3A3 & G3P4, machine gun 12.7 mm type 54, and small arms ammunition.
- Mortar bombs: 60 mm mortar HE, 60 mm smoke WP, 122 mm smoke WP M44A1, 120 mm HEM44A2.
- Artillery ammunition.
- Air and anti-aircraft ammunition.
- Tank and anti-tank ammunition.
- Hand grenades, pyrotechnics and demolition store, fuses, detonators and primers, propellants and explosives.
- Clothing.[10]

The POF also produces a large variety of commercial explosives, dynamites and detonators, inclusive of industrial chemicals, in its Wah Nobel subsidiary, a joint venture with Nobel of Sweden.[11] Its manufacturing capabilities also include hunting ammunition, brass, copper and aluminium ingots, extrusions and sections for non-military applications. The garments factory in the POF complex manufactures military uniforms and can potentially cater to the civilians' demands. All the 14 factories and 6 departments within the complex of the POF are ISO 9001 certified.[12] The POF also provides commercial services which include, technical and professional training and laboratory testing.[13] In fact, this industrial complex stands as the largest reservoir of a technical workforce and professional engineers in all fields of engineering in the country. The deplorable status of the foreign exchange situation and the Western sanctions on the export of raw material to the country led the defence planners to develop the indigenisation programme. The aim of this programme has been to be self-sufficient in raw materials and semi-finished goods. The POF has been encouraging the development of the local vending industry in order to utilise their assets for manufacturing parts of arms and ammunition.[14] Setting up joint ventures in and outside the country has also been motivated by the need to acquire knowhow, materials and finances.

The POF has always been seen to engage in joint ventures starting with the Royal Ordnance Factories, UK, in 1951, and set up the first plant for the production of .303 ammunition and the corresponding weapons.[15] Small arms production facilities for 7.62 calibre ammunition to NATO standards was set up with Germany. This was followed by various other joint ventures with China and Czechoslovakia. The Heavy Ammunition Factory at Sanjwal, located 25 km from Wah, was initially set up with help from Czechoslovakia and manufactures heavy artillery ammunition. This factory produces "shell bodies, cases, and major components for 105 mm howtizer HE, 100 mm HE and 10 mm HESH for tanks, 60 mm and 81 mm mortars and smoke grenades and aircraft bombs."[16] Since 1988, low drag bombs (US pattern) started being manufactured under US licence. Plans were reported for the manufacture of Pakistan Air Force (PAF) F-16 aircraft related ammunition.[17]

Another example of a joint venture is the Propellant Factory at Havelian (60 km northeast of Wah). This was set up with Czech assistance and equipment for the production of single base propellant. After 1965, this facility was expanded with Chinese assistance and the plant was to produce double based propellant at a capacity of 1,500 tons/year.[18] The POF also has a joint venture with M/s SAAB of Sweden for the production of commercial explosives such as dynamite, etc.

Pakistan established its first joint venture abroad with Saudi Arabia at the facility at Al Kharg. This facility manufactures arms and ammunition of different types, including 7.62 calibre machine guns and G-3 rifles. Reports suggest that the POF is now more confident and keen to undertake joint ventures outside Pakistan and, thus, more such joint ventures will be established in the future.[19] However, these are likely to be focussed more on the Islamic countries which are capable and willing to make the necessary financial investments.

Arms export has been adopted as a major policy measure for the development of the POF. Lt Gen Abdul Qayyum, chairman of the POF Board, in his interview with *Military Technology*, stated, "POF is primarily responsible to meet the defence needs of our armed forces. Its secondary mission, however, is utilisation of surplus capacity of machines and plants for commercial purposes, including exports."[20] The POF has been effectively participating in the defence exhibitions in the UK, Far East (including Southeast Asia), South Africa, etc. It has established sales agents in all the potential world markets. This has led to enhanced attention of international traders to buy POF produced arms and ammunitions. It has been exporting to more than 30 countries across the world. POF exports ranged between $15 million to $30 million a year by 2002 and they have the potential of earning from $50 million to $100 million annually through exports of arms and ammunition.[21] Nations importing from the POF include: Bahrain, Bangladesh, Cambodia, Canada, Denmark, Germany, Hong Kong, Switzerland, Singapore, Sri Lanka, UAE, Indonesia, Jordan, Kuwait, Malaysia, Myanmmar, Saudi Arabia, UK and USA.

The POF has been consistently making efforts toward increased cooperation between the public and private sectors. Lt Gen Abdul Qayyum, chairman of the POF Board, on a visit to the Karachi Chamber of Commerce and Industry (KCCI), invited the private sector to come forward and identify the areas of cooperation. He also agreed to support the private sector in the manufacture of textile machinery and parts in Pakistan.[22] The POF is keen on cooperation with the private sector because, firstly, it would be helpful in attaining self-sufficiency; secondly, the private sector would benefit with the transfer of technology; and thirdly, the POF would extend its linkages in the international market and, thus, the POF exports will benefit through a wider market. The POF has also apparently extended an invitation to the Islamic countries to benefit from Pakistan's defence production potential. It has invited the business community of the Islamic countries to join and utilise the surplus capacities of the POF for manufacturing defence equipment.[23]

Heavy Industries Taxila (HIT)

This facility, located near Taxila, was set up with the help of China. Until the mid-1960s Pakistan was receiving imported tanks, initially from the US (the M-47 and M-48 Patton class in the 1950s and the 1960s) and then from the Chinese (the T-59, which was produced in China from the Soviet T-54 design built under licence).[24] In 1971, Heavy Rebuild Factory Project (P-711) was conceived with Chinese assistance and technology to rebuild T-59 tanks. As the fleet of T-59 tanks manufactured by China grew, the Heavy Rebuild Factory (HRF) was established in Taxila in the late 1970s, mainly to undertake rebuilding and modernisation of tanks.[25] The facility is spread over 48 acres of land and is capable of rebuilding tanks and power packs as well as manufacturing individual optical and electrical components. When the production started in 1981, the HRF had the capacity to rebuild 100 tanks and 250 engines every year and by October 1990, that capacity had been able to service 1,000 tanks and 2,000 engines.[26] It is claimed that out of 11,000 components used in the overhaul of the T-59, approximately 8,000 are now manufactured locally.[27] More recently, the HRF at Taxila was renamed Heavy Industries Taxila (HIT). The overhauling of the Patton tanks and the upgrading of the T-59s was being done in critical areas, with technical assistance from China, America and Britain in the five key areas[28]

(i) The 100mm tank gun which fires standard NATO ammunition and is manufactured by the POF.

(ii) The fighting compartment fitted with a fire/explosion, detection and suppression system which was lacking earlier.

(iii) Thermal sights fitted in place of the first generation infrared devices.

(iv) A computerised fire control system with a laser range finder.

(v) A stabilisation system fitted to all stationary and moving targets to be engaged with a high probability of first round hit.

HIT, which employs over 7,000 workers, and is basically devoted to land combat systems, witnessed a rapid growth in the 1980s when it started to produce the T-69 MBT(main battle tank) with Chinese help. The T-69 11MP tank is fitted with a special engine and also special armour to enhance armour protection.[29] In the beginning of 1989, the then Army Chief, Gen Mirza Aslam Beg made an announcement that Pakistan would come out with its own indigenously built tank within a period of two years. A prototype of the T-69 11 MP was to come out "by the end of December 1990. A protocol was signed with China that included the establishment of the five factories: Hull Fabrication Factory (HFF), Turret Manufacturing Factory, Engine Manufacturing Factory, Gun Barrel Manufacturing Factory and Flexible Machining Centre."[30] HRF's capabilities were substantially enhanced with the acquisition of skills and experience in the field of production facilities and covering firepower, mobility and protection. As a result, it grew into a multi-factory complex and was renamed Heavy Industries Taxila in 1992. The current and future planned production of the HIT include the following products:

(a) **Tank "Al Khalid".** The Al Khalid was the outcome of the decade-long Sino-Pakistan efforts. In 1988, the announcement for manufacture of a new MBT (MBT 2000- Al Khalid) with the assistance of China was followed by the agreement signed in 1990 with China North Industries Corporation (NORINCO).[31] A four phased approach was adapted by Pakistan instead of building a new MBT, which involved: (i) upgrade of the existing Type 59 MBT; (ii) assembly/manufacture of the Type 69-II MBT (this has 50 per cent of its component from the Type 59, and 50 per cent new components); (iii) co-production and manufacture of the Type 85 MBT (this has 20 per cent components from the Type 59, 30 per cent from the Type 69-II MBT, and 50 per cent new components); (iv) production of the MBT 2000 with 45 per cent of its components taken from existing vehicles (10 per cent Type 59, 15 per cent Type 69-II and 20 per cent Type 85) and 55 per cent new components.[32]

Al Khalid was to operate in areas with high ambient temperature and dust and, thus, special emphasis was placed on the design and installation of high capacity cooling and efficient air clearing systems. The first prototype of the MBT-2000, also referred to as the P-90, was completed in 1991, and, subsequently, the trials were carried out in 1992. In many respects, the MBT 2000 appears to be almost identical to the Chinese NORINCO Type 90-II MBT. During the development phase of Al Khalid, a number of prototypes of the vehicles were built and tested in various configurations. The first 15 pre-production Al Khalid MBTs were handed over to the Pakistan Army in July 2001.[33]

(b) **Tank "Al Zarrar".** The Al Zarrar, again a product of Chinese assistance, came into being to keep the fleet of T-59 and T-69 tanks technologically and operationally compatible with modern tanks. The Al Zarrar configurations were built to give the user the maximum possible flexibility in making a decision on the systems to be installed in production vehicles. It carried the upgrades which not only are an improvement on the combat capabilities of the Type 59 but also an improvement on overall reliability of the vehicle and reduced maintenance.[34] The first batch of 80 indigenously modernised and upgraded Al Zarrar tanks was handed over to the Pakistan Army at the Heavy Industries Taxila in February 2004, symbolising the contribution of the facility towards Pakistan's self-reliance in defence production.[35]

(c) **APC "Talha".** The Heavy Industries Taxila has extensive experience in the local production and assembly of the American LP M113 series of armoured personnel carriers (APCs) and also a number of locally developed variants. Exploring this experience, the facility has developed to a prototype stage, a new armoured personnel carrier called the Talha.[36]The Talha is an indigenously designed and manufactured all-terrain, amphibious infantry support vehicle with the 12.7 mm machine gun as its main armament.[37]

(d) **Local Production of M113A2.** In 1989, Pakistan signed an agreement to build 775 APCs M113A2 MK1 under licence from United Defence LP of the United States. Initially, the pilot production commenced with hulls provided by the United Defence facility at San Jose, California. Curiously, this agreement was not suspended/terminated when US sanctions were imposed in 1990. Subsequently, local manufacture of hulls started and also the assembly of the vehicle was done in the Heavy Industries Taxila, with the materials supplied from California. This vehicle has a number of additional features, including a new cooling system and improved suspension. Recently, Pakistan has developed at least two additional variants of the M113 series APC for the usage of the Pakistan Army. [38]

(e) **APC "Saad".** Pakistan has reportedly developed a six-wheeled road version APC called Saad. This has a 400 hp engine and can carry 13 personnel.[39] This vehicle will provide "mounted fighting capability" to the Pakistan Army.

(f) **Logistic Vehicle "Al Qaswa".** The Al Qawsa is a logistics vehicle, expected to enter production in the near future. According to Heavy Industries Taxila, the vehicle has a combat weight of 14.5 tonnes of which six tonnes is cargo and can be used for a wide range of other specialised roles such as gun platform, anti-tank missile launcher, radar carrier, mortar carrier and ambulance.[40]

(g) **Infantry Fighting Vehicle "Al Hamza".** This has been developed with a Chinese made one-man turret and 25 mm cannon.

(h) **WZ 653 Series ARV.** In 1995, NORINCO (from China) supplied 20 WZ 653 series armoured recovery vehicles (ARVs) to Pakistan. According to reliable sources, Pakistan obtained the licence to manufacture these and the initial batch of 45 vehicles, also referred to as the ARV-W653 in Pakistan, has been completed at HIT.[41]

Pakistan Aeronautical Complex (PAC)

The Pakistan Aeronautical Complex at Kamra, north of Islamabad was established in 1973. This facility is the nucleus of the aeronautical industry in Pakistan and is dedicated to overhaul and repair of Chinese and French aircraft in the PAF inventory. It also undertakes the manufacture of light aircraft and assembly of ground-based radars. The PAC consists of the following factories.

Mirage Rebuild Factory (MRF)

This facility began operation in 1978, when it started to overhaul the Mirage III EP combat aircraft and their SNECMA engines. The MRF has a site area of more than 810,000 square metres and employs approximately 2,000 engineers and technicians. It can undertake complete overhaul of the Mirage III/5 aircraft, Atar 9C turbojets, and all associated aircraft components and engine accessories.[42] It has been engaged in overhauling Mirage aircraft of the UAE (United Arab Emirates) Air Force and has the capacity to overhaul 8-10 aircraft and over 30 engines per year.[43] The MRF has been further updated and modified. In 1988, the technical capability to undertake the overhauling of Pratt & Whitney F100-PW-220 engines of the F-16s, acquired from the United States at a cost of $ 40 million was located in the MRF, thus, modifying the capacity of the facility.[44]

F-6 Rebuild Factory (F-6RF)

The F-6 Rebuild Factory i.e. the F-6RF, is an important facility at Kamra, established with Chinese assistance in 1980. The primary purpose of the F-6RF has been the overhaul of the PAF's Shenyang F-6 aircraft and their accessories (Soviet MiG-17 built under licence in China and sold to Pakistan). Apart from the machine tools, this establishment possesses modern technical capabilities for several engineering processes employed in aircraft manufacture such as surface treatment, heat treatment and casting.[45] The F-6RF has been expanded to a workforce of over 2,500 personnel, including professional engineers and technologists, and has been overhauling and rebuilding the PAF's FT-5s (MiG-15 trainers), FT-6s (MiG-17 trainers) and A-5Cs (MiG17 modified by China), FT-7P (Chinese MiG 21 trainer) combat aircraft, their components and instruments. It also manufactures metallic/rubber parts required during overhaul of aircraft.[46]

Aircraft Manufacturing Factory (AMF)

The Aircraft Manufacturing Factory, was established in 1975, with the objective of assembling the Mushshak (MFI-17) light aircraft/ basic trainer with knockdown kits received from foreign sources. It is the only aircraft manufacturing concern in Pakistan and since 1981, it has been engaged in the manufacture of the light, robust, basic trainer-cum-surveillance aircraft Mushshak and the Super Mushshak – a variant with a more powerful engine cockpit air conditioning, electric instruments and several other improvements.[47] The AMF bought the sole manufacturing rights from Sweden and built aircraft for Pakistan's military and also for export to Iran, Oman and Syria.[48] By early 1989, the Pakistan Army and Air Force had around 175 Mushshak aircraft in service, and the AMF was producing around 16 aircraft per year.[49] The AMF also developed the Super Mushshak with a more powerful engine and new facilities. It has excellent facilities to rebuild and repair the Mushshak at factory level and also cater to the after sales spares support to the existing Mushshak operators.[50] The AMF also entered into the production of the Karakoram-8 jet trainer, in collaboration with the China National Aero-Technology Import & Export Corporation (CATIC). The jet trainer was initially launched as the NAMC L-8 in 1987 in the Paris Air Show and subsequently proposed to be co-developed in partnership with Pakistan (with 25 per cent share). The jet trainer was redesignated K-8 and named after the mountain range in Jammu and Kashmir.[51] It is also manufacturing low speed target drones, the Baaz and Ababeel, for aerial target practice. The AMF is capable of designing and manufacturing complicated aircraft due to the latest CAD/CAM and silicon graphics facilities[52]

The Joint Fighter (JF-17) Thunder, also known as the Fighter–China-1 (FC-1) Fierce Dragon in China, is a single-seat multi-role fighter aircraft co-developed by Pakistan and China. The first two aircraft were delivered to the Pakistan Air Force on March 12, 2007. The JF-17 is designated to be a low cost fighter to meet the tactical and strategic requirements of the Pakistan Air Force. There have been reports that the design was developed by the MiG complex in Russia and transferred to

China after the Russian Air Force cancelled procurements.[53] It is fitted with the RD-33 engine (also installed in MiG-29 fighters). The project is expected to cost about US $500 million, divided equally between China and Pakistan. Each individual aircraft is expected to have a fly-away cost of less than US $ 15-20 million.[54] Although Pakistan has plans to procure 150 aircraft, there are signs of the number going up to as high as 300. According to reports, the JF-17 will replace Pakistan's Nanchang A-5 (Q-5) and Mirage III/V currently in service in the PAF, and Chinese supplied F-7 (MiG-21) at a later date. The first 150 aircraft are expected to be in service by 2015.[55] Potential importers for JF-17 are Egypt, Bangladesh, Burma and Algeria.

Kamra Avionics and Radar Factory (KARF)

The Kamra Avionics and Radar Factory (KARF) began operating in 1987 and deals with radar manufacturing, radar overhauls, building complex components and doctrine modules, Caterpillar/Siemens power generators and high-tech air-borne avionics for the PAF. The key production areas for the KARF cover:

Radar Warning Receiver. The RWR BM/KJ 8602 system is designed to provide the pilot with real-time and unambiguous threat warning over 360 degrees, thus, reducing vulnerability of the combat aircraft to radar associated weapons.

Grifo-7 Radar. The Grifo-7 radar was launched at IDEAS 2000 and is a joint venture of the Italian firm M/S FIAR and Kamra Avionics and Radar Factory, Pakistan Aeronautical Complex. The production equipment used for the Grifo-7 is generic in nature and can also be utilised for the production of other electronics/avionics systems.[56] The Grifo-7 radar is a coherent digital fire control system, designed to improve the air-to-air and air-to-ground performance of the F-7 PG (Chinese MiG 21 version) combat aircraft. The radar system provides an air combat mode with two different acquisition modes which are "bore-sight" and "super search."[57] The Grifo-7 radar has been produced with the objective of equipping 46 F-7 PG aircraft with the radar, together with approximately 45 Mirage IIIOs. The facility has also been offering the radar for Mirage III upgrade programmes "worldwide."[58] The radar is expected to be installed on the Russia-China-Pakistan JF-17 Thunder multi-role light combat aircraft.

Heavy Mechanical Complex (HMC) Ltd.

The Heavy Mechanical Complex (HMC) Ltd., located in Taxila is not officially part of the defence production establishment since it is a major heavy engineering subsidiary of the State Engineering Corporation (SEC), controlled by the Ministry of Industries and Production, Government of Pakistan. This was established in 1979 with Chinese assistance and is the largest undertaking of this type in Pakistan.[59] But the Heavy Forge Factory at this complex is significantly important for Pakistan's defence production requirements. The HMC is capable of undertaking the designing, engineering and manufacturing of industrial plants and machinery. This also possesses the largest fabrication and machining facilities in the nation with computer aided designing (CAD) capabilities. It manufactures equipment for a large variety of areas, including, hydro-electric power plants, thermal power plants, oil and gas processing plants, steel structure and railway equipment, etc. [60]

Institute of Optronics

The Institute of Optronics was established to assemble/manufacture the night vision devices for the armed forces in 1985, at Rawalpindi. The institute has established production and testing facilities "based on second generation image intensifier tubes" to meet a series of military specifications and needs for night vision devices.

Pakistan has being pursuing an indigenous programme for the development and manufacture of components of the night vision devices. The institute has also been working on the development of facilities for night vision devices based on thermal imaging techniques for all types of armoured vehicles and helicopters.[61]

Margalla Electronics (ME)

Based in Islamabad, Margalla Electronics was established in 1984 as a self-reliance project under the Defence Production Division to support the defence Services in the field of electronics. The facility undertakes:

- Repair and rebuild of electronic equipment used by the Services.
- Applied research to improve equipment performance and reliability.
- Original design and production.[62]

This facility has been working at a slow pace and its utility has been under question. In the 1990s, there was a debate about closing this facility; but due to some technical reasons, possibly due to its potential role in nuclear weapons, it was not wound up.[63]

Air Weapons Complex (AWC)

The Air Weapons Complex (AWC) was established in 1992 with the main focus on the generation of indigenous capabilities for evolving core technologies. Pakistan claims that the AWC has reduced its dependence on foreign sources not only for state-of-the-art weapon systems but also for weapons with modern technologies.[64] However, this is highly improbable given the complexity and technological sophistication of modern air weapons. At best, it can undertake licensed manufacture and overhaul. All the same, the AWC has a blend of professional and dynamic skills and has established itself as a key player in the field of air delivered weapons/ systems in the country. Its products include battlefield interdiction and tactical support weapons, airfield attack and denial weapons, navigation and communication systems, electronic warfare (EW) systems, infantry support equipment, unmanned aerial vehicles (UAVs) and air defence systems.[65] Its products include battlefield interdiction and tactical support weapons, airfield attack and denial munitions, navigation and communication systems, unmanned aerial vehicles, electronic warfare systems, and command, control, communications, intelligence (C4I) systems.[66]

Naval Dockyard

While the Pakistan Navy's position has received varied attention over time, overall it has been accorded low priority in the country till recent years. The navy's share is believed to be around 10 per cent in the defence budget of Pakistan.

The Pakistan Naval Dockyard is the main facility for naval weapon systems production and maintenance. It was established in 1952 and undertakes repair works, modernisation and refit of Pakistan Navy ships, submarines and craft. The first major construction work began in 1971 with the building of a floating dock. The facility has developed the capability for warship construction projects and extensive overhaul/refitment work of the naval fleet.[67] The dockyard provides technical assistance and repair of a wide variety of equipment. It is instrumental in fleet modernisation and upgradation programmes, such as installation of surface-to-surface missiles on ships and submarines, EW equipment on ships and aviation units, anti-aircraft guns, and command and control systems onboard Pakistan Navy ships. The Pakistan Naval Dockyard has a workforce of 8,000 men and has one graving and four floating docks. In the last two decades, the naval dockyard claims to have completed the overhaul/refit of 22 submarines, 27 warships, 101 missile boats, and other small naval craft.

In 1971, the naval dockyard began indigenous construction activities with support craft (1,000 tons floating dock). Over a period of time, the dockyard has produced various auxiliary and naval vessels. These include midget submarines, demagnetiser ships and 200 tons missiles craft-mines counter-measure vessels. The most prestigious production of the dockyard is the assembly under licence of the French submarine Agosta 90-B, which is a state-of-the-art submarine with the latest sensors and combat systems. *Saad*, was the first submarine to be built in Pakistan and it completed its deep sea dive test on September 19, 2003, and was commissioned on December 12, 2003. The *Hamza* (ex *Ghazi*), submarine, built at the Pakistan Navy Dockyard, was launched in December 2005 and commissioned in 2006. The parts for the two submarines, *Saad* and *Hamza,* were supplied by France in the late 1990s.[68]

The Pakistan Naval Dockyard has successfully built the Jalalat class (fast attack craft-missile) (PTG), named *Jalalat* and *Shujaat*, commissioned in 1997 and 1999 respectively. The Larkana class (large patrol craft) was also commissioned in 1994.[69] Although, China has supplied the majority of the Pakistani naval capabilities from China, France, Japan and Turkey have also been regular contributors.

Karachi Shipyard and Engineering Works (KSEW)

Karachi Shipyard and Engineering Works, was established in 1975 with the help and technical assistance of West Germany, to boost the naval manufacturing industry and fulfil Pakistan's indigenous shipbuilding and heavy engineering requirements. It undertakes shipbuilding, ship repairs, submarine and warship construction, and other engineering such as construction of infrastructure of power plants.[70]

The services of the KSEW include:

1. **Ship Building.** KSEW is actively involved in the construction of vessels of various sizes with maximum shipbuilding capacity of up to 26000TDW at its three berths. The shipbuilding activities in the KSEW fall under three categories: merchant ships, naval ships and submarines.[71] The KSEW has been manufacturing the submarine Agosta 90-B for export purposes. It has manufactured four ocean going vessels for China, two tugs for Saudi Arabia, two tugs and cargo vessels for the UAE, and Iran has received 19 naval support craft (both big and small).[72]

The capabilities built by the KSEW include:

- *Jurat and Quawwat* – Jalalat class (fast attack craft-missile) (PTG), launched in September 2004 and commissioned in 2005. These have been designed with Chinese assistance. Further development of similar craft is reportedly in process, in cooperation with the Thai company, Marsun.[73]
- *Gwadar and Kalmat* – Coastal tankers (AOTL), commissioned in 1984 and 1992 respectively.[74]
- *Janbaz and Joshila* – Coastal tugs (YTB) , commissioned in 1990 and 2000 respectively.[75]

2. **General Engineering and Foundry.** KSEW is also involved in large and well-equipped engineering workshops in the country, producing and catering to national and international clients. The main general engineering products include: sugar plant/machinery, industrial boilers, pressure vessels, cement plant spares and components, cranes, equipment for petroleum and petrochemical industry, drilling rigs, iron, steel and non-ferrous castings.[76]
3. **Ship Repairing Facilities.** KSEW undertakes under-water/above-water ship repair and maintenance work for national and international clients.[77]

National Development Complex (NDC)

The foundation of the National Development Complex (Integrated Defence Systems) was laid in 1993 with the object of developing infrastructure for indigenous development and production of modern weapon systems. The aim of the NDC has been to deliver reliable and state-of-the-art weapon systems and military hardware. The NDC, in fact, consists of a cluster of research, development, and manufacturing units under the aegis of the Pakistan Atomic Energy Commission (PAEC). The units were consolidated for the indigenous development and manufacture of modern weapon systems for Pakistan.[78] The complex manufactures a large variety of products which include missile systems, launchers, specialised aerial weapons like the area denial bomb PSD-1 and fuel-air explosive bomb FAE-1 and defence electronics [79]

In the late 1980s, Pakistan signed an agreement with China for the purchase of M-11 (estimated range of 300 km) and possibly M-9 ballistic missiles. China, in turn, facilitated the agreement by building a turnkey facility in Pakistan where such missiles could be produced.[80] In 1994, US intelligence agencies detected the construction of such a facility in Fatehjung, 40 km west of Islamabad. The configuration and design of the Fatehjung plant matched the M-11 missile facility in Hubei province in China. Technicians and engineers from the China Precision Machinery Import/Export Corporation were sighted at the plant.[81] The facility was completed in 1997-98 and is believed to produce the Hatf-III/Ghaznavi (M-11) and Hatf-IV/Shaheen-I (possibly M-9) solid fuelled ballistic missiles. Some reports suggest the sourcing of the missile parts from the cities of Lahore, Karachi and Gujranwala and finally their assembly at the Fatehjung plant. It is believed that the facility now manufactures the Chinese M-11 and M-9 ballistic missiles. The facility is developing the medium-range Shaheen-II with Chinese assistance.[82]

National Radio Telecommunication Corporation (NRTC)

The National Radio Telecommunication Corporation was established with Japanese collaboration (Nippon Electric Company) and has been producing high quality telecommunication equipment for the defence Services, Pakistan Telecommunication Corporation Ltd (PTCL) and other organisations since 1965-66.[83] Some of the important products in the field of defence are: digital electronic field telephone exchanges PFX-3208 and PFX-6416 for usage in a harsh environment, Automag 412, HF and VHF military version radios, digital radio communication systems-Fquad-450, inter-trench communication ITC 2000, etc. In the commercial field, its products include: VHF single channel radio, VHF / UHF dual channel radio, VHF mobile / base radios, DP boxes and towers.[84]

Pakistan Machine Tool Factory (PMTF) (Pvt) Ltd

The PMTF is a precision engineering goods manufacturing facility, established in technical collaboration with M/s. Oerlikon Buhrle & Co. of Switzerland and commenced production in 1971. The PMTF, with a work-force of approximately 1,900 personnel, is engaged in the production of machine tools, automotive transmissions and axles components, gears for locomotives, pressure die cast parts and other products. Facilities in the factory include, designing, machining, forging, heat treatment, assembly, die casting, etc.[85]

Research and Development (R&D) Establishments

The main research and development organisations include:

- Defence Science and Technology Organisation (DESTO)
- Armament Research and Development Establishment (ARDE)
- Military Vehicles Research and Development Establishment (MVRDE)

- Naval Research and Development Authority (NRDE)

The *Defence Science and Technology Organisation* (DESTO) was established in 1963, to conduct research on weapon systems and also to render professional advice on the applications of science and technology. The R&D areas of this organisation include: aerodynamics, computer systems, engineering, explosives and chemical and biological defence.[86] The facility has a staff of around 1,000 people and around 33 per cent of its annual budget is spent on pay and allowances.[87]

The DESTO Headquarters are located at Chaklala for providing policy advice, liaison and organisational management. DESTO's R&D infrastructure is located at the following different physical locations:

- DESTO Laboratories Complex, Chattar.
- DESTO Laboratories, Karachi.
- DESTO Laboratories, Chaklala.[88]

The *Armament Research and Development Establishment* (ARDE), was established in 1974 and undertakes research and development in the field of arms and ammunition. It has also been collaborating with other public and private sector units. Its major accomplishments are weapons and tank ammunition.[89]

The *Military Vehicles Research and Development Establishment* (MVRDE, came up in 1972, mainly with the objective to explore and build upon Pakistan's indigenous technical and industrial potential. The establishment is capable of conducting research and development in defence related mechanical systems, and military vehicles.[90] It basically supports the build-up of self-reliance capability in the field of defence production as it undertakes absorption of technology, broadening of the defence production base and creation of a technical manpower pool. The establishment has developed and placed in production the M47M armoured vehicle-launched bridging system.

The *Naval Research and Development Authority* (NRDE) was established in 1998 as Prime Minister Nawaz Sharif was keen to have a naval R&D organisation. The Pakistan Naval Dockyard provided the staff for the NRDA, but the organisation did not lay down any clear objectives to fulfil.

Arms Export/Promotion

The defence industry has been a large employer in Pakistan and has assisted the development of numerous sister industries. In the past few years, Pakistan has stepped up its efforts to boost its arms exports. It has followed a new and rigorous strategy to find markets for the weapon production with the aim of increasing export earnings in order to offset the high import bills. Most arms experts in Pakistan believe that the global arms export market "is a big market of about $ 20 billion and even a modest beginning or a certain percentage of the annual figure could lead to a major breakthrough as far as Pakistan is concerned."[91]

Pakistan commenced export of small arms after 1971 as noted above. In recent years, it stepped up its efforts by organising a naval show in Karachi in 1998. In 1999, against this background, the Joint Chiefs of Staff Committee under the chairmanship of Gen Pervez Musharraf, took a decision to conduct an international defence exhibition and seminar (IDEAS) in December 2000. As a result, a coordination cell was set up in the JSHQ (Joint Services Headquarters) to execute this project.[92] The exhibition, IDEAS 2000, was conducted on commercial lines and was supported by the Ministry of Commerce and the Export Promotion Bureau (EPB). The exhibition was apparently attended by 43 delegations from 31 countries, and 58 foreign exhibitors displayed their products.[93] The Pakistani military hardware demonstrated included the K-8 fighter trainer, Super Mushshak trainer aircraft, Al Khalid tank, air defence system ADS 37, and Anza and Baktar Shikan missile systems. To give a feel of the products and also in order to attract arms sales, a permanent Defence Products Exhibition Centre has been established at Rawalpindi.

The second International Defence Exhibition and Seminar, IDEAS 2002, was hosted in September 2002 at Karachi. Thirty different countries participated in the seminar which provided a platform to the international research scholars to exchange views on security issues. During 2002, KSEW received export orders, including the construction of various marine craft from Germany, UAE, Saudi Arabia, Bangladesh and Iran. The Pakistan Aeronautical Complex (PAC) signed export contracts worth $ 517 million, including with the Royal Oman Air Force worth $2.27 million for Super Mushak aircraft.[94] The third International Defence Exhibition and Seminar, IDEAS 2004, was hosted in 2004 in Karachi under the slogan of "Arms for Peace."

The Defence Export Promotion Organisation (DEPO) came into being in 2001 and exports under it started in 2002. The DEPO has been established to facilitate customer inquiries and coordinate export of defence products and services with marketing support, in coordination with the defence manufacturing sector.[95] Reports suggest that the DEPO has formulated plans to increase the volume of Pakistan's defence exports to $250 million in five years from the mark of $ 40 million in the year 2002.[96] DEPO Planning and Development Director, Air Commodore Mansoor Malik believes that this can be achieved only with the cooperation of both public and private sectors in the field of defence production. Efforts are being made to improve the products of low value range and promote the sales of high value products.[97] The traditional high value products include the Agosta 90-B and other naval craft, basic and advance jet trainers, tanks and air launched weapons systems. Non-traditional products consist of aerial target systems i.e. "drones and UAVs, radars and avionic systems modules, chaff and flare dispensers, laser range finders and optical instruments, training simulators for land, naval and air systems, mine breaching and lifting equipment."[98] According to Air Commodore Mansoor Malik, the DEPO aims to increase defence product exports to $ one billion in 10 years, thus, making defence the second largest exporting sector after textiles. Pakistan produces around 100 products which have the potential for exports whereas the number of products presently exported is 12.[99]

Pakistan has identified a number of countries in the Gulf states, Southeast Asia, Africa and South Asia as potential markets for its products. It is also trying to explore the markets in Europe and the United States where it expects to exploit the close defence cooperation between the two. According to the DEPO Director General, Maj Gen Syed Absar Hussain, most of the country's defence related export went to the Middle East, Africa and South Asia. Defence related exports have increased to over $150 million in 2006 from the figure of $20 million in 2000.[100] Pakistan seems to be having an aggressive marketing strategy for its defence related products and has an ambitious plan to capture at least one per cent share of the global arms market by 2007.[101] Pakistani defence exports are likely to expand in the future with the commercial production of the Super Mashshak air trainer, Al Khalid MBT, Al Zarrar MBT, and the co-production of the JF-17 fighter with China.

Conclusion

Pakistan's indegenous defence production has been expanded significantly in the last two decades. Pakistan was concentrated heavily on the manufacture of small arms and light weapons after 1965 owing to the fact that the military almost ran out of ammunition during the 1965 Indo-Pak War. This was the major driving factor behind the development of the small arms industry in Pakistan's and insistence towards self-reliance. Eventually, the small arms and light weapons industry has been developed, fulfilling the requirements of not only Pakistan's military but also of more than 30 nations, presently, reportedly importing weapons from Pakistan. Small arms export from Pakistan has also expanded over the years, due to the following factors:

1. Pakistan Ordnance Factories follow both the NATO/US standards and the Chinese (and erstwhile Eastern Bloc) standards, specifications and calibres in their production. This provides Pakistan with a larger market for its products. Presently, two types of nations are importing from Pakistan – countries which follow NATO/US specifications like Kuwait, Saudi Arabia, UAE and Turkey, and a second set of countries which follow the Chinese specifications like, Bangladesh, Thailand, and Egypt (which follows both standards).
2. Pakistan, from the very beginning, pursued the objective of building its image as the leader of the Islamic world and has been engaged in military cooperation at different levels with various Muslim countries. Pakistan's policy of providing military support and arms exports to the Islamic world has expanded the market for Pakistani defence products in the Muslim countries.
3. Pakistan has been following a clear strategy of expanding its export earnings in order to offset the increasing weapon import bills and

also with the (aspirational) objective of creating the defence sector as the second largest export sector after textiles which currently comprises 60 per cent of the exports in Pakistan.

Pakistan has been projecting itself as a major defence manufacturer. But as far as weapons systems and military equipment are concerned, Pakistan's defence industry has yet to come up with an indegenous design and development capability. Most of the major weapon systems which are reportedly manufactured by the Pakistani defence industry are limited to overhaul/repair, assembly of the major components and licensed manufacture of some of the weapons. Research and development in the Pakistan defence industry still needs to grow in order to get to the final steps in indigenous defence production, which implies the "design and development of the weapon systems." Few developing countries, in fact, can do this, and Pakistan's national science, technology and industrial capabilities are fairly limited even by developing countries' yardsticks. This is what Pakistan is trying to correct through building a defence industrial base. Pakistan, for example, has no capabilities to design and develop and engine for automobiles leave alone for a main battle tank. This is why the Heavy Industries Taxila manufacturing the MBT-2000 Al Khalid MBTs. The JF-17s are currently being manufactured in China with the basic design and technology having come from Russia. However, the fact remains that Pakistan is undertaking repair and overhaul of its weapons systems, especially the platforms, with an increasing proportion of defence production under license. This definitely reduces the cost of importing the defence equipment in totality and adds to the capabilities of the local defence industry. Co-production of equipment will gradually assist in building the production base of military systems in Pakistan.

To sum up, Pakistan has been engaged in the expansion of the indigenous defence industry by expanding its production as well as exports mainly to serve three identifiable goals.

- Increasing indigenous capabilities for production (under licence, etc) of major weapons to provide for some element of self-reliance.
- Initially concentrating on building small arms/light weapons production capabilities and export capacity in order to:

- Ensure sufficient arms/ammunition for a prolonged war against India.
- Enable sufficient small arms supplies to jihadi organisations without having to depend on outside supplies (as was the case in the Afghanistan War of the 1980s).
- Expand exports to offset costs of production of these weapons by increasing the economies of scale.
- Pursue foreign policy goals and ideological support in Muslim countries.

- The defence sector in Pakistan presently stands as one of the important sources to absorb the limited professional and the technical skills in Pakistan. Expansion in defence production and exports in the long run would, directly or indirectly, contribute to economic and industrial development. This, in turn, would also provide Pakistan's military with a techno-economic reason to continue deepening its role in the country's political, and social fabric as the dominant factor.

Notes

1. Message by Gen Abdul Waheed for the seminar on "Self-Reliance in Defence" by the Ministry of Defence at Rawalpindi on January 16-17, 1993, p.11, as cited by, Ayesha Siddiqa-Agha, *Pakistan's Arms Procurement and Military Buildup, 1979-99, In Search of a Policy* (New York: Palgrave, 2001) p.109.
2. Abdul Qadeer, " POF- Through The Decades," *Defence Journal*, vol. XIX, no. 9-10, 1993, as cited in *Strategic Digest,* April 1994, pp. 564-567.
3. Aabha Dixit, "Defence Production in Pakistan," *Asian Strategic Review 1991-92* (New Delhi: Institute for Defence Studies and Analyses, 1992), p.287.
4. Hasan Askari Rizvi, "Factors Shaping Pakistan's Arms Production Programme," *Defence Journal*, no. 11, 1988, pp.38-39, as cited by Dixit, Ibid., p.287.
5. Dixit, Ibid., p.287.
6. YEARBOOK 2004-2005, at http://www.pakistan.gov.pk/divisions/defence production_division/images/YEARBOOK2004-05.pdf
7. Internet site, http://www.pof.gov.pk/history.htm
8. Internet site, http://pofwah.com.pk/products.htm

9. Golden Jubilee of Pakistan Ordnance Factories (POF), Wah, at, http://www.pakpost.gov.pk/philately/stamps2001/pof.html
10. Internet site, http://pofwah.com.pk/products.htm
11. Internet site, http://www.army-technology.com/contractors/machine_guns/pakistan/
12. "POFs History" at http://www.pof.gov.pk/history.htm . The POF top management signed a contract with M/s AOQC Moody International of the UK, requesting them to send their team of experts to assess POF production potential, quality state, documentation and housekeeping standards. After a scrutiny, M/s Moody international awarded ISO-9001 certificates to all fourteen industries of the POF
13. For details, see http://pofwah.com.pk/products.htm
14. "50 Years of Pakistan Ordnance Factories," *Military Technology, MILTECH*, Special Supplement, 2002, p.16.
15. http://www.globalsecurity.org/wmd/world/pakistan/wah.htm
16. Dixit, n.3, p.291.
17. Dixit, Ibid.
18. Dixit, Ibid., pp.292-293.
19. *Dawn*, August 17, 2001.
20. n.14, p.7.
21. *Dawn*, February 28, 2002.
22. Internet site, "POF Invites Private Sector for Investment," http://www.pakistaneconomist.com/database1/Inv-Opp/inv-opp6.htm
23. Ibid.
24. John Kaniyalil, "Defence Industries in Pakistan," *Strategic Analysis*, May 1993, pp.229-247.
25. Internet site, FAS, Taxila, http://www.fas.org/nuke/guide/pakistan,facility/taxila.htm
26. Mushahid Hussain, "Pakistan's Heavy Armour; Upgradation/Modernisation Programme," *Defence Journal*, October 1990, p.7, as cited by Dixit, n.3, p.293.
27. Kaniyalil, n.24, pp.229-247.
28. *Muslim* (Islamabad), July 25, 1991, as cited in Kaniyalil, Ibid.
29. Dixit, n.3, pp.293-94.
30. Maj Gen Farhat Ali Burki, "A Step Towards Self-Reliance," *Defence Journal*, October 1990, p.28, as cited by Dixit, Ibid., p.294.

31. "MBT 2000 (Al Khalid)," *Jane's Armour and Artillery 2005-2006*, p.74.
32. Ibid.
33. Ibid.
34. Ibid., p.77.
35. http://pakistanidefence.com/news/MonthlyNewsArchive/2004/ March2004.htm
36. n.31, p.358.
37. Ibid., p.359.
38. Ibid., p.359.
39. Ibid.
40. Ibid., p.360.
41. Ibid., p.77.
42. "Indigenisation of Pakistan Air Force's Weapon Systems," at Internet site, http://www.geocities.com/CapitolHill/3023/defence_production.html
43. Ibid.
44. Siddiqa-Agha, n.1, p.127.
45. "Indigenisation of Pakistan Air Force's Weapon Systems," at Internet site, http://www.geocities.com/CapitolHill/3023/defence_production.html
46. Ibid.
47. n.31, p.357.
48. Internet site, http://www.fas.org/nuke/guide/pakistan/facility/kamra.htm
49. n.46. The 156.6 KW upgraded variant, first flown in June 1988, has completed its flight trials. All new production aircraft are expected to conform to this standard. It was reported in early 1989 that about 20 Mushshaks had been ordered by the UAE Air Force, and procurements by other countries are being discussed.
50. n.31, p.357.
51. Ibid., p.89-90.
52. Internet site, http://www.fas.org/nuke/guide/pakistan/facility/kamra.htm
53. n.31, p.81.
54. "JF-17 Thunder," at http://en.wikipedia.org/wiki/JF-17_Thunder
55. Ibid.
56. Internet site, http://www.ideaspakistan.com/2000/day_two.htm
57. *Jane's Radar and Electronic Warfare Systems 2006-2007*, p.230.
58. Ibid.

59. Internet site, FAS, Taxila, http://www.fas.org/nuke/guide/ pakistan,facility/ taxila.htm
60. Ibid.
61. Pakistan Military Consortium, Armed Services of Pakistan, at Internet site, http://www.pakdef.info/pakmilitary/army/companies.html
62. Ibid.
63. For details, see Siddiqa-Agha, n.1, pp.123-124.
64. "Air Weapons Complex," at Internet site, http://www.awc.com.pk/main.html
65. Ibid.
66. Ibid.
67. "P N Logistics" at, http://www.paknavy.gov.pk/ram.htm
68. *Jane's Fighting Ships 2005-2006*, p.538.
69. Ibid., pp.543-544.
70. "Karachi Ship Yard and Engineering Works Ltd" at, http://www.depo.org.pk/index.php?a=profile&id=13
71. http://www.depo.org.pk/index.php?a=showallproducts&id=13
72. http://www.pakistaneconomist.com/database1/Industry/Ind158.htm
73. n.68, p.543.
74. Ibid., p.545.
75. Ibid.
76. n.70.
77. Ibid.
78. "Missile Facilities: National Defence Complex (NDC)," at, http://www.nti.org/e_research/profiles/Pakistan/Missile/3294_3327.html
79. Internet site , http://www.fas.org/nuke/guide/pakistan/facility/ fatehjung.htm
80. Ibid.
81. Ibid.
82. Ibid.
83. Internet site, http://www.nrtc.com.pk/index_1.htm
84. Ibid.
85 Internet site, http://www.pmtfl.com/profile.htm
85. " Pakistan Arms Industry" at http://www.pakdef.info/pakmilitary/army/companies.html

87. Siddiqa-Agha, n.1, p.132.
88. "Pakistan Arms Industry" at http://www.pakdef.info/pakmilitary/army/companies.html
89. Ibid.
90. Ibid.
91. Muhammad Aslam, "Breakthrough in Arms Exports," *Dawn*, November 13, 2000.
92. Maj Gen S. Ali Hamid, "Defence Export and Arms Merchants," *Dawn,* July 29, 2002.
93. Hamid, Ibid.
94. "Pakistan Aeronautical Complex (PAC) Signs $517 Million Export Contracts," at http://pakistanidefence.com/news/MonthlyNewsArchive/2002/Septe,ber2002.htm
95. http://www.depo.org.pk/index.php?a=about
96. "Defence Exports to Swell Six Times," *Dawn*, January 3, 2002.
97. Ibid.
98. Ibid.
99. Ibid.
100. "Pakistan Defence Export Reached $ 150 Million, jf-17 Will be on Display in Next Ideas Expo," at http://pakistanidefenceforum.com/index.php?showtopic=57682
101. See http://pakistanidefence.com/news/MonthlyNewsArchive/2006/March2006.htm

3

Current Trends in Nuclear Weapons Thinking and Strategies

Manpreet Sethi

The year 2001 was significant for more reasons than just being the first year of a new millennium. It also marked ten years of the end of the Cold War and reflected a perceptible change of mood from the heady days of hope and optimism of the early 1990s.[1] Fast developing cooperative relations between the USA and Russia then had almost led a few international strategists to write obituaries of nuclear weapons and war in general.[2] One notable report published by the Stimson Centre recommended, "The ultimate objective of US national security policy should be the elimination of all weapons of mass destruction from all states – not the preservation of nuclear deterrence in perpetuity."[3] Taking a cue from the prevailing spirit of bonhomie, even the United National Security Council concluded in a 1992 Summit Meeting, "The world now has the best chance of achieving international peace and security since the foundation of the United Nations."

By 2001, however, these expectations had come to nought as international relations developed along a completely different trajectory. It was on May 1, 2001, that President Bush had made a landmark speech at the National Defence University, and given US leadership on most matters of nuclear security, this was significant. Rather dramatically he declared, "Today, the sun comes up on a vastly different world. The wall is gone and so is the Soviet Union… Yet this is still a dangerous world, a less certain, a less predictable one...."[4] These words proved prophetic when only four months later, a singular event on 9/11 transformed thinking on international security issues. Terrorism, possibly with weapons of mass destruction (WMD), facilitated by proliferation of WMD and delivery system technologies to 'rogue states' was immediately identified as the predominant threat.

While a new cache of foreign policy tools and military strategies were quickly crafted by the US to meet the emergent challenges, one concept of the old guard that was reinvented to suit contemporary threat perceptions was nuclear deterrence. This continued to perform its traditional task of holding peace between nuclear states, though this requirement appeared non-existent, while also donning a new role, justification and form. The US Nuclear Posture Review (NPR) of January 2001 took the new strategic reality into account and sent out a clear message – that nuclear weapons were here to stay. This thread was picked up by the Russian military doctrine that followed in November 2003 and together they set the tone for others. And so, today, every nuclear weapon state (NWS) covets its nuclear arsenal and maintains it at the heart of national security.

This paper examines current trends in nuclear weapons thinking and strategies in NWS with a view to drawing some implications for India's nuclear strategy. It must, however, be stated at the outset that this paper confines itself to examining ongoing developments, whether in the form of actual research and development (R&D) or at a conceptual level in the US, Russia, UK and France. Given the more direct implications of nuclear strategies and capabilities of China and Pakistan, they merit an individual examination that shall be undertaken subsequently. For this essay, the analysis of nuclear trends is based on four parameters – nuclear deterrence, ballistic missile defence, nuclear arsenals and weapons infrastructure, and arms control. The second section of the paper identifies the trends that can broadly be discerned from current developments and provides some indicative implications of these for India's nuclear strategy.

Parameters of Analysis

Nuclear Deterrence

Over the last six years, threat perceptions of the US have altered significantly. Official statements clearly exclude the possibility of war with Russia. It was in recognition of this change that George Bush, during his election campaign in 2000, promised to leave the Cold War behind and "rethink the requirements of nuclear deterrence." While this was then interpreted as holding the promise of a gradual reduction in the role of nuclear weapons in US defence strategy, 9/11 and the emergence of two new threats – those arising from WMD proliferation to "rogue states", in American parlance, and from the avowed interest of terrorist organisations in acquiring WMD – actually pushed Bush in the other direction.

US conceptualisation of a new strategic framework and the role of nuclear weapons therein were articulated by the NPR[5] in 2001. It was premised on three assumptions:

1. The US must *retain a robust nuclear arsenal* because nuclear weapons provide a broad range of benefits to US defence and foreign policy. Firstly, they provide deterrence against nuclear attack, and also against chemical and biological weapons. Secondly, they deter other equivalent powers from launching or winning a major conventional war. And lastly, with some modifications, they could help in destroying targets hidden deep underground.
2. *Significant cuts in nuclear weapons are possible* because Russia is no longer the major threat confronting the US. The NPR, therefore, projected a scaling down of operationally deployed warheads to 3,800 by 2007, and their further reduction to 1,700-2,200 by 2012.
3. The size and composition of the US arsenal should be governed by the principle of "*strategic adaptability*"[6] to meet threats arising from multiple potential opponents and sources of conflict that may include rivals for global or regional leadership, rogue states, and terrorists. The USA should also prepare for the

possibility of rapid escalation of existing threats or sudden emergence of new ones. This risk held back the NPR from recommending a complete destruction of dismantled weapons. Rather, it suggested that the downgraded weapons be moved as reserves in the nuclear force structure, where they could remain intact, and ready for recall, if necessary. Termed the Responsive Force, this would augment an already existing "hedge" of some 2,500 active and inactive nuclear weapons[7] and serve three purposes: act as replacement for warheads destroyed each year in routine reliability and safety tests; provide a safeguard against failure of operationally deployed weapons; and, enable a quick increase in the size of the operational arsenal in the face of unexpected developments.

Based on the direction provided by the NPR, American nuclear deterrence today rests on flexibility to quickly respond to the changing strategic, technical, operational and political environments. Taking this a step further, the Quadrennial Defence Review (QDR) of 2006 recommends a shift in emphasis from a "one size fits all" nuclear deterrence to a more "tailored deterrence" that can handle threats from rogue powers, terrorist networks as well as near peer contingencies. While classical nuclear deterrence is believed to be capable of handling the latter, deterrence coupled with defence, counter-proliferation and preemption are expected to provide security against small WMD capable nations, as well as against non-state actors. In fact, Ryan Henry, deputy undersecretary of defence for policy had opined in 2005 that though deterrence of terrorists was most difficult, it was not impossible if the US could identify what they held dear and hold that at risk. For instance, Islamic terror groups may be deterred by the threat of retaliation against Muslim holy sites. Also, as these groups did not operate in a vacuum, it was possible to identify governments or territories that supported their operation and threaten them with preemption or retaliation.[8] But, he did concede that deterrence had to be complemented by other measures to be more effective in the present circumstances.

Therefore, in the face of new threat perceptions, nuclear deterrence is today considered one, but not the sole, arrow in the US security strategy quiver. In a move towards operationalising this synergy, the Department of Defence has been upgrading its nuclear strike plans to reflect a transition from the Single Integrated Operational Plan (SIOP) of the Cold War to smaller and more flexible strike plans for modern adversaries. For instance, one such plan, the CONPLAN 8022, developed by STRATCOM (the Pentagon's strategic command) in coordination with the US Air Force and Navy provides "prompt global strike options to the President with nuclear, conventional, space and information warfare capabilities to destroy time urgent targets."[9]

If the US is in no hurry to reduce the role of nuclear weapons, neither is Russia. In fact, Russian nuclear muscle flexing in the post-Cold War era has largely coincided with the souring of the dream of a cooperative partnership with the West.[10] In December 1999, during his visit to China, President Boris Yeltsin underlined Russia's nuclear status when he said, "It seems Mr. Clinton has forgotten Russia is a great power *that possesses a nuclear arsenal*… I want to tell President Clinton that he alone cannot dictate how the world should live, work and play. It is us who will dictate."[11] Only four months later, in April 2000, President Vladimir Putin reminded the world that Russia is a "mighty nuclear power" and, in a similar vein, said just an year later, "Either Russia will be a great power or it will not exist at all."[12] Such statements reflect a need on the part of Russia to convince itself and the world that despite its economic disarray, political turmoil and reduced conventional might, it remains a power of international standing.

Russia's nuclear status is of crucial importance for the country at this present juncture for two main reasons. First and more obviously, its nuclear weapons fill an internal void by serving as an overt symbol of strength and power at a time when other determinants of national status and international prestige are found wanting. They give Moscow the requisite strength to pursue domestic policies of the kind that it deems fit. Nuclear weapons form a sort of shield to insulate external criticism on matters Russia considers its own, such as the Russian policy in Chechnya.[13]

At the same time, the Russian nuclear arsenal also serves an external need. It fortifies an otherwise weak nation against the relative strength of some of the other international players that Moscow perceives as security concerns. For instance, the expansion of the North Atlantic Treaty Organisation (NATO) to areas traditionally considered a Russian preserve, as also the likely deployment of ballistic missile defence (BMD) outposts in these countries, or the increasing US tendency towards unilateralism are viewed with grave concern, and Russia's nuclear status, it is hoped, would hold them from proceeding beyond a point.

Placed in such a security matrix, Russia perceives great value in its nuclear weapons to underscore its status as a powerful nation. Not surprisingly, therefore, over the last five years, the Russian government has sought to reassert its nuclear strength through plans for new nuclear weapons systems, upgradation of existing ones, as well as the conduct of well-publicised military exercises that contemplate the use of nuclear weapons. The good news for Russia is that the constraint of limited resources that until recently had prevented it from overhauling its old military equipment is now changing. Increased oil revenues allow greater defence spending, including on modernisation of the strategic rocket forces, a trend that had stopped in 2000.[14] This process is aided by the basic premise of contemporary Russian security strategy that maintenance of a robust nuclear deterrent is critical for Russia.

In fact, while the country's new military doctrine is expected to be released some time this year, it would most likely echo, perhaps even more vehemently, what the doctrine of April 21, 2000, had stated: "Under modern conditions, the Russian Federation relies on a need to possess nuclear capabilities enabling it a guaranteed possibility to inflict damage of predetermined scale to any aggressor under any circumstances."[15] It also mentioned Russia's right to use nuclear weapons in response to the use of not just nuclear weapons but the use of other WMD, as well as in the case of conventional weapons. It may be recalled that Russia had abandoned its no first use (NFU) nuclear doctrine in 1992 in the wake of a dramatic decline in its conventional capabilities.

Obviously then, nuclear deterrence remains central to Russian military and political strategy, and it is still largely conceived in the traditional sense of bipolar deterrence. Unlike the US, current Russian threat perceptions do not particularly revolve around non-state actors or WMD terrorism or even the need for deterrence of small nuclear nations. Russian fears still emanate from NATO expansionism and US unilateralist tendencies, both of which compel Moscow to sustain its nuclear deterrence capabilities.

Meanwhile, an overt debate on the need and role of atomic weapons is back on the agenda in British politics with a vengeance. In October 2006, Prime Minister Tony Blair had initiated a public debate on the future of the independent British nuclear deterrent. Two months later, in a White Paper entitled "The Future of the UK's Strategic Deterrent", Blair underlined his government's belief that "an independent British nuclear deterrent is an essential part of our insurance against the uncertainties and risks of the future."[16]

After three months of debate, on March 14, 2007, the British Parliament approved, albeit with a fractured vote (409 to 161), the replacement of the country's submarine-based nuclear deterrent. This approval came in the face of significant opposition from within the ruling Labour Party, as also from non-governmental organisations (NGOs). The opponents argued that the UK did not need to replace the existing four Vangaurd submarines and the Trident missile systems mounted on them and should instead live up to its commitments under the nuclear Non-Proliferation Treaty (NPT) by scrapping nuclear weapons. But Blair and his likely successor Gordon Brown, have favoured the move because they believe that nuclear deterrence is a key "insurance policy in an uncertain world,"[17] inhabited by states like North Korea and Iran, and by non-state terrorist organisations. Blair stated in Parliament, "The government's judgment, on balance, is that though the Cold War is over, we cannot be certain in the decades ahead that a major nuclear threat to our strategic interest will not emerge."[18] And if the UK was to maintain a credible nuclear deterrent, then he argued for immediate action since the SSBNs (nuclear-powered submarines) are due to become obsolete in the mid-2020s and it would take until then to design, build and deploy new versions. However, he conceded the possibility of reducing the number of submarines from four to three, and the stockpiled warheads by 20 per cent from 200 or so to 160, in order to reduce potential replacement costs.

With the decision now taken in favour of Trident replacement, the UK is set to retain nuclear deterrent capabilities, even if in a scaled down version. France appears to be in no different a mood. It was in 1960 that France acquired autonomous nuclear deterrence against Soviet nuclear and conventional superiority, and for the sake of its prestige and influence in Europe and beyond. Since then, the *force de frappe* (nuclear strike force) has been central to French security and foreign policy. On January 19, 2006, President Chirac further reaffirmed this when in an address at the headquarters of the Strategic Air and Maritime Forces, he said that nuclear weapons "continue, and will continue tomorrow to be the ultimate guarantor of our security." In fact, this speech was particularly remarkable for defining the French concept of nuclear deterrence in the post-Cold War world. Four points stood out[19]:

(a) It provided new missions of deterrence to nuclear weapons while retaining old ones. These included safeguarding broader French interests, ranging from territorial to strategic supplies (mainly energy); and deterring leaders of states that sponsor terrorism by hitting at their centres of power and capacity to act.

(b) It spoke of more flexible nuclear forces through enhancement of submarine and air launched nuclear weapons to address new situations and "cover threats wherever they arise and whatever their nature." Quite like the US, France expressed the need for quick and responsive nuclear forces that presented the option of decapitating a regime without causing civilian casualties. In fact, a report to the Senate Foreign Affairs Committee in 2003 sought an adaptation of nuclear deterrence from just "anti-city deterrence" to one that could provide a more variegated response through weapons with "selective yields and improved penetration of the nuclear warheads and a larger variety, enhanced range and higher precision of the carrier system."[20]

(c) It maintained that nuclear weapons give France "the ability to keep our freedom to act, to control our policies, to ensure the durability of our democratic values."

(d) It cast nuclear weapons as a matter of national pride since it reflected the "marshalling of all energies, development of our research capabilities and finding innovative solutions… Nuclear deterrence thus, became, the very image of what our country is capable of producing."[21]

Ballistic Missile Defence

In his speech of May 2001, President Bush had stated, "Deterrence can no longer be based solely on the threat of nuclear retaliation," and, hence, the need for "new concepts of deterrence that rely on both offensive and defensive forces."[22] Meanwhile, the NPR too had outlined missile defence as a crucial leg of the New Triad, the other two being the development of a combination of non-nuclear and nuclear strike capabilities to enhance deterrence; and, a revitalised defence and nuclear infrastructure. As explained by J.D. Crouch, US assistant secretary of defence and official spokesperson for the NPR in 2002, the BMD aimed at creating a "broader array of capabilities… to deter and, if deterrence were to fail, to defend against potential adversaries."[23] It was described as an imperative in the new security environment in which risks emanated more from a few ballistic missiles of rogue states rather than the many in the Russian arsenal. [24]

Over the last five years, the US has been engaged in aggressive R&D as well as phased deployment of an active, integrated and multi-layered missile defence. Having abandoned the Anti-Ballistic Missile (ABM) Treaty in June 2002, the US BMD programme envisages interception of incoming enemy missiles at all stages of flight: boost phase interception to attack them while still over enemy territory; mid-course ground-based interception; as well as terminal stage interception through Patriot PAC 3 point defence of critical facilities and forces.

It is not within the scope of this paper to recount the details of the three programmes. Suffice it to say that while these have seen their share of successes and failures, over the last couple of years, the success rate has been comparatively higher. In fact, 2006 was an exceptionally good year for the BMD. Most tests, fifteen of the last sixteen,[25] proved successful, engineering challenges were met and more nations signed on as a result of these successes, as also because of growing threat perceptions. The North Korean test in October 2006 pushed Japan and South Korea to reinforce their commitment to missile defence. The ongoing stalemate over Iranian nuclear intentions is pushing other countries in Europe to seriously consider the option. Meanwhile, in September 2006, NATO launched the Active Layered Theatre Ballistic Missile Defence Programme to protect troops in the field against short- and medium-range missiles by approving the construction of a $ 90 million command and control system. It is scheduled to have an initial operational capability by 2010 and to be fully operational by 2016.

None of this has been watched by any comfort by Russia. Moscow was always critical of US BMD plans.[26] But by the time the US left the ABM Treaty, it had become reconciled to the idea of an elementary missile defence, and crafted its own responses along two lines: a political response, such as rethinking the role of nuclear weapons and deterrence, and scrapping START II; and a technological one, through modernisation of its nuclear forces and the simultaneous development of BMD counter-measures. Perhaps it was a potent reflection of both responses that a Ministry of Defence Policy Paper of 2003 reemphasised the importance of the nuclear triad in Russian military strategy. Revising an earlier radical reduction of the land-based intercontinental ballistic missiles (ICBMs) in favour of naval submarine-launched ballistic missiles (SLBMs), Russia indicated its decision to retain the former till the end of their service lives, including all extensions. It also hinted at maintaining the option of arming its Topol Ms (SS-27s) with multiple independently targeted reentry vehicles (MIRVs) as well as maintaining MIRVed ICBMs outlawed under START II.

By 2004, Russia claimed to have developed three new long-range missile systems as part of its modernised strategic force. These included the mobile version of the Topol M ICBM, the sea-launched Bulava and a new, hypersonic manoeuvrable reentry vehicle to defeat BMD. In fact, the latter has been referred to several times by the Russian president with immense pride from 2003 onwards, the latest mention being in his state of the nation address in 2006, wherein he indicated that "work is already under way on creating… maneuverable combat units that'll have an unpredictable flight trajectory for the potential opponent."[27] While few details are available, these are believed to be hypervelocity scramjet systems capable of destroying targets at intercontinental range (10,000 km), with high accuracy and capability of a deep manoeuvre in altitude as well as direction. On counter-measures as well, Russia has worked to improve fast burn boosters, lofting or depressing ICBM trajectories, spoofing the interceptor missile's tracking sensors, and protecting the missile body with reflective or ablative coatings.

In keeping with the imperative of maintaining a robust nuclear deterrent to defeat US BMD, the budget for such programmes has also been increased. On February 7, 2007, Sergei Ivanov, Russia's deputy prime minister and defence minister, told the Duma that the Defence Ministry would receive $ 30.98 billion in 2007 as against $ 8.08 billion in 2001.[28] During 2007-15, the State Armament Programme estimates to spend $ 188.68 billion for a complete reequipment of Russia's strategic forces. It plans to commission 34 silo-based missile launchers and command centres and 66 mobile Topol M ICBM systems, as also increase the number of strategic bombers, procurements that would largely go towards replenishing Russian nuclear forces that had degraded their capability in the initial years of this decade. It is also planned that eight new strategic missile submarines would be built and commissioned, besides the development of space-based reconnaissance, telecommunications, data relay and early warning capabilities.

While Russia has quietly worked at maintaining its nuclear deterrent vis-a-vis a missile defended US, it is in the more recent months that disquiet over the BMD has increased. This is largely a result of the US decision to deploy BMD elements – ten interceptors in Poland and a radar in Czechoslovakia – both former allies of the USSR. Russia perceives this move as having the potential to "raise tensions in Europe to a level they have not reached since the last great showdown in the Cold War…."[29] Russian analysts have questioned the real motivations behind this. Mikhail Barbanov, editor of *Arms Export* magazine believes the real intent to be "the desire to expand US military and strategic capacities and constrict those of other states that have nuclear missiles, Russia and China most of all."[30] According to him even a limited BMD "injects a high degree of indeterminacy into the strategic plans of other countries and undermines the principle of mutual nuclear deterrence."

The head of the Russian Defence Ministry's international military cooperation department, Yevgeny Byzhinsky, described the American move as "unfriendly" and warned that Russia would be compelled to respond with "adequate retaliatory measures of military and political character."[31] Col Gen Boris Cheltsov, chief of the air force, has opined that deployment of ABM in Europe "will give the Pentagon and its NATO allies the potential to destroy Russian strategic nuclear forces at the most vulnerable stage: the initial ascending leg of the trajectory."[32] Though most Russian pronouncements dismiss the possibility of these deployments eroding nuclear deterrence with the US, they do express two fears: one, of a possibility of the present rudimentary infrastructure leading to a build-up of military presence in Europe; and second, of the system acting as a lodestone for other countries such as Ukraine, Georgia or Moldova to invite the US to their territories. Not only would this bring US forces much closer to Russian borders but also into countries that Moscow still considers fall in its area of influence. Therefore, Moscow has refused to see these moves as "limited preventive measures" that the US describes them as and instead looks at them in the general context of the strategic and military-political environment, and its relationship with the West, which is not going through the best of times. Moscow has also expressed scepticism over American overtures for a joint missile defence system and has suggested instead a joint analysis of threats first.

Among its political responses to the expanding BMD, hints have been dropped by senior Russian military and government officials on the abandonment of the 1987 Intermediate Range Nuclear Forces (INF) Treaty which is widely considered the cornerstone of detente and peace and security in Europe. The Russian foreign minister indicated this in February 2007 when he said that Russia would stay within the INF Treaty only if the US abandoned BMD plans in Eastern Europe. In a more strident and direct response, Gen Solovstov, commander of the the strategic missile forces, said that Russia could resume construction of intermediate and short-range nuclear missiles.[33] Meanwhile, President Putin has cryptically said Russia's response would be "asymmetrical and low cost," without providing any details. This could well refer to increasing the number of warheads on Russian missiles, which has been mentioned in the past as a low cost option to saturate US defences.

Meanwhile, the UK and France are, for the moment, bit players in the BMD game. Both were initially sceptical of US moves in this direction. Their doubts were based upon considerations about the seriousness of the threat that the BMD sought to address, its technological feasibility, the financial cost of the exercise, the future of the ABM Treaty and international arms control, and the impact on relations with Russia and China. But once Bush's resolve to push ahead with the technology became clear, as also his desire to hold complete and close consultations with the allies on the issue, the two countries considerably toned down their rhetoric.

The subject has many facets for the two countries, given their membership of the European Union (EU) and NATO, both of which have different perspectives on missile defence. While the European security and foreign policy of the EU has little focus on BMD or even a unified approach, NATO is engaged in a theatre missile defence system. But the US sees BMD as a national programme and seeks bases in Eastern Europe on the basis of bilateral agreements. In fact, the head of the US Missile Defence Agency has said that US missile defence components could become a national contribution toward an alliance-wide defence system if and when NATO decides to establish such a system.

At the root of the differences among the US, EU and NATO positions is lack of unity on how much to rate the Russian threat and how to deal with it. On the one hand, is the position voiced by the French president who warns that "we must be very careful, as regards this project, not to encourage the creation of new dividing lines in Europe or the return to an obsolete order. To my mind, this project raises many questions to which thought will have to be given before responding."[34] Therefore, France is largely neutral on NATO deployments but is a stakeholder in European theatre missile defence (TMD) efforts and is itself investing in early warning satellites. On the other hand, the British government is involved in talks with Washington, already hosts a radar which feeds information to the US missile defence system, and is willing to discuss the potential deployment of interceptors in the UK. But the US itself is hesitant to take up this offer since missile defence bases on British territory would improve American ability to intercept Russian ICBMs, thereby raising more problems.

Nuclear Arsenals and Weapons Infrastructure

The health of nuclear weaponry (operational forces) and the infrastructure (development and production capabilities) provide a good indication of the nuclear thinking and strategies of a nation.

In his official briefing on the NPR, J.D. Crouch pointed out that there are no recommendations in the report about developing new nuclear weapons. But more significant was his qualification of this statement with, "We are trying to look at a number of initiatives," including modifying existing nuclear weapons to give them "greater capability against…hard targets and deeply buried targets."[35] Indeed, contemporary US nuclear strategy clearly recommends an upgrade of strategic offensive arms and the development of smaller nuclear munitions for possible use along with other smart weapons against hardened, underground facilities housing command centres or nuclear, biological, chemical (NBC) weapons related infrastructure. The NPR, in fact, identified 1,400 underground sites worldwide that required targeting by the nuclear force because conventional weapons were inadequate to destroy them.[36] In order to perform this function, it recommended the development of a robust nuclear earth penetrator or an earth penetrating bunker buster mini nuclear weapon. The director of Sandia Laboratories too argued in 2001 that, "…the yields of weapons left over from the Cold War are too high for addressing the deterrence requirements of a *multi-polar, widely proliferated world. Without rectifying that situation, we would end up being self-deterred.*"[37] US military experience with Iraq, and the Taliban in Afghanistan who have effectively used caves as their hideouts, only strengthened the case for mini nukes.

For several months after this recommendation, the debate raged over the feasibility and desirability of such a weapon. Supporters of these small, nuclear bunker busters argued that "precise" nuclear strikes with low yield warheads would minimise, if not obviate radioactive fallout and, hence, restrict collateral damage. This, however, may not be true given that even a precise, low yield nuclear weapon cannot be expected to carry out as surgical a strike as is claimed. There are several imponderables that must be taken into account. Errors could arise from a number of factors such as slippages on pinpoint accuracy because of faulty target intelligence, problems with navigation or guidance systems, as well as reentry challenges. Dangers inherent in such an operation are therefore, no less likely to lead to a catastrophe of unimaginable proportions. In fact, a report prepared for the Federation of American Scientists (FAS) concludes,

> No earth-burrowing missile can penetrate deep enough into the earth to contain an explosion with a nuclear yield even as small as one per cent of the 15 KT Hiroshima weapon. The explosion simply blows out a massive crater of radioactive dirt, which rains down on the local region with an especially intense and deadly fallout.[38]

In view of the deep divisions on the subject, specific approval for R&D of such a weapon was never forthcoming in the form of Congressional approval or funding.[39] However, the attraction of newer warheads never waned in the US. In 2005, the Reliable Replacement Warhead (RRW) Programme was initiated when Congress allocated $9 million to explore making existing nuclear warheads last longer without diminishing their explosive power. This programme is euphemistically described as aiming "to improve the reliability, longevity and certifiability of existing weapons and their components,"[40] besides also enhancing their safety and security. It is also endowed with a more 'benign' purpose of providing research and engineering problems to the "unchallenged" nuclear workforce in labs that were also to be refurbished as part of the RRW programme. In fact, the National Nuclear Security Administration (NNSA) has argued that the programme would be of great service towards revitalising the existing "decrepit" nuclear infrastructure, which it claims had suffered under "decades of neglect, intense Congressional scrutiny and legal enforcement actions in the late 1980s and 1990s." In an October 2006 report, the NNSA stated that a revamped complex would "improve the capability to design, develop, certify, and complete production of new or adapted warheads in the event of new military requirements."[41]

This refurbishment is the third leg of the new triad, and is expected to repair and replace nuclear weapons production and development facilities. Known as the Complex 2030 programme, for the year it is to be realised, it would enable the US to increase reliable warhead production capabilities while reducing actual numbers. In the process, it would achieve what Linton Brooks, administrator of the NNSA, wanted in the first place, not "a smaller Cold War era nuclear stockpile," but "capabilities appropriate for 21st century threats."[42] In his testimony before the Senate Armed Services Sub-Committee, Brooks said, "Today's Cold War legacy stockpile is the wrong stockpile from a number of perspectives"[43] because it contained too many high yield weapons that offered little or no capability against hard and deeply buried targets, provided no way to limit collateral damage, and could not destroy chemical or biological munitions. The RRW then sought to rectify these limitations by matching nuclear weapons to the new threats. Moreover, in the biggest coup of arguments, it is claimed that the RRW would ensure security of warheads against physical attack by terrorists, thus, reducing security costs of manpower and equipment at nuclear facilities.

Premised on such 'lofty' objectives and deriving more credibility from the QDR that recommended the development of nuclear weapons that are "accurate, safe and reliable and tailored to meet modern deterrence requirements,"[44] the RRW programme is today an ambitious effort to produce new warheads. In order to make this possible, the Department of Defence has been working with the Department of Energy to finalise a new warhead design. Nuclear weapon laboratories were tasked to this effect and in early 2006, the Lawrence Livermore National Laboratory in California and the Los Alamos National Laboratory in New Mexico submitted competing designs for a new warhead. A period of review followed during which, in January 2007, Bush even hinted at the possibility of a hybrid of the two designs to arrive at one that would be more robust and resistant to accidental or unauthorised use. But, in March this year, the NNSA chose the Livermore Laboratory design since it invoked greater confidence of being certified without nuclear testing. While announcing the decision on the new warhead design which will initially replace the W76 warhead for submarine-launched ballistic missiles, NNSA's acting administrator, Thomas D'Agostino said that the RRW programme would use a warhead design that was tested in the 1980s but package it with new features, such as insensitive high explosives less liable to explode by accident, as well as locking devices that would prevent the warhead from being used if it fell into the hands of terrorists.[45]

While the selection of RRW seems to maintain the US moratorium on testing, it may not be forgotten that the NPR had reiterated opposition to American ratification of the Comprehensive Test Ban Treaty (CTBT), while recommending that the country should reduce the time necessary to prepare its nuclear test sites from the current period of two years to one year. This was despite the fact that the US has a Stockpile Stewardship Management Programme (SSMP) that is a virtual nuclear testing facility that ensures the continued viability of US nuclear weapons, trains a new generation of weapon scientists, and takes up refinement of weapon designs and production processes. Yet, the NPR had proposed accelerating test site readiness.

As expected, the move invited international criticism and that may have been one of the reasons for the US selecting a new warhead design that would need no new tests. Yet, it must be pointed out that the US deputy secretary of energy, on a visit to Russia in early March 2007, soon after the selection of the new design, said that the US reserved the right to conduct nuclear tests in the future, though he hoped these would not be necessary.[46] The head of the US Strategic Command, Gen James Cartwright also told the Senate Armed Services Strategic Forces Sub-committee on March 28, 2007 that the RRW programme would not be terminated even if a need for testing was felt.[47]

In its proposed budget, the Administration is seeking $6.4 billion in nuclear weapons spending for 2008. This figure, which is about $100 million more than current spending and one and half times the average Cold War spending on nuclear weapons, would continue the current SSMP programme while ramping up the RRW process and the overhaul of Complex 2030.[48] The NNSA is seeking to have the first warhead of the series available by 2014 at the latest and hopes to begin full-scale RRW production by 2025. Meanwhile, the NNSA and the Pentagon are also reported to begin a study for an RRW that would be carried by an air force ICBM.

These developments are obviously not lost on Russia. Though there is not much information available on the exact work underway on nuclear weapons in Russia, statements indicating "Russia's strategic forces are the main priority on the national defence agenda," by nobody less than the president, convey the general trend. In mid-December 2006, Putin called for the "development of cutting edge strategic weapons" and emphasised "quality over quantity."[49] Among some of the other major modernisation efforts underway in Russia, the launch of a new generation nuclear submarine in April 2007 deserves a special mention not only because it seeks to upgrade Russia's undersea nuclear strike force, but because it is for the first time in 17 years that the country has launched such a vessel.[50]

With the decision on replacement of its SSBNs, the UK nuclear weapons infrastructure is naturally expected to be in a state of animation. Meanwhile, France too has been shoring up its nuclear deterrence capabilities. Having dismantled its land-based nuclear missile silos in 1996, the French nuclear deterrent is now based only on a dyad of submarines and aircraft. Hence, the French government has engaged in a more focussed approach towards modernisation of its nuclear forces. In November 2006, it conducted the test firing of its new 8,000 km range M-51 ballistic missile which is to carry submarine-based nuclear weapons. Expected to replace France's existing SLBMs by 2010, the new missile would be capable of carrying six nuclear warheads.

Arms Control

Given the current mood as discussed in the above paragraphs, it should come as no surprise that arms control is nowhere in the picture, at least in the form known during the Cold War. The CTBT has been in a state of limbo from 1999 onwards. In 2002, once the US walked out of the ABM Treaty, Russia announced its abandonment of START II. Recent Russian pronouncements on the INF Treaty have put it under a cloud and the Fissile Material Cuttoff Treaty (FMCT) is still awaiting direction in the Conference on Disarmament (CD). Last May, there was a sudden spurt of activity when the US put forth a draft FMCT that other countries promised to study. But nothing substantive has occurred since then. All these indicate a general trend away from arms control, particularly of the multilateral variety.

Instead, the US, normally the leader in these matters, has displayed greater inclination for unilateral initiatives in an attempt to reduce redundant weapons while keeping the option of reversibility. This was best evident in the negotiations and conclusion of the Strategic Offensive Reductions Treaty (SORT) in 2002. The brief (only 500 words long) US-Russia bilateral treaty codifies cutbacks but in a very loose and flexible fashion. It legally binds the two countries to a reduction of their nuclear arsenal to a range between 1,700-2,200 by 2012 but allows each side to determine the manner, sequence and time-table that it would follow and also how the dismantled warheads should be disposed of. The flexibility in this regard has obviously been maintained to uphold the US desire to reduce deployed weapons, but stockpile them in a reserve or responsive force. Also, the treaty contains no provisions for limiting delivery vehicles. Rather, it allows the two countries to retain as many delivery vehicles as they like—without exceeding the limits of

START I, which itself will remain in force until 2009 only, and expire before SORT reaches its targets.

SORT also does not include the elimination of MIRVed missiles, a step that START II had stipulated. This is obviously a concession to Russia since it deploys a greater proportion of its strategic warheads on MIRVed ICBMs and is likely to MIRV the new Topol M missiles too in response to the BMD. Neither have the USA and Russia laid down any verification procedures to establish the veracity of the cutbacks.[51] In fact, a move away from verification appears to be the current American tendency. The draft on the FMCT proposed by the USA in May 2006 at the CD also steers clear of enforcing any verification mechanism, leaving it instead to National Technical Means to detect non-compliance.

Trends and Implications for India's Nuclear Strategy

Continued Salience of Nuclear Deterrence

While the world may have moved on from the centrality of the Cold War and its bilateral conception of nuclear deterrence, the underlying rationale of deterrence nevertheless remains valid and relevant. It is, of course, viewed differently and no longer straitjacketed only in mutually assured destruction (MAD). Rather, to cater for the new range of threats and uncertainties, it has been endowed with greater flexibility that allows for a tailored response instead of a one size fits all approach. While classical deterrence prevails against other major nuclear powers, it is enforced through additional instruments such as active and passive defence, counter-proliferation, and prevention of WMD proliferation against the smaller arsenals of rogue states and against non-state actors. Deterrence, therefore, is no longer the sole keeper of security, but is one among an array of potential approaches.[52] There are several trends here that need to be considered in the Indian context.

Given India's threat perceptions, primarily from nuclear-armed neighbours with comparable or better nuclear forces, classical nuclear deterrence will have to remain an important pillar of national security for the foreseeable future. Since weapons of the same kind can only deter the use or threat of use of nuclear weapons, and since these WMD are here to stay, India cannot afford complacency in the build-up of its nuclear deterrent capabilities. Meanwhile, though terrorism, including of the WMD kind, is perceived as a major threat, India does not seek to address it through counter-proliferation or preemption but with improved intelligence, export controls and better preparedness.

Secondly, given the current trend of emphasis on flexibility in deterrence enforcement, it needs to be debated whether India too would need some changes in its nuclear doctrine to reflect this better. Right now, the doctrine is based on "massive retaliation." Does this restrict the choice of response and, hence, detract from the credibility of deterrence? Would it be better to define the nature of retaliation more generically as "punitive," thus, allowing for a more graded response? While it cannot be denied that the Indian nuclear doctrine is premised on deterrence by punishment and, hence, on counter-value targeting to hold large targets at risk, it is nevertheless debatable whether massive retaliation would qualify for every contingency. For instance, in deference to the larger trend, the present nuclear doctrine threatens nuclear retaliation against chemical and biological weapons use, but is it credible that such use should/could provoke massive retaliation?

Thirdly, the NWS are seeking flexibility also in terms of the yield of nuclear warheads, mostly making them smaller, to meet different contingencies. For India, given its current capabilities, this is a non-issue since in any case it does not have the large megaton monsters of the Cold War period. But, it would be of greater relevance for India to seek a range of options through the triad – or the dispersion of nuclear forces on land-based missiles, sea-based missiles and air-delivered warheads. Diverse basing would provide greater freedom of deployment as well as enhance survivability, which is so critical with India's no first use posture.

Deterrence with Defence

Unlike the situation in the Cold War when deterrence and defence were seen as mutually exclusive, the trend today indicates their cohabitation. This, however, means a change in the operation of deterrence from deterrence by punishment, which was based on MAD, to the same by denial.[53] This is expected to shore up deterrence by signalling to the enemy that not only would he lose a nuclear war, but the other would win it too. Counter-proliferation, preemption and missile defence are the components of denial strategies and emphasise the war-fighting role of the nuclear weapon. However, this applies only in the context of asymmetric threats from small WMD capable states or non-state actors.

In the case of India, given that it perceives only a political role for its nuclear weapon and does not consider it militarily usable, deterrence by denial shall not only be irrelevant, but also since its security challenges arise from comparable or larger nuclear forces, deterrence by denial will also not be feasible. This may have to be true even after the country has acquired a rudimentary BMD capability because it would at best only provide point or area defence. Therefore, deterrence by punishment would have to be the basic premise for the Indian nuclear strategy.

Reduction, but Refinement of Nuclear Weapons

All the NWS have accepted reductions in their arsenals, whether in the number of warheads or delivery platforms, or both. But also, in all cases, these cutbacks are to be accompanied by moves towards refinement and modernisation of nuclear forces. The overall trend is generally towards a leaner and meaner nuclear force, including the development of small and more usable nuclear weapons.

As a country with a minimum nuclear deterrence strategy and still engaged in building and operationalising a credible deterrent, the trend of reductions in stockpiles does not apply to India. But New Delhi must be attuned to the latest developments in the field of new nuclear warheads and delivery systems. It is also important that the country develops an adequate infrastructure that is capable of building and maintaining a credible force posture, and also sufficiently forward looking to provide new capabilities as required. While India obviously need not match the scale of the nuclear weapons infrastructure of the larger powers, it must build it as a flexible and responsive one that can address the uncertainties of the future. At this juncture, when India is contemplating and planning the separation of its nuclear facilities as a commitment under the Indo-US civilian nuclear cooperation, this consideration must be kept in mind. The formulation of an overall roadmap that lays down priorities and guides actions would go a long way in increasing the credibility of deterrence.

As far as the trend towards smaller nuclear weapons goes, it has little relevance for India, given its counter-value targeting philosophy and deterrence by punishment doctrine. However, India will have to take into account the tendency to project small nuclear weapons as more usable in some scenarios. India has always maintained that any use of the nuclear weapon would not only be a disaster, but, more importantly, also irreparably damage the moral taboo against nuclear use. This, then, could have serious repercussions for Indian security. For instance, Pakistan may interpret this development as it being acceptable to undertake a demonstration/small nuclear strike against India to check the advancement of conventional forces in case of a crisis[54]. In such case, if India responded with a nuclear strike, it would inevitably lead to a larger nuclear exchange that would be disastrous for both, and if it did not, it would seriously undermine the credibility of its deterrence. Therefore, it would be best if the nuclear weapon was not seen as a slightly more dangerous conventional weapon, and never brought into use. It is in India's interest to urge a high nuclear threshold for all.

Possibility of Nuclear Testing

Though for the moment, the US has displayed a reluctance to conduct nuclear tests, it has not categorically ruled out such a move. Not only has the US not ratified the CTBT, American officials have hinted at the conduct of nuclear tests if required, as mentioned earlier in the paper. Meanwhile, President Putin too had stated while visiting one of the Russian nuclear labs in 2003 that his country would refrain from nuclear testing "under certain obligatory conditions, one of the most important of which is a similar attitude on the part of other nuclear states…" Engaged as both are in a process of nuclear modernisation, and having zealously retained the option of underground nuclear testing, there is no guarantee that one or the other may not do so in response to a perceived need to restore strategic stability in an insecure environment. China's response in such a situation would have to be factored into India's nuclear deterrence.

This issue is particularly relevant for India in the context of the ongoing negotiations on the Indo-US civilian nuclear cooperation agreement. While the Hyde Act already passed by the US makes it mandatory that the bilateral agreement of cooperation (the 123 Agreement), presently being negotiated, should include an Indian commitment to abjure any nuclear tests in the future, India has refused to go beyond its unilateral moratorium. While there is nothing to indicate that New Delhi would undertake a nuclear test without any provocation, it is loath to surrendering the option not only because it provides insurance against future uncertainties, but also because an open option has symbolic value.

Unilateral Nuclear Cutbacks

On nuclear reductions, the general tendency seems to be in favour of parallel but unilateral reductions in the US and Russian nuclear arsenals without any mutual agreements or prior consultations. These cuts arise more from technical or economic expediency factors and are more by way of rationalisation of arsenals in the face of changed threat perceptions. Unilateral decisions on the composition and size of the national nuclear arsenal also help retain the option of reversibility since the reductions do not enforce any legal commitments.

Given this trend, India cannot count on China being involved in any multilateral nuclear reduction exercises led by other NWS, a possibility that has been referred to in the past. It was expected that bilateral nuclear arms control between the USA and Russia would eventually bring in other countries, as arsenals dropped to their levels. But the present move is from bilateral to unilateral instead of towards multilateral controls. New Delhi shall, therefore, have to base the calculation of its own nuclear deterrent on current estimation and future projections of the Chinese arsenal, discounting the possibility of their coming down from the present numbers, and not being surprised if they actually went up in response to the US BMD. China has expressed that it would maintain "pace not race" with the US, but it is determined to hold Washington to the deterrence equation. India too will have to maintain the same with China.

Dwindling Faith in Multilateral Treaties

A corollary of the above is an overall decrease in faith in the efficacy of multilateral treaties of arms control. This is of little direct implication for India since it was never a part of any of these, not even of the treaties that constitute the non-proliferation regime. However, the overall trend has indirect implications to the extent that New Delhi has always laid great score by multilateral arrangements as a measure of confidence-building. In the present environment, however, there appears to be greater propensity towards more bilateral or "coalition of the willing" type of arrangements such as the Proliferation Security Initiative (PSI), Container Security Initiative (CSI)[55] or the United Nations Security Council Resolution (UNSCR) 1540[56]. While wary of such US led initiatives in the past, an economically resurgent India now finds it less threatening to accommodate these, if it considers them in its security interest.

While there is no reason why India must stop pressing for more multilateral initiatives on arms control such as the negotiation of a universal, verifiable FMCT or the conclusion of a no first use (NFU) treaty, and also on disarmament since a nuclear weapon free world (NWFW) is best suited to its security, the country will have to be more patient and realistic on the chances of their acceptance. Meanwhile, India must also be prepared for eventualities such as the FMCT being exclusively negotiated by the five NWS through bargains that suit them and then put forth before the others for their signature. Given US frustration with multilateralism, this could be a possibility and India must weigh its options well before it becomes a reality.

Blurring Lines Between Conventional and Nuclear Weapons

Until now, a clear distinction between conventional and nuclear weapons in terms of their doctrine, role, and delivery systems ensured a certain degree, however perverted, of stability. With the increase in lethality of conventional arsenals and the decrease in size and estimated damage of nuclear weapons, the lines could get hopelessly blurred. The impact of a weapon is determined on the basis of its power of destruction and as fuel air explosives (FAE), thermobaric bombs and electro-magnetic pulse (EMP) weapons show, they are not far behind nuclear weapons.

In fact, advances in conventional weapons technology suggest that by 2020, precision long-range conventional weapons may be capable of performing some of the missions currently assigned to nuclear weapons. For instance, uncertainty in the location of road mobile missiles carrying WMD requires a nuclear weapon for assured destruction today, but future real-time imagery and battle management, combined with precision strike long-range missiles, could use a conventional weapon to effectively destroy such targets tomorrow.[57] Hence, the Bush Administration is interested in incorporating new conventional capabilities as being made available by the revolution in military affairs (RMA) into the US strategic doctrine and force structure. Accordingly, the QDR promises an initial capability to deliver precision-guided conventional warheads using long range Trident SLBMs within the next two years.

However, this trend could prove highly destabilising. In fact, several in the US were themselves unconvinced of the prudence of a global strike capability, fearing particularly that Russia or China might mistake the launch of a conventional ballistic missile for a surprise nuclear attack requiring instant retaliation. But the Pentagon is pressing the Congress for $175 million to proceed with an initial phase of substituting conventional warheads for nuclear warheads on two SLBMs for each of the dozen deployed SSBNs, for targeting "fleeting, high-value, high-regret factor-type threats."[58]

The other problem arises from the fact that strategic arms reductions treaties do not cover strategic offensive weapons with non-nuclear warheads and it would be impossible to find out how many US strategic submarines have such warheads. For the time being, Russia has decried this move as "unfortunate".[59] But it might only be a matter of time before it and others follow suit, vastly complicating security scenarios and changing the nature of warfare.

Increased Tussle Between Offence and Defence

The US has seen sagacity in complementing its deterrence capabilities with erection of missile defence in order to counter the current range of WMD threats. However, despite all the hyperbole over the BMD, the fact remains that there can be no foolproof guarantee that every incoming missile shall be intercepted in time, and every time. A certain amount of residual uncertainty would always remain.

Meanwhile, military history purports that there is no defensive system that cannot be breached given sufficient time, technology, and perseverance and offensive action by the adversary. In fact, defensive capabilities often promote offensive behaviour and there is no reason why this situation will not be played out in the context of events set into motion by the BMD. Russia and China are striving to establish some sort of strategic stability by matching their nuclear weapons and missile defences to the US. This includes vertical nuclear proliferation and the simultaneous development of BMD and counter-BMD technologies.

However, what also needs to be considered is that the US is factoring these measures into its BMD. For instance in one R&D exercise, the Defence Advanced Research Projects Agency (DARPA) has conducted tests of a hypersonic projectile powered by a supersonic combustion ramjet (scramjet) engine burning hydrocarbon fuel.[60] This marked a step towards realisation of flight at hypersonic speeds, which could be used for powering long-range hypersonic missiles, gun launched kinetic energy weapons and access to space vehicles. Such developments indicate a race to seek superiority in offence and defence. The impact of this on inter-state relations is certain to be not all benign. Suspicious attitudes and actions premised on mistrust can naturally be expected to breed more of the same.

For India, the implications of the US BMD come in an indirect manner in the form of instabilities generated by the Russian and Chinese responses. Particularly, as China improves its offensive and defensive nuclear capabilities, it would have an impact on India's nuclear deterrence. While this aspect shall be studied in greater detail while examining the Chinese nuclear thinking and strategy, it must, however, be said that India will also be forced over time to sharpen both the offensive and defensive aspects of its nuclear arsenal.

Increased Insecurities and Proliferation

Given the trends highlighted until now, it is hardly surprising that insecurities seem to be generally on the rise. At one level, the US-Russian relationship is going through turbulence unseen since the end of the Cold War. While the USA and UK feel the need to keep a "weather eye open for a resurgent Russia,"[61] Moscow is wary of NATO's expansionist overtures and the US' BMD forays into its sphere of influence. In fact, Russia's discomfiture was clearly evident in a rather aggressive speech made by President Putin at the Munich Conference on Security Policy on February 10, 2007. While generally lambasting the US for its unilateral approach to issues and disregard for international law, Putin specifically attributed destabilisation of nuclear relations to two factors: one, the obvious stagnation in disarmament; and two, the plan to expand BMD into Europe.[62]

At another level too, the continued centrality of nuclear weapons in the security strategies of the NWS and the US propensity towards preemption have generated an extended impulse for the acquisition of nuclear weapons by countries that feel threatened by the US. According to an FAS report of 2006, eight countries launched more than 26 ballistic missiles of 23 types in 24 different events.[63] Along similar lines, a report by the WMD Commission put forth in 2006 estimated that ten new nuclear powers could emerge within the decade. While motivations for nuclear acquisition are mostly regional, it is, nevertheless, a fact that contradictions between what the NWS are pursuing themselves and demanding of others is a dangerous game that will breed proliferation.

Not surprisingly, therefore, an assessment of the United Nations in the year 2005 was as pessimistic as, "The early 21st century is characterized by deteriorating relations among major powers, the unraveling of treaty-based security regimes, an increased sense of vulnerability to terrorist attack, and crisis of legitimacy and credibility on national and international institutions of governance... Such developments are important factors in creating a fear filled security environment…."[64]

Such an environment then cannot be conducive to peace, economic development and social justice, the primary national security objectives of India. As the country is in a region prone to proliferation (state to state, as well as non-state to state or vice versa, with or without government complicity) and terrorism, it faces real and urgent security challenges. While the country must address these challenges through different means at different levels, as has been mentioned earlier, the only sustainable way out of the nuclear action-reaction cycle is continued effort for a nuclear weapon-free world and India must use every opportunity and forum to keep the issue alive, notwithstanding its dim prospects in the light of current trends in nuclear thinking and strategies.

CONCLUSION

Most NWS today concede that the role of nuclear weapons is very, very limited. However, the standard argument goes, "As long as other nations have stockpiles of nuclear weapons, we will need a robust nuclear deterrent to defend ourselves and maintain a balance of power that stabilises the nuclear-armed world."

Indeed, the world of nuclear weapons has existed as a globalised entity, in cause and effect, from much before the term acquired the modern day economic connotation. Any development in the nuclear arena of one country has normally had direct or indirect (through a cascading chain reaction) implications on another or more. This has normally resonated with a proportionate or disproportionate response, leading to more of the same.

As is evident from the examination of current nuclear developments, the end of the Cold War and the sweeping changes it brought in international relations brought no significant change in the nuclearised mindsets that still envisage nuclear weapons at the centre of national security. New threats have meant additions and modifications to the concept of nuclear deterrence, not its removal from security strategy. Amongst the most significant changes to the original conceptualisation of deterrence has been that brought about by the deployment of BMD. This has made nuclear deterrence operative in both the punishment and denial modes. While punishment remains the *modus vivendi* between the NWS, denial strategies are expected to work against weaker adversaries from where the threat of retaliation is non-existent or manageable. The asymmetrical relationship, however, holds the temptation of preemption and, in turn, not only raises insecurities for others, but also increases the attractiveness of the nuclear weapons and breeds proliferation. With multilateral treaties no longer able to hold countries to compliance with their commitments, the attraction of nuclear weapons could prove fatal.

Current trends in nuclear weapons thinking and strategies, therefore, are hopelessly removed from the distinct possibility created in 1991 of actually discarding the weaponry as detritus of the Cold War. From the way the wind blows today, it is highly unlikely that another such opportunity will present itself any time soon. India's nuclear strategy must, therefore, take cognisance of this reality and gear up to meet the challenges of the future – both by way of establishing a credible nuclear deterrent, as also pushing for more long-term security in a nuclear weapon-free world.

Notes

1. Much of this optimism emanated from a reassessment of threats on the part of the US and Russia. The predominant view among American security analysts of the time was that Russia lacked the capacity or even the intention to threaten or attack Western territories. CIA Director Robert Gates even told the US Congress in 1992 that "the threat to the US of deliberate attack from the [former Soviet Union] has all but disappeared for the foreseeable future." The then Russian foreign minister echoed the same very sentiments when he stated in the same year that his nation "no longer views the US as a foe." Tom A. Zamora, "Put A Safety Cap on Testing," *Bulletin of Atomic Scientists*, vol. 48, no.2, March 1992, p.25.

2. The spirit of the changing times was aptly caught by an international analyst in these words, "These are the days of hope, not despair… It is time to strip away the complex and arcane strategic theory of the Cold War and start from scratch." Lincoln Wolfenstein, "End Nuclear Addiction," *Bulletin of Atomic Scientists*, vol. 47, no. 4, May 1991. Also see William Arkin, Damian Durrant and Hans Kristensen, "Nuclear Weapons Headed for the Trash," *Bulletin of Atomic Scientists*, vol. 47, no. 10, December 1991, p. 16.

3. Barry Blechman and Cathleen Fisher, "An American Legacy: Building a Nuclear Weapon-Free World," *The Final Report of the Steering Committee*

Project on Eliminating Weapons of Mass Destruction (Washington D.C.: Henry L Stimson Centre, March 1997).

4. President Bush's speech on missile defence delivered at the National Defence University (NDU), Washington, May 1, 2001. Available at http://www.acronym.org.uk

5. The NPR is a comprehensive review of US strategic nuclear policies, doctrine, force structure, command and control, operations, supporting infrastructure, safety, security, and arms control. The Congressionally mandated report, prepared by the secretary of defence, also examines the selection of targets, stockpile levels, and new and potential threats to the United States and its allies and interests worldwide.

6. Term as used by Ivo H. Daalder and James M. Lindsay, "A New Agenda for Nuclear Weapons: On Nuclear Weapons, Destroy and Codify," *The Brookings Institution Policy Brief*, no. 94, 2002.

7. The present hedge comprises mainly retired warheads from the 1987 INF Treaty and the 1991 START I accord, which required destruction of delivery vehicles (bombers and missiles) but not the warheads.

8. As cited by Pamela Hess, "Bring Back the Nukes," http://www.spacewar.com, December 14, 2005.

9. Robert S. Norris and Hans M. Kristensen, "US Nuclear Forces, 2006," *Bulletin of Atomic Scientists*, vol. 62, no.1, January-February 2006.

10. In the initial aftermath of the USSR's break-up, President Yeltsin and Foreign Minister Andrei Kozyrev sought a close relationship with the West. However, this tendency had dissipated by the end of the decade of the 1990s as a result of soured relations over the war in Bosnia, expansion of NATO and growing Russian unhappiness over the American tendency to unilaterally use power.

11. "Yeltsin Rattles Nuclear Sabre After Criticism Over Chechnya," *Disarmament Diplomacy*, Issue no. 42. Emphasis added.

12. "A Gladiator's Victory" reproduced in What the Papers Say, March 27, 2001 and cited by Thomas Ambrosio, *Challenging America's Global Preeminence: Russia's Quest for Multipolarity* (Hampshire: Ashgate Publishing Ltd, 2005), p. 162.

13. "Russia Calls NATO 'Cynical' Over Chechnya," *Reuters* (Moscow), December 3, 1999. It may be recalled that the first wave of "nuclearisation of Russian military thinking" surfaced after the end of the first war in Chechnya in 1997, when Russian Defence Minister Igor Sergeyev commissioned programmes for the development of the Topol M ICBM and the Iskander dual-use tactical land-based ballistic missile. For more on this, see Alexander A. Pikayev, "Speculations on Russia's Deterrence Policy," in Ian Kenyon and John Simpson, eds., *Deterrence and the New Global Security Environment* (Oxon: Taylor and Francis, 2006), p. 102.

14. This had been the result of the unhappiness of the conventional armed Services over the imbalanced procurement policy in favour of nuclear forces that had been initiated in 1997 after the first Chechen War, but which threw up the inadequacies in the conventional capabilities in the Chechen War in 1999. Therefore, in the early years of the new decade, Russian nuclear forces were largely ignored.
15. As cited in Pikayev, n. 14, p. 107.
16. Richard Cobbold, "Comment: A Debating Society," *RUSI Journal*, vol. 152, no.1, February 2007.
17. "Blair Faces Backlash Over Nuclear Deterrent Replacement," http://www.spacewar.com, December 3, 2006.
18. Lachlan Carmichael, "Blair Unveils Plans to Keep Nuclear Arsenal, Cut Warheads," http://www.spacewar.com, December 4, 2006.
19. "Chirac Reasserts French Nuclear Weapons Policy," *Disarmament Diplomacy*, no. 82, Spring 2006.
20. Dominique Lalanne, "New Nuclear Strategy, New Nuclear Weaponry," *INESAP Bulletin*, no. 23.
21. Chirac's speech, n.19. The last two points were criticised for providing a rationale for nuclear weapons acquisition to other states, most notably Iran, which already perceives its nuclear programme more for status and pride than security.
22. Bush's speech, n. 4.
23. As derived from the official briefing of the US Department of Defence, dated January 9, 2002, and made available by BASIC on http://www.basicint.org.
24. For more on rationale of BMD, see Manpreet Sethi, "Ballistic Missile Defence" in Jasjit Singh and Manpreet Sethi, *Nuclear Deterrence and Diplomacy* (New Delhi: Knowledge World, 2004) pp. 92-101.
25. "US Releases Technical Details on Missile Shield in Central Europe," http://www.spacewar.com, April 19, 2007
26. A report entitled, "US-Russian Relations in Nuclear Arms Reductions: Current State and Prospects," prepared by the Russian Centre for Arms Control, Energy and Environmental Studies had stated in June 2001 that the US move was aimed at devaluing the Russian nuclear arsenal and warned that Russia would have to take adequate measures in response. As quoted in Eugene Miasnikov, "Russian Perceptions of US-Russian Security Relations and Responses to NMD," *INESAP Bulletin*, no. 18, 2001.
27. Sergei Kortunov, "Russia Must Stay Nuclear," http://www.spacewar.com, November 29, 2006.
28. As cited by Alexander Bogatyrov, "Russia Should Renew its Nuclear Arsenal," http://www.spacewar.com, February 13, 2007.

29. Martin Sieff, "Rumblings From Russia," http://www.spacewar.com, October 19, 2006.
30. Mikhail Barbanov, "Why Russia Fears BMD," http://www.spacewar.com, February 15, 2007.
31. As cited by Sieff, n. 29.
32. Dmitry Danilov, "Europe's BMD Turmoil," *The Post Chronicle*, April 12, 2007
33. Martin Sieff, "Russian Threat to Withdraw From INF Not Bluff," http://www.spacewar.com, February 21, 2007.
34. Chirac's remark during a Press conference on March 9, 2007, and as cited by Oliver Meier, "Europeans Split over US Missile Defence Plans," *Arms Control Today*, April 2007.
35. BASIC, n.23.
36. James J. Wirtz and Jeffrey A. Larsen, *Nuclear Transformation: The New US Nuclear Doctrine* (Hampshire: Palgrave Macmillan, 2005).
37. Robert W. Nelson, "Low-Yield Earth-Penetrating Nuclear Weapons," *FAS Public Interest Report*, January-February 2001. http://www.fas.org. Emphasis added.
38. Nelson, Ibid.
39. It may be mentioned that the Spratt-Furse Amendment of 1994 prohibited the US Administration to undertake R&D on low yield nuclear weapons, which were technically defined as those with a yield of less than 5 kilotons.
40. Jonathan Medalia, "Nuclear Weapons: The Reliable Replacement Warhead Program," *Congressional Research Service*, May 24, 2005, p.6
41. Wade Boese, "New US Warhead Design Selected," *Arms Control Today*, April 2007.
42. As cited in Walter Pincus, "Plan to Study Nuclear Warheads Stirs Concern," *Washington Post*, April 6, 2006.
43. Statement at cited in Stephen I. Schwartz, "Warheads Aren't Forever", *Bulletin of Atomic Scientists*, vol 61, no. 5, September/October 2005. pp. 58-64.
44. Department of Defence, *Quadrennial Defense Review Report 2006*, p. 49
45. Walter Pincus, "Nuclear Warhead Plan Draws Opposition," *Washington Post*, March 4, 2007
46. "US Retains Right for Nuclear Tests if Necessary," http://www.spacewar.com, March 14, 2007.
47. John Fox, "Nuclear Testing Would be Debated, US General Says," *Global Security Newswire*, March 30, 2007.
48. Wade Boese, "Bush Seeks Budget Boost for Future Warhead," *Arms Control Today*, March 2007. It is estimated that since the NPR, there has been more than

a billion dollar jump in nuclear weapons spending. See Frida Berrigan, "Nuclear Hypocrisy and Iran," http://www.justinternational.org, March 2007.

49. "Russia Against US MD Plans for Europe," http://www.spacewar.com, December 27, 2006.

50. "Hi-Tech N-Sub Launched by Russia After 17 Years," *Times of India*, April 16, 2007.

51. The onerous and complicated task instead has been left to a Bilateral Implementation Commission that is expected to meet at least twice a year to deal with issues of compliance.

52. A similar viewpoint has been expressed by Kenyon and Simpson eds., n. 3, p. 9ff.

53. For an informative analysis of this shift, see Rajesh Rajagopalan, "Nuclear Deterrence: The Return of the Denial Strategy," *Asian Strategic Review* 1998-99 (New Delhi: IDSA, 1999), pp 151-167.

54. Interestingly, some Pakistani literature points to the same logic being used by India to mount a small nuclear attack against them.

55. The PSI and CSI are US led counter-proliferation initiatives that seek to conduct intelligence-based operations to detect or intercept cargo suspected of carrying WMD usable material. While India is yet to join the PSI, some of its ports are already CSI compliant.

56. The resolution was adopted in April 2004, soon after the revelations of the extent of the A.Q. Khan proliferation network. It mandated all countries to promulgate national legislation criminalising WMD proliferation and enforce effective export controls to minimise chances of WMD proliferation. National reports to that effect are to be submitted to a UNSCR 1540 Committee.

57. For more on this, see Stephen M. Younger, "Nuclear Weapons in the 21st Century," Los Alamos National Laboratory document no. LAUR-00-2850, June 27, 2000.

58. Wade Boese, "Global Strike Still on Pentagon Wish List," *Arms Control Today*, April 2007.

59. Viktor Litovkin, "New American Non-Nuclear ICBM Creates Global Dangers," http://www.spacewar.com, June 16, 2006.

60. "Hypersonic Scramjet Projectile Flies in Missile Test," http://www.spacedaily.com, September 04, 2001.

61. Cobbold, n. 16, pp 6-7.

62. Putin's Speech at the 43rd Munich Conference on Security Policy, February 10, 2007. As available at http://www.securityconference.de.

63. Martin Sieff, "8 Nations Now Building ICBM Nuclear Missiles," http://www.spacewar.com, December 26, 2006.

64. Report of UN Secretary General, 2005.

4

Nuclear North Korea: Shifting Strategic Calculations?

Monika Chansoria

The North Korean nuclear issue constituted a key nuclear non-proliferation crisis of the post-Cold War era. The crisis over North Korea's nuclear programme raised an essential query as to whether the global non-proliferation regime, symbolised by the nuclear Non-Proliferation Treaty (NPT) was inescapably breaking down. The North Korean nuclear crisis hogged considerable limelight since the post-Cold War years and continues to do so, with Pyongyang repeatedly pleading that it has been a victim of US hostility. Significantly, the United States' rhetoric towards Pyongyang too is far from being conciliatory. The US refused to discuss formulating a non-aggression pact or replacing the 1953 armistice with a peace treaty[1] until the North reassured it that the nuclear programme had been stopped.

Yet, North Korea not only exists, but also attracts global prime time coverage, with its nuclear and missile brinkmanship diplomacy, deftly demonstrated by its conducting the nuclear test on October 9, 2006. North Korea started its nuclear programme in the early 1950s when North Korean scientists began cooperating with the Soviet and Chinese nuclear programmes. Pyongyang acquired its initial nuclear facilities in the 1960s, mostly from the Soviet Union, and built a significant nuclear complex in the 1970s and 1980s. Most experts believe that the main purpose of North Korea's nuclear programme has been to acquire nuclear weapons.[2]

The Soviet-supplied, 25 megawatt (MW) reactor at Yongbyon, a city located about 85 km north of the capital Pyongyang, was well suited to the production of plutonium for weapons. North Korea probably produced and separated in the range of 6 to 12 kg of plutonium before the reactor was shut down in 1994 in the context of the 1994 Agreed Framework with the United States.[3]

Though North Korea's nuclear programme started well before 1985, it was only after it joined the NPT in the same year that global attention was focussed on its activities in this field, especially since the country pursued an active programme in violation of the treaty. These violations centred on a number of facilities at the Yongbyon Nuclear Research Centre. The key facilities at Yongbyon included an operational 5 MW electric nuclear power reactor, a large-scale reprocessing plant for plutonium extraction that was partially completed, a number of radiochemistry laboratories that could be used for plutonium extraction, a high-explosive testing facility, and a fuel fabrication plant.

Meanwhile, the United States' intelligence agencies had come to the conclusion in the early 1990s that North Korea had extracted plutonium at the Yongbyon reprocessing plant, and possibly at a number of radiochemistry laboratories, using irradiated fuel rods from the 5 MW reactor, which was thought to have been partially or fully refuelled in 1989.

It is technically feasible that North Korea could have obtained as much as 12 kg of plutonium, enough to manufacture one or two nuclear weapons. It was assessed by most US intelligence agencies at that time that the amount of plutonium recovered by the country was more than it declared to the International Atomic Energy Agency (IAEA) and that this amount would have been enough to make one or possibly two nuclear weapons.[4] In May 1992, the IAEA initiated a series of inspections and visits to verify North Korea's initial inventory of nuclear facilities and materials and during the process and course of the year, the agency found discrepancies in the country's declaration of levels of past plutonium production. In an effort to resolve the discrepancies, the IAEA in 1993 called for a "special inspection" of two undeclared sites near the Yongbyon nuclear complex. Moreover, the North Korean decision to withdraw from the NPT took the international community by surprise and sprung the US Administration into action. It immediately initiated negotiations with North Korea, and by June 1993, had succeeded in persuading the country to suspend its withdrawal. Nevertheless, North Korea refused to have itself considered a full party to the NPT and, hence, refuted the right of the IAEA to conduct even ad hoc or routine inspections.[5] Consequently, the director general of the IAEA stated by the end of 1993 that IAEA safeguards could no longer provide "any meaningful assurances" that nuclear materials were not being diverted for weapons production.[6]

Thereafter, by any reckoning, 1994 was a rare year for North Korea, both the best and the worst of times in Pyongyang's chequered international image. The year started with the continuation of nuclear brinkmanship — an endless end game, as it were — but closed with what promised to be a "grand bargain," if implemented, or the prospect of cooperative security of two-plus-four[7] (the two Koreas plus Japan, China, Russia, and the United States).

Pyongyang initially agreed to an IAEA inspection of its declared facilities in March 1994, as part of a complicated package deal, but later blocked the agency from taking radioactive samples at the plutonium extraction plant at Yongbyon on the ground that key elements of the deal had not been fulfilled. The crisis grew by mid-May 1994, when the country started to de-fuel the 5 MW reactor, while refusing to implement procedures placed by the IAEA to segregate 300 fuel rods, which had been carefully selected from the 8,000-rod core. If an analysis had been made of the radioactive signature of the segregated rods, it could have indicated how long the rods had been in the reactor, which would have permitted the IAEA to determine whether North Korea had the capacity/capability to obtain plutonium for one or two nuclear devices.[8]

Crucially, the United States understood the stakes at play vis-à-vis the nuclear crisis in Pyongyang and thereby appeared to be willing to offer a package deal to the cloistered Kim Jong Il regime, and on August 12, 1994, following a week of intense discussions in Geneva, the US and North Korea issued a joint statement of principles for settling the dispute via a package deal. On October 21, 1994, after a month of difficult rounds of discussions, both parties signed a landmark Geneva Accord or what also came to be known as the Agreed Framework and a confidential document as appendix. The accord provided a roadmap to an overall solution of the Korean nuclear issue through a comprehensive *quid-pro-quo* package deal. According to Samuel S. Kim, it was a carefully choreographed "swim or sink together" joint venture of reciprocal steps that both sides were expected to take in a nine-year implementation process rotating through five distinct stages, with specific measures to be completed on specified dates.[9]

It would be apt to say here that the Kim Jong Il regime managed to translate nuclear brinkmanship into diplomatic breakthrough, and in terms of foreign policy, North Korea harvested substantially. However, the enigma of North Korean politics continued largely unabated in the times ahead, characterised by a lack of policy-making transparency and despite all signs pointing to the need for urgent structural reforms of the economy, a continued hesitancy to do so. Each side retained a veto as the accord gave both sides more or less equal leverage, against reneging. Accordingly, North Korea agreed to freeze, halt, and eventually dismantle its 5 MW graphite-moderated reactor in operation and the 50 MW and 200 MW graphite-moderated reactors under construction, and related facilities, in addition to remaining a party to the NPT and fully complying with its safeguards agreement with the IAEA. In return, Pyongyang, too, got a fine deal from Washington — a comprehensive security, political and economic package whereby the US agreed to organise under its leadership, an international consortium to finance and supply two light water reactors (LWRs) with a total capacity of 2,000 MW by 2003 (worth around $4 billion) in addition to delivering alternative energy in the form of heavy fuel oil shipments to offset the energy forgone due to the freeze, at a rate of 500,000 tonnes annually during the transition period. Moreover, it was also assured that the barriers to trade and investment would be reduced.[10]

The signing of the Geneva Accord was followed by a flurry of US-Democratic People's Republic of Korea (DPRK) talks in Pyongyang,

Beijing and Washington. On November 28, 1994, the IAEA publicly stated that its team visited the nuclear facilities in Yongbyon and Taechon and "confirmed that these facilities were not in operation and that construction work had stopped."[11] In early December 1994, US and North Korean officials met at the State Department and announced that they had resolved most of the technical issues required to open liaison offices in their respective capitals and that a US delegation would soon go to Pyongyang to examine potential sites for an office. Thus, the first stage of Washington-Pyongyang rapprochement began and ended on an upbeat note.

Even though the implementation of the 1994 Agreed Framework on the nuclear issue preoccupied US-North Korean relations for a few years, by late 1997, Pyongyang began to accuse Washington in increasingly strident terms of failing to abide by the agreement. It cited three concerns: continuing economic sanctions, delayed delivery of heavy fuel oil, and delays in the construction of LWRs by the KEDO. The key elements on the US side were a formal statement of non-aggression, providing a light water reactor and making progress toward normalisation of ties. However, the US was four years behind schedule in providing the reactor.[12] When these pleadings did not elicit the desired responses from Washington, Pyongyang halted work on the canning of spent nuclear fuel and threatened to reopen the reprocessing plant and nuclear reactor at Yongbyon.[13]

The conflict between Washington and Pyongyang resurfaced to the forefront by late 1997 and policy-makers in Washington expressed concerns about intelligence information, indicating that North Korea was constructing a secret underground facility. When the Clinton Administration briefed Congress that North Korea was constructing a secret underground facility, which appeared to be associated with nuclear weapons development, many in Congress raised their concerns over the very viability of the Agreed Framework. It became increasingly evident that the North Koreans were making progress in developing a threatening nuclear weapons capability. All of the above efforts, though, did not succeed in bringing out anything substantial.

Since the framework was not a formal treaty but rather a set of guidelines designed to help the two countries that were deeply mistrustful of each other, it became evidently clear that both sides began backing out of the framework well before autumn of 2002, with each side accusing the other of not fulfilling its framework obligations, leading to the corrosion of the Agreed Framework. The subsequent collapse of the Agreed Framework dealt a serious blow to the security situation in the Korean Peninsula and plunged it into yet another impasse, marked by suspicion and mistrust.

Collapse of the Agreed Framework: Nuke Crisis Resurfaces

Against the backdrop of the clear and continuing proliferation threats from Pyongyang, along with a Republican-dominated Congress in Washington, in November 1998, President Clinton established a North Korea Policy Review Team, led by William J. Perry, to conduct an extensive review of US policy toward the DPRK. The Perry Report recommended a comprehensive and integrated two-path strategy, having profound implications for the future of the US-DPRK relations[14] wherein the report stated that acquisition of nuclear weapons or long-range missiles by North Korea and especially the combination of the two (nuclear weapons and long-range missiles) could undermine the relative stability and cause extensive damage if deterrence failed. Acquisition of such weapons by North Korea could also spark an arms race in the region, undermine the relative stability of deterrence on the Korean Peninsula and would surely do grave damage to the global non-proliferation regimes covering nuclear weapons and ballistic missiles. A continuation of the DPRK's pattern of selling its missiles for hard currency could also spread destabilising effects to other regions such as the Middle East.

The Perry Committee recommendations, which went on to become the Clinton Administration's key policy on North Korea, rejected the strategy of "buying objectives." It argued, for example, that the DPRK offered to cease its missile exports if the US agreed to compensate it for the forgone earnings from missile exports. The policy review team firmly believed that that such a policy of trading material compensation for security would only encourage the DPRK to further blackmail, and would encourage proliferators worldwide to engage in similar blackmail.

The apprehensions gained strength when the Report of the North Korea Advisory Group, submitted to Congress in October 1999, stated that North Korea has at least enough plutonium for one to two nuclear weapons and reported, "There is little reason to believe that North Korea has not or could not make a nuclear explosive device capable of producing a significant nuclear yield...North Korea's ongoing nuclear programme activity raises the possibility that it could produce additional nuclear weapons."[15] Moreover, the US Department of Energy acknowledged that about 6 kg of plutonium was enough to make a nuclear explosive device.[16] Significantly, these estimates were consistent with the US Administration's statements that North Korea probably had enough plutonium for one or two nuclear weapons in addition to the findings of the Rumsfeld Commission which concluded that North Korea's ongoing nuclear programme activity raised the possibility that it could produce additional nuclear weapons.[17]

At the turn of the millennium, the DPRK set off a crisis with its October 2002 admission of an active nuclear weapons programme, in violation of the Agreed Framework with the US. The US and North Korea have been at loggerheads since October 2002, with the George W. Bush Administration confronting Pyongyang about breaking the terms of the 1994 agreement. It would also be imperative to mention here that this was also the time when the 2002 US Nuclear Posture Review (NPR) targeted North Korea with a preemptive strike. The Bush Administration had made its disdain for the Kim Jong Il regime evident from the time it took office. President George W. Bush clubbed North Korea, Iran and Iraq as the "axis of evil"[18] to give expression to that disdain. The 2002 US NPR advocated the construction of a unilateral nuclear deterrence set-up on three legs of a "New Triad": nuclear and non-nuclear offensive strike systems; active and passive defences; and a responsive infrastructure with new capabilities to meet emerging threats. The 2002 US NPR[19] seemed to have substantiated the Bush Administration's new nuclear weapons policy, apparently incorporating renewed concepts that should have been formulated by reviewing the implications of the 9/11 incident. The levels of mistrust were extremely high. With the September 2002 National Security Strategy moving the US towards a stated policy of preemptive strikes, the DPRK appeared apprehensive that if it agreed to disarm and abandon its deterrent posture, the United States would eventually move and destroy it.

Moreover, various officials of the Bush White House, including former National Security Advisor Condoleezza Rice, stated that North Korea had "aggressively pursued a covert programme since 1999," citing a Department of Energy report that indicated that the DPRK tried to buy frequency converters to be used in a gas centrifuge facility to enrich uranium.[20] The North Koreans, led by Vice Foreign Minister Kang Sok Ju, promptly responded to the allegations and asserted that they had the right to pursue nuclear capabilities since the US president had already placed them in the "axis of evil."[21] Acting in accordance with its statements, the North expelled the IAEA inspectors in December 2002 and backed out of the agreement, leading to a nuclear stand-off between the two nations.

The North Koreans went ahead by taking a series of steps at the Yongbyon nuclear site. They removed the seals at all frozen facilities (experimental reactor, storage building, and reprocessing laboratory), dismantled the IAEA monitoring cameras, and expelled the three IAEA international inspectors. The subsequent North Korean actions included tampering with the stored fuel rods, which were a source of weapons-grade plutonium; announcement of plans to restart the experimental reactor; and conduct of ballistic missile tests. These developments apparently suggested deliberate and purposeful moves in the direction of producing nuclear weapons.[22] It was also discovered in October 2002 that North Korea, while freezing its plutonium-based programme, had admitted having taken secretly to using a different route to nuclear weapons, helped by Pakistan. North Korea began seeking nuclear weapons fuel through uranium enrichment that was given a boost by A.Q. Khan, the father of Pakistan's nuclear bomb, who in 2004, admitted proliferating nuclear technology to North Korea and other countries. According to US reports, he made as many as thirteen trips to North Korea in the 1990s and helped supply uranium enrichment equipment and possibly even warhead designs[23] in return for missiles.

Significantly, the North Korean deal opens a window on to the much broader network of illicit proliferation between key states in which A.Q. Khan (Pakistan) was just one of the many players blurring the lines between the actions of states and those of individuals. In the early 1990s, it was revealed that the Chinese had supplied M-11 missiles to Pakistan, the result of a suspected 1987 deal, but these were left in their crates at an air force base west of Lahore to try and avoid sanctions and growing international pressure on China's activities. China also helped Pakistan build an M-11 factory near Rawalpindi. In the mid-1990s, when the intelligence leaked publicly, there were calls from Congress to sanction either China or Pakistan but the Clinton Administration was desperate to avoid taking such actions as it was trying to improve relations with both countries. Even China itself was nervous about going too far and risking US wrath and, consequently, Beijing began to edge away from its active role in missile proliferation.[24]

Islamabad was left looking elsewhere for a missile with a longer range and which could carry a larger payload. The North Korean "Nodong" fitted the bill. North Korea was also more likely to be a reliable vendor of ballistic missile technology. It was known to be willing to sell pretty much anything for hard cash, of which it was desperately short.[25] This was also the time when Pakistani Prime Minister Benazir Bhutto adamantly declared that the deal with the North Koreans was for cash and said, "When I went to North Korea, A.Q. Khan told me we can get their (missile) technology (so) that we can compare to our own. So I took (it) up with Kim Il Sung...December '93 I talked to him, he agreed...and it was in cash, they needed money and so it was done for cash, with no exchange of nuclear technology. Exchanging nuclear technology for missiles was never even discussed during my visit."[26] As a result of the deal, Khan got the Nodong and rechristened it the Ghauri.

In the years after Benazir Bhutto's visit, between January 1997 and March 1998, North Korea exported components for twelve Nodong missiles to Pakistan. In April 1998, Khan finally tested the Ghauri, claiming that his contribution to Pakistan's security extended far beyond simply enriching uranium. The money for the missiles was paid in instalments, under the cover of conventional arms purchases. It has been estimated that the Nodongs would have cost at least $3 billion.[27] But by 1997, cash was getting harder to come by for the Pakistani government, with foreign reserves nose-diving to critically low levels, almost putting the country on an edge of default.[28] Could they have looked for an alternative form of payment? The US government source leak to *The New York Times* in October 2002 that Pakistan was the likely source of the North Korean gas centrifuge uranium enrichment programme[29] fuelled to the notion of an exchange, since by the mid-1990s, North Korea was looking for help vis-à-vis its clandestine enrichment programme. Barter was in the interest of both countries, as each had technology the other desperately wanted and neither had the cash to pay for it. The nuclear-for-missile barter trade between Islamabad and Pyongyang probably began in 1997 and continued at least until July 2002.[30]

Crucially, following Pyongyang's declaration in 2002 of its nuclear capability, in addition to the US, several Asian countries, including China, recognised that a nuclear-armed North Korea presented a threat to regional stability. Prominently, Beijing's concerns focussed primarily on potential ripple effects throughout Northeast Asia in reaction to a nuclear-armed North Korea. In addition, Beijing had a strong interest in avoiding disruptions in its beneficial economic relations with South Korea.

Since the very beginning, China appears to have been reluctant to pressurise North Korea intensely, fearing a collapse of the Kim Jong Il regime would cause serious economic and social problems for China. China does not seem keen to stretch the limits too far by alienating its Communist ally. As a matter of fact, the relationship between China and North Korea was solidified early during the years of the Korean War in the 1950s. In addition to this, Beijing and Pyongyang have also shared ideological affinity, having weathered the collapse of Communism in Eastern Europe and the Soviet Union. As two of the handful of the world's "Last Leninists,"[31] the continued existence of the other is of considerable importance to both these nations. Pyongyang is economically dependent on Beijing, which provides most of its food and energy supplies. Furthermore, North Korea gets about 70 percent of its food from China that, incidentally, is the provider of 70 to 80 percent of North Korea's conventional fuel. China currently provides tens of millions of dollars' worth of aid to North Korea, with two-way trade with China constituting about one-third of North Korea's entire trade. In addition, numerous reports have pointed out that considerable official and unofficial cross-border trade between North Korea and China goes unreported, and North Korea's weapons sales too, are not included in most trade estimates. More critically, the period between 1995-98 saw massive floods devastate an already weakened North Korean economy, with China contributing an estimated $200 million worth of food aid annually. Keeping in mind all these statistics, there are overriding concerns in Beijing to prevent economic or military crises that would lead to thousands of North Korean refugees fleeing across the 1,400-km border into China, with an estimated 300,000 North Koreans already residing illegally in China, in addition to economic refugees continually crossing the border to seek opportunities in China, placing increased pressure on the Chinese economy.

Therefore, China appears to be fretful that isolating North Korea might cause its regime to collapse, which, in turn, could witness harmful strategic consequences. From Beijing's perspective, if there comes a moment which leads to the collapse of the Kim Jong Il regime in North Korea, it could prospectively leave China with a unified neighbour and US troops placed right next to its border, a situation that Beijing in all probability would be absolutely averse to.

In a way, the Chinese diplomatic prestige is being tested here, with Foreign Minister Li Zhaoxing asserting time and again, that the six-party process was the only "realistic and viable course" for resolving the nuclear stand-off. A crucial factor in the future would be to judge as to how far Beijing would go to persuade Pyongyang. Significantly, Washington realises that getting support from Beijing would be crucial to deal with Pyongyang, since China is North Korea's main ally and trading partner. In all possibility, China would like to see the Kim Jong Il regime survive in North Korea, and, in addition to this, Beijing envisages itself in a position of having brokered some sort of agreement in Northeast Asia, leading to enhancement of its stature as a peace-maker, a regional power and, most significantly, a responsible player on the global platform. In the above-mentioned backdrop, it appears abundantly clear that China indeed is in the driver's seat more than ever, with the added responsibility of becoming part of the solution and averting conflict with the newly shifted strategic ground in Northeast Asia courtesy Pyongyang going nuclear.

Keeping the above-mentioned aspects in mind, after much diplomatic deliberations, and a significant role played by China, the six-party talks that included North Korea, South Korea, Japan, China, Russia and the United States, hosted by Beijing, got underway in 2003 to resolve the North Korean nuclear impasse. The six-party talks harnessed the diplomatic leverage of the parties most directly affected by the DPRK's proliferation to Washington's effort to dismantle in a permanent, thorough and transparent manner all of North Korea's nuclear programmes. There is an emerging sense that whatsoever may be the orientations, whether hawkish or dovish, the US always appeared to want to engage North Korea by elevating dialogue and treading towards orchestrating international pressure to force North Korea to dismantle its nuclear weapons programme.

The option for a negotiated solution seemed to be the only pertinent solution to resolve the North Korean nuclear crisis, and the six-party talks have been viewed as a step in the right direction in this regard. The US insisted that North Korea dismantle its nuclear programme before receiving any benefits, but Pyongyang wanted to receive major concessions, including obtaining a formal security guarantee from Washington, and removing political and legal obstacles to economic assistance from Japan, South Korea, and international financial institutions, before giving up its most important negotiating leverage. Apparently, this has been the sticking point in every negotiation witnessed in the case of North Korea. Though the creation of the six-party negotiating mechanism in 2003 was a positive development and, subsequently, various rounds of talks have been held, it has not as yet yielded tangible results. While the talks did enable the United States to more closely engage China on the issue of North Korea's nuclear future, it remained unclear how far Beijing could, or was willing to, go in pressuring North Korea to abandon its programme. China appeared averse to the idea of regime collapse in Pyongyang or a war between the United States and North Korea that could result in US troops being placed on the Chinese border. Moreover, North Korea repeatedly boycotted the six-nation nuclear arms talks on numerous occasions, citing a "hostile" US policy. The six-party talks made stringent efforts to make progress towards a statement of basic principles for negotiations aimed at persuading Pyongyang to disarm. However, the deliberations ran into rough weather with Pyongyang restating its rejection of a US demand that it disarm its nuclear weapons. On the other hand, Washington too was categorical that it would not lift economic sanctions or provide security assurances until it could be verified that North Korea had dismantled its nuclear programme. Against this backdrop, chances to secure a diplomatic solution to the North Korean nuclear crisis appeared bleak after nearly three years of deadlock. There has been a sense of cynicism vis-à-vis the six-party talks owing to the fruitless trajectory of the multiple rounds of talks, which failed to yield a breakthrough.

Pyongyang Goes Nuclear

October 9, 2006, went down in history as the date on which the world community witnessed what had long been suspected, speculated, and to a certain extent, feared, when North Korea successfully tested a nuclear device by conducting an underground nuclear test and thereby changed the orientation of the crisis altogether. The North Korean Foreign Ministry somewhat grandly claimed that the country had made a great leap forward in the building of a great, prosperous, powerful socialist nation,[32] characterising the test as "a self-defensive counter-measure against the United States' daily increasing nuclear threat and financial sanctions against it."

On the other hand, the US reacted to the nuclear tests by stating that it would continue to strive for implementation of the September 2005 Joint Statement[33] which resulted from the six-party talks, offering North Korea a clear path to a positive future and concrete benefits in return for carrying out its commitment to denuclearise. "We call on all five members of the Six-Party Talks and the United Nations Security Council—as stated in United Nations Security Council Resolution 1695 — to exert every effort to persuade North Korea that the test of a nuclear weapon would only bring its further isolation and would not be in the interest of the North Korean people."[34] Earlier, sensing the reality of a nuclear North Korea, there were apprehensions that such a situation would upset East Asia's entire military balance, causing South Korea, Japan and even Taiwan to consider developing equivalent deterrents.[35] However, this indeed became a reality and the entire Korean Peninsula was pushed into a period of grave uncertainty.

Since the announcement of the resumption of the six-party talks by Assistant Secretary of State and chief US negotiator Christopher Hill on January 19, 2007, it is expected that Pyongyang would follow through on its disarmament agreement made subsequently on February 13, with Hill expressing the hope that Pyongyang would meet the mid-April 2007 deadline set by the deal to halt operations at its Yongbyon nuclear reactor and readmit IAEA inspectors.[36] In return, North Korea would reportedly receive 50,000 tonnes of heavy fuel for energy use initially and eventually receive one million tonnes of heavy fuel or equivalent energy aid if it permanently closed its nuclear facilities and completely disbanded its atomic weapons programme. The US, China, Japan, South Korea and Russia reportedly reached tentative agreements to provide North Korea with $400 million in fuel oil and aid in return for the North's starting to dismantle nuclear facilities and allowing inspectors back into the country. The North would for now hold onto the arsenal that the US believes contains more than six nuclear weapons or fuel. It has to be acknowledged that North Korea has successfully manoeuvred to bring the region back to its former status quo.[37]

As of February 2007, North Korea had a total estimated plutonium stock of between 46 and 64 kg, of which about 28-50 kg are estimated to be in separated form and usable in nuclear weapons. The vast majority of North Korea's separated plutonium—at least 80 per cent—was produced since North Korea's freeze on production and reprocessing ended in late 2002.[38]

The North Korean negotiators yet again repeated the pattern of hard bargaining by refusing to participate in the latest round of multilateral negotiations launched in early 2007, saying they were waiting for the transfer of $25 million that had been frozen at a bank in Macau since 2005 due to US accusations of North Korean money laundering and counterfeiting. North Korea has repeatedly said it will not begin implementing the six-nation disarmament accord signed on February 13 until the money is safely back in its hands. This could well be considered as an erroneous move since giving new incentives and pulling sanctions off would be perceived by Pyongyang and the world as a reward for defying the world and going nuclear. This might just be a triggering point for nations such as Iran that are tipped to be on the edge of going nuclear. The crisis continues unabated and what appears lucid is that any likely solution would have to fall in the category of a grand bargain. A steep uphill task is around the corner with the only difference being that the North Koreans now have actually gained nuclear ability as opposed to the earlier situation of possessing the capability to perhaps go nuclear.

The Likely Road Ahead

A nuclear-armed North Korea fundamentally alters the geo-political picture in Northeast Asia. A nuclear arms race among Japan, South Korea, and even Taiwan could ensue to the detriment of China's own long-term security interests, which would, in turn, weaken the global non-proliferation initiative. Given North Korea's record of selling weaponry and nuclear technology abroad, its proclivities for brinkmanship and the likely domino effect of nuclear proliferation in East Asia,[39] in all it makes the state of affairs even more hazardous. There is increasing belief among some Western analysts that the US and its regional partners, South Korea, Japan, China and Russia, should offer Pyongyang carrots but threaten sticks if it remains obstinate.

Indeed, the balance of equations in the Asian context has shifted noticeably in the aftermath of North Korea going nuclear, with the insecurities of nations such as Japan having risen many notches higher since Pyongyang went nuclear as well as the after the July 2006 missile tests conducted by the Kim Jong Il regime. This sentiment was visibly demonstrated in the statement issued by the Japanese Foreign Ministry when it announced, "In view of the development, deployment and proliferation of ballistic missiles in the region, and the clear and present threats such as the recent missile launches by North Korea in particular, the Government of Japan will continue to do its utmost to build up its BMD capabilities in close cooperation with the USG (United States Government) and with a sense of urgency."[40] The Japanese government decided to fund joint technical research on theatre missile defence (TMD) with the US, followed by an agreement in August 1999 to launch a five-year research and development programme, focussing on a navy theatre-wide defence (NTWD) system, which would be deployed on Aegis ships.

Japan initially was reluctant to be a participant in the US TMD programme primarily because it had doubts regarding the technical feasibility and effectiveness of these missile defence components.[41] However, North Korea's missile launch over Japan's main islands in August 1998 proved to be a major catalyst in convincing Japanese policy-makers of the potential danger of ballistic missile attacks.

Going by this argument, a plausible means for the Japanese to maintain and consequently strengthen their existing deterrent against North Korea in the immediate case and against China in the long-run would include the acceleration of US-Japan cooperation in the field of ballistic missile defence (BMD). In addition to this, the Japanese Navy held its annual fleet review on October 29, 2006, with rather comprehensible striking capabilities, with Japanese Prime Minister Shinzo Abe deftly stating, "Our country's Self-Defence Forces are being called upon to play a more crucial and varied role...I believe this is an excellent opportunity to demonstrate our readiness."[42] Crucially, Abe singled out North Korea as a major threat to Japan, saying its recent ballistic missile test launches and its claim to have exploded a nuclear device on October 9 are "grave and unforgivable."[43]

The pivotal question now is whether the Kim Jong Il regime can survive the political fallout as the world's newest nuclear power in that any shift in policy by China or South Korea would be at least partly based on the anticipated reaction of Japan, the nation that today feels most threatened by North Korea's ballistic missiles. Analysts have assumed that a nuclear-armed North Korea would lead Tokyo to accelerate plans to redraft its pacifist Constitution and rearm itself with a more aggressive military.[44] North Korea may be prepared to restrict some nuclear activities in return for guarantees and commitments from the US and other powers. It would not be prudent, however, to anticipate an early end to Pyongyang's programme or to dangers this programme poses both for security in East Asia and for the future viability of the non-proliferation regime.[45]

These developments have hastened the reactions of the missile defence advocates who feel that the time is ripe to accelerate the process of deployment of the US missile defence systems. In the wake of all these developments, Riki Ellison, president of the Missile Defence Advocacy Alliance (MDAA), made a call to action by the United States based on the lessons learned of the long-range missile testing of North Korea. "Reflecting on the July 4 incident of the launching of multiple missiles from North Korea, against international sanctions, agreements and world opinion last month, a reality that seems to be getting apparent... the people of Hawaii, Washington, Oregon and California are more vulnerable than previously thought and need additional missile defence protection."[46] Clearly, these trepidations have got strengthened since the successful conduct of the nuclear test, in addition to Iran's active participation with North Korea adding ominous ramifications to the international proliferation of ballistic missiles. Therefore, an understanding that seems to be becoming apparent in the backdrop is that there is increasing reason for the United States to expand missile defence bases in other countries so that the US and its allies with their populations will have protection against possible ballistic missile attacks stemming from the Middle East and Northeast Asia.

The situation in the post-October 9 scenario raises the stakes many notches higher in that Pyongyang is in possession of both the nuclear weapon and its means of delivery. In addition, North Korea might threaten to sell its nuclear technology to other states that are of considerable proliferation concern or even terrorist organisations in order to fund its regime and revive its collapsing economy. The picture seems bleak and the stakes have never been higher given North Korea's record of selling weaponry and nuclear technology abroad. Will all these possibilities ultimately plunge the entire Asian continent in general and the East Asian region in particular into an (nuclear) arms race? Apparently, this possibility very much exists and cannot be ruled out entirely. The toughest proliferation cases will get tougher in that there are concerns that Iran is taking its cues from the North Korea playbook. Furthermore, in South Asia, India for sure, can take the credit for being conscientious in ensuring that its weapons material and technology are guarded against commercial and illicit export to other countries. New Delhi, indeed, has a spotless record in this arena, very much in contrast with the position of Pakistan, whose enrichment technology has been diverted to Iran, North Korea and Libya and, in return, Pyongyang has provided adequate aid to Pakistan's missile programme.

Considering all these factors, the regional balance undoubtedly has been upset by the October 9 nuclear blasts and the dust is not expected to settle any time soon. Pyongyang would not take the road to disarmament and relinquish its nuclear capabilities as is expected by a sizeable section of the world community unless and until it secures massive economic bargains as well as security guarantees for itself from the nations that have been in deliberations with the cloistered Northeast Asian nation. However, what really needs to be watched and judged is how far the US and its allies would be willing to go, so as to disarm North Korea. Critically, Pyongyang's going nuclear brings in a new sense of urgency, making it imperative for the concerned parties to strike out a solution to the long-drawn crisis and ensure that strategic stability prevails in the Korean Peninsula as well as in Asia.

Notes

1. More details available at http://usinfo.state.gov/xarchives/display.html?p=washfile-english&y=2007&m=April&x=20070403171303esnamfuak0.9407465
2. For more details, see Joseph Bermudez, "Exposing North Korea's Secret Nuclear Infrastructure Part I," *Jane's Intelligence Review*, July 1, 1999.
3. For open source estimates of DPRK plutonium production, see *CIA Report to Congress on the Acquisition of Technology Relating to Weapons of Mass Destruction and Advanced Conventional Munitions*, July 1 through December 31, 1998, pp. 5-9.
4. "Tracking Nuclear Proliferation, 1998: North Korea," at: http://www.ceip.org/programs/npp/korea.htm.
5. Manpreet Sethi, "Post-Cold War Nuclear Proliferation: Patterns and Possibilities," *Asian Strategic Review 1997-98* (New Delhi: IDSA), p. 196.
6. More details available at http://www.carnegieendowment.org/files/Tracking_Ch06nkorea.pdf
7. Samuel S. Kim, "North Korea in 1994: Brinkmanship, Breakdown and Breakthrough," *Asian Survey*, vol. 35, no. 1, January 1995, p. 13.
8. Kalpana Chittaranjan, "North Korea: Nuclear Issues," *Strategic Analysis*, vol. 23, no. 8, November 1999, p. 1308.
9. For details, see Kim, n. 7.
10. For the full text of the Geneva Accord, see News and Negotiations, "US, Pyongyang Reach Accord on North's Nuclear Programme," *Arms Control Today*, vol. 24, no. 9, November 1994.
11. For viewing the entire statement visit, http://www.armscontrol.org/factsheets/dprkchron.asp
12. For details, see Jay Solomon and Gordon Fairclough, "Troubled Power Project Plays Role in North Korea Showdown", *Wall Street Journal*, January 30, 2002.
13. David G. Brown, "North Korea in 1998: A Year of Foreboding Developments," *Asian Survey*, vol. 39, no. 1, January/February 1999, p. 130.
14. For details, see William J. Perry, *Review of US Policy toward North Korea: Findings and Recommendations, Unclassified Report*, US Department of State, October 12, 1999.
15. *North Korea Advisory Group Report,* submitted to the US House of Representatives, US Congress, October 29, 1999.

16. US Department of Energy. "Drawing Back the Curtain of Secrecy," RDD-5, January 1, 1999, p II-27, no. 33.
17. For more details, see Rumsfeld Commission Report, Findings and Recommendations, Executive Summary, July 15, 1999, p. 12.
18. Text of the State of the Union Address, Release from the Office of the Press Secretary, January 29, 2002, Washington D.C.
19. Department of Defence, *Nuclear Posture Review 2002* [Excerpts], Submitted to US Congress January 8, 2002.
20. Cited in Brian Knowlton, "North Korea Arms Pact is Now Dead, Powell Says," *International Herald Tribune*, October 21, 2002.
21. For details, see David C. Kang, "The Avoidable Crisis in North Korea," *Orbis*, vol. 47, no. 3, Summer 2003, pp. 503-04.
22. Walter Pincus, "Hints of North Korean Plutonium Output," *Washington Post*, January 31, 2003.
23. For more details, visit http://www.spacewarexpress.com, July 26, 2005.
24. Gordon Corera, *Shopping for Bombs: Nuclear Proliferation, Global Insecurity and the Rise and Fall of the A.Q. Khan Network* (London: C. Hurst & Co. Ltd., 2006), p. 88.
25. Joseph Bermudez, "A Silent Partner," *Jane's Defence Weekly*, May 20, 1998.
26. Peter Roff, "Bhutto Missile Story Raises Hill Hackles," *United Press International*, March 7, 2005.
27. "Pakistan," *Foreign Missile Developments and the Ballistic Missile Threat Through 2015*, Unclassified Summary of the National Intelligence Estimate (Washington D.C.: US Central Intelligence Agency, December 2001), pp. 24-25.
28. Corera, n. 24, p. 90.
29. David E. Sanger, and James Dao, "US Says Pakistan Gave Technology to North Korea," *The New York Times*, October 17, 2002.
30. Gaurav Kampani, "Second Tier Proliferation: The Case of Pakistan and North Korea," *The Nonproliferation Review*, Fall-Winter 2002, p. 108.
31. For more details, see Andrew Scobell, "China and North Korea: From Comrades-in-Arms to Allies at Arm's Length," at http://www.nautilus.org/DPRKBriefing Book/china/PRC_Scobel.pdf, March 2004, p. 2.
32. Official North Korean announcement of the nuclear tests by the Korean Central News Agency, October 9, 2006.
33. The joint statement at the conclusion of the fourth round of the six-party talks, released in Beijing on September 19, 2005, by the Ministry of Foreign Affairs of the People's Republic of China, stated that the six parties unanimously reaffirmed

that the goal of the six-party talks was the verifiable denuclearisation of the Korean Peninsula in a peaceful manner. The DPRK committed to abandoning all nuclear weapons and existing nuclear programmes and returning, at an early date, to the Treaty on the Non-Proliferation of Nuclear Weapons and to IAEA safeguards. The United States affirmed that it has no nuclear weapons on the Korean Peninsula and had no intention to attack or invade the DPRK with nuclear or conventional weapons. The DPRK and the United States undertook to respect each other's sovereignty, exist peacefully together, and take steps to normalise their relations subject to their respective bilateral policies. For more details of the text, visit http://www.state.gov/r/pa/prs/ps/2005/53490.htm.

34. Official US Statement reacting to the North Korean Nuclear Test of October 9, 2006, at http://www.whitehouse.gov/news/releases/2006/10/20061003-10.html.

35. Byung-joon Ahn, "The Man Who Would Be Kim," *Foreign Affairs*, vol. 73, no. 6, November/December 1994, p. 107.

36. For more details, visit http://www.nti.org/d_newswire/issues/2007_3_23.html#A8A72DDF.

37. Jim Yardley and David E. Sanger, "In Shift, A Deal is Being Weighed by North Korea, *The New York Times*, February 13, 2007.

38. For more details, see David Albright and Paul Brannan, "The North Korean Plutonium Stock till February 2007," Institute for Science and International Security, February 20, 2007.

39. Michael E. O'Hanlon, "Pyongyang: Reform or Abyss, *Financial Times*, October 11, 2006.

40. "Deployment of US PAC-3 to Kadena," Press Release by Ministry of Foreign Affairs (MOFA), Japan, July 20, 2006 at http://www.mofa.go.jp/announce/announce/2006/7/0720.html

41. Takeshi Yuzawa, *Japan's Security Policy and the ASEAN Regional Forum: The Search for Multilateral Security in the Asia-Pacific* (New York: Routledge, 2007), p. 138.

42. "Japanese Navy Holds Annual Fleet Review," Associated Press, *Taipei Times*, October 30, 2006 at http://www.taipeitimes.com/News/archives/2006/10/30/2003334012

43. Ibid.

44. Anthony Faiola and Maureen Fan, "North Korea's Political, Economic Gamble," *The Washington Post*, October 10, 2006, p. A12.

45. Jonathan D. Pollack, "North Korea's Nuclear Weapons Program to 2015: Three Scenarios," *Asia Policy*, no. 3, January 2007.

46. For more details visit, http://www.missiledefenseadvocacy.org/

5

Financing "Transformation" of Military Forces: An Overview

Amiya Kumar Ghosh

Despite a large literature, uncertainty remains about exactly what transformation is. A transformed military thinks differently about the art of war and about preparation for battle than the one which is not transformed... Financing the Armed Forces is presumably also affected: transformation might make militaries more or less expensive, either per unit of effect or relative to other components of state budgets.

- Stephen J. Cimbala, *Joint Forces Quarterly*,
issue no. 38, June 2005.

We witness transformation when we see airmen traveling by horseback with tools of trade (GPS and laser range inders) hanging from a saddle. With secure satellite and radio links, they pass target coordinates to bombers, or fighters from the Air Force, Navy or Marines flying miles overhead. We see venerable 40-year-old B-52 precisely place a JDAM just 800 meters from our friendly positions. No single piece of this equation is transformational but together it yields a transformational asymmetrical advantage over any enemy.

- General John P. Jumper, Chief of Staff, US Force in an interview,
Military Aerospace Technology,
Online Edition vol. 1, issue 2, May 2001.

Transformation as a Process

As the first quotation shows, that there is a degree of ambiguity about what transformation of the military is, what kind of investments are required to bring it about and in what timeframe. Accordingly, there is bound to be uncertainty about how much is required to finance it.

The second quotation, which underlines the point that transformation is not just about new technology and acquisition, is also very relevant in this context. Even existing technology and platforms used innovatively can be transformational. It is the dramatic effect on operations that is the hallmark of transformation.

As per the dominant view, the cultural aspects are more important in bringing about transformation of the armed forces than the technologies. The emphasis is on cultural change where "innovation and informed risk taking are encouraged and rewarded – a culture that is characterized by information age." This calls for an "increased emphasis on concept development and experimentation, a change in personnel system and information structure."[1] A cultural change is also required to make the armed services work together. This requires joint doctrine, joint training and interoperability of equipment and systems.

Viewed in this way, the issue of how much to spend on transformation becomes a secondary issue, if not somewhat irrelevant. The financing aspects get more importance when modernisation gets linked to transformation. To provide the link, modernisation is to be viewed as capability building in the context of transformational requirements. Here the most important strategy that has emerged is that of reallocation of resources rather than augmentation of resources.

Defence transformation has preoccupied the US Department of Defence (DoD) for more than a decade. In US defence, two competing views about "transformation" have emerged. Some have defined transformation as a discontinuous or leap-ahead change. This view supports those who believe it is necessary to move money, manpower, and doctrine away from current manpower systems and methods to entirely new technologies and procedures. This is the radical approach. Others tend to define transformation as incremental change using current and modernising technologies in new ways, with the end result of radical improvement.

A conference was held by the Asia-Pacific Centre for Security Studies in February-March, 2004 to discuss defence transformation. No strong consensus emerged during the conference as to what "defence transformation" exactly entailed. Some saw defence transformation as a process, others as an objective. Most definitions of defence transformation, however, see it largely fed by current breakthroughs in information technology (IT), creating new synergistic capabilities, and involving significant and fundamental changes in military doctrine, organisations, and institutions.[2]

Vice Admiral (Retd) Arthur Cebrowski the first director of the office of Force Transformation in US Defence, stated, "Transformation is foremost a continuing process. It does not have an end point. Transformation is meant to create or anticipate the future. Transformation is meant to deal with co-evolution of concepts, processes, organisations and technology. Change in any one of these areas necessitates change in all."[3]

Cebrowski's argument that military transformation is a process not a destination, means it cannot be achieved through sequential planning. If transformation comprised linear sequential planning, the issue of financing it could be addressed methodically. Nor can "co-evolution of concepts, processes, organisations and technology" be given a financial content.

Even for the US, which is supposed to be in the process of defence transformation for more than a decade, it is difficult to answer the question of how much they are spending on transformation. To quote the Assistant Director of the Office of Force Transformation, Walter Fairbanks, "A frequent question is how much DoD spends on transformation. That is hard to say, because transformation is far more than a list of programs. The concepts, capabilities, and organizations developed through innovative ideas, experimentation, major training exercises, and assessment of lessons learned on the battlefields of Afghanistan and Iraq cannot be categorized under a transformation line item in the defense budget."[4]

Issues pertaining to processes have come increasingly into prominence under transformation initiatives in US defence since 2001. It has been recognised that transformation of the armed forces really involves a revolution in management technology and business practices. The attempt is to reform with the aim of capability enhancement, focussed on three primary processes: requirements assessment; programming and budgeting; and system acquisition.

For the assessment of requirements, the most important change was the formation of the Joint Capabilities Integration and Development System (JCIDS) in 2003. The JCIDS process was aimed to achieve two objectives. The first was greater jointness in requirements analysis, taking opportunities to bring about closer links among related Service missions. The second objective of the JCIDS process was to develop requirements using a broad "capabilities-based" approach, rather than the platform-based or system-based approach. "JCIDS would force the DoD to consider whether a new airplane was the best alternative to fulfilling the capability requirement at all; perhaps, there was a more effective or efficient means of creating a given effect on the battlefield."[5]

To bring about this shift in thinking, six Functional Capabilities Boards (FCBs) were set up to look into the requirements for generically defined military capabilities, intended to cover the full range of battlefield needs.

In the area of programming and budgeting, instead of the Planning, Programming and Budgeting System (PPBS), where the 'planning' aspect did not get adequate attention, a revised process called the PPBE process ("E" standing up for execution) was installed in 2003. In the revised process, the Office of the Secretary of Defence (OSD) began the process by setting firm goals in the secretary of defence's Strategic Planning Guidance (SPG). "The SPG was followed by a period of intense analysis, aimed at providing specific programmatic guidance to the Services, rather than leaving them to develop their program objectives memoranda (POM) in isolation."[6]

As regards the DoD acquisition system, past reform efforts tended to focus narrowly on the acquisition procedures and rules, rather than on the whole system of requirements assessment, programming and budgeting. Now the acquisition system is composed of three overlapping processes, including the JCIDS process for requirements assessment, processes of programming and budgeting and the acquisition process.

The concept of transformation as a process also draws attention to modernisation, which is always considered an ongoing process. But would this ongoing process of modernisation bring about transformation of the armed forces? Or can the process of modernisation be so designed as to bring about transformation? We shall attend to this aspect subsequently.

Transformation and Culture of Innovation

In implementing the transformation process in US defence, the major emphasis now is on bringing about change in human behaviour and creating a *culture of innovation* within the DoD. Another major emphasis is on development of new concepts in meeting asymmetric challenges. That is why they view transformation as a process.

The challenge for us is of a slightly different kind. We are yet to induct revolution in military affairs (RMA) technologies in a significant manner in our military. There are gaps in our technological base. For sophisticated weapons, we are overwhelmingly dependent on imports. In our procurement policy, there is a predilection for imports. While this may be necessary to some extent where there are a lot of technological gaps, it is to be realised that large scale imports are inimical to innovative thinking and would not allow domestic research and development activities to grow. This will prove to be a great hurdle in bringing about transformation of the armed forces. It will baffle many analysts that a country, which could be self-reliant in development of strategic weapons and innovative in its approach, has to depend so much on imports for weapon systems in non-strategic areas.

Therefore, our strategy for transformation in the military would be through adopting a strategy for RMA, based on development of indigenous capabilities. This may involve selective imports of sub-systems, incorporating cutting edge technology to be integrated within the country.

Regardless of how transformation may be defined, Cebrowski has identified some criteria by which military modernisation programmes may be judged for their transformational qualities. *His top criterion is that the weapon system or operating procedure be interoperable.* Interoperability means that the system can function with a variety of other systems, including from other Services. Other criteria Cebrowski has named are judgments as to whether the system helps users to change war-fighting methods as opposed to merely improving existing methods; and whether the system can deal with a wide range of threats.

There is general agreement on these criteria. It is felt that these criteria should be kept uppermost in mind in acquisition of systems in the modernisation process, so that the modernisation effort itself leads to transformation of military forces.

To ensure interoperability of weapon systems, it is important to go through the indigenous route of technological development as the criterion of interoperability can be kept in view in all cases of weapon development, and a system once developed, can be used by more than one Service by some adaptations which would be comparatively easy if the indigenous route of development of the system was taken. Ensuring interoperability of systems leads to cutting down on the duplication of systems.

Barriers to Transformation

It is important to recognise that there are important organisational barriers to bringing in transformation of the armed forces. This can be illustrated with reference to the US armed forces where the top leadership was enthusiastic about transformation. President George Bush, speaking at the US Naval Academy in May 2001, called " for a future force that is defined less by size and more by mobility and swiftness, one that is easier to deploy and sustain, one that relies more heavily on stealth, precision weaponry, and information technologies." He also committed himself "to fostering a military culture where intelligent risk-taking and forward thinking are rewarded, not dreaded, and to ensuring that visionary leaders who take risks are recognized and promoted."[7]

The US armed forces have also accepted the need to transform so as to meet the demands of information-age warfare and have fielded new capabilities such as stealth and precision strikes, new approaches like network-centric warfare and effects-based operations. "Nevertheless," as pointed out by Thomas G. Mahnken, "significant organizational barriers to the adoption of new technology, doctrine and organizations exist. The Services have been particularly reluctant to take measure that are disruptive of Service culture, such as shifting away from traditional platforms and toward new weapon systems, concepts, and organizations. The Army's efforts to field a medium-weight ground force, the Navy's development of network-centric warfare, and the Air Force's experience with unmanned air vehicles illustrate such difficulties. In each case, efforts at transformation have faced opposition from service traditionalists who perceive threats in new ways of war. For the Defence Department to succeed in transforming the US armed forces, it must both reallocate resources and nurture new constituencies."[8]

The budget data on acquisition programmes suggest that the US military Services continue to have strongly platform-centric approaches to procurement.

This may be true for the militaries of most countries. Therefore, funds for introducing systems which can transform would be "insufficient." This poses more problems for those who feel enthused about bringing about transformation. Mahnken suggests, "The Defence Department should begin redistributing resources away from legacy systems of declining utility and toward new ways of war. The Pentagon should scale back or cancel weapons that are heavy or have limited mobility, highly detectable signatures, and limited range; it should increase funding for long range precision strike, stealth, and C4ISR systems. The department should increase substantially the funds it devotes to research and development."[9]

This prescription would not be easy to follow because of organisational resistance. All the same, a few important points come out about financing transformation:

(i) There has to be reallocation of resources from legacy systems to resources to transformational systems. Because of constraints of resources, one cannot fund legacy systems with the same vigour as before and, at the same time, fund the new systems which are to bring about transformation.

(ii) The Defence Department should increase substantially the funds it devotes to research and development (R&D) as more and more experimentation is required to pursue potentially important technologies through basic research.

Mahnken makes the third point which is more specific:

(iii) In order to meet new challenges, "*the secretary of defense should set aside a significant portion of the military's procurement budget for innovative programs.*"[10]

As transformation of the armed forces would depend heavily on innovation and experimentation, it would call for more resources being invested in carrying on basic research on science and technology, leading to development of mature technologies which can be exploited militarily. This would also call for a new procurement procedure.

A New Strategy of Investment

In the transformation process, one has to look for investments which are most critical to its success. One cannot proceed on an incremental basis. In the strategy for investment for bringing about transformation, one has to concentrate on a few critical areas for investment. To quote Stuart Johnson, "While there is not one-to-one correspondence between investment spending and force transformation, the process is supported by targeted investment in those technologies that enable force transformation: command, control, and communications: reconnaissance; surveillance; and precision strike, to name four."[11]

The first and most important step could, therefore, be to develop an integrated joint programme through indigenous research and development, for all the three Services in the area of command, control, communication, computers, intelligence, surveillance, reconnaissance (C4ISR). "An interoperable C4ISR suite is critical to seamless operation of forces that will depend on strong information dominance over the enemy, a shared operational picture and targeting data."[12] It is not easy but will have a very high pay-off.

For obvious security reasons, as also for developing the right operational capability suited to our requirements and cost-effectiveness, one cannot but follow the indigenous route for developing such a major integrated system. The experience of Plan ASCON and Plan AREN of the Indian Army, though two decades old, clearly points to this direction. Following the indigenous route of technological development, with the leadership and management role adopted by the army, was the key to their success. Innovativeness is present in our Service culture which requires the right incentive to flourish.

In recent years, project Samyukta, though it took more time than originally envisaged, indicates the ability of indigenous R&D to take on challenges in the difficult technology of electronic warfare and its ability in system integration. The advantage of undertaking the domestic (R&D) route is that these systems can be constantly upgraded in the light of new operational challenges, which cannot be done for imported systems, even when domestic production is undertaken through the transfer of technology (ToT) route.

To develop the C4ISR suite would provide much more challenges to technology development than ever before. Several agencies can collaborate in this endeavour, with a team of Service officers taking a leadership role.

All the three Services have to undertake transformation in a coordinated manner, as *jointness and interoperability is the key to transformation*.

Capabilities-Based Planning (CBP) Approach for Transformation

The CBP has been recognised as the most important transformational initiative in defence.

Capability is the ability to achieve desired operational effects under specified standards and conditions through a combination of means and ways to perform a set of tasks. As Ryan Henry puts it, "A capability is not a platform or an asset. It's the ability to achieve desired effect in the battle space…Our first task is to determine conceptually what capabilities we need: what we need to be able to do. We will then apply normal decision-making process."[13]

Defence strategy has to visualise the kind of war the country has to be prepared for, in deciding about the capabilities it needs to develop. That is why the periodic comprehensive defence reviews are so very essential from the strategic point of view. It is necessary to visualise the kind of war or security challenges that the country would be faced with, or is currently engaged in, what should be the "objectives" in meeting these challenges, and consider the "ways" of meeting those challenges, and the means available.

Many organisations will say that they are transforming when they are not considering their purpose. In the transformation process, one has to be clear about the "ends" to be met, the "means" that are available and the "ways" of meeting them. To introduce capability-based planning and to bring about transformation of the armed forces, we need a framework where the "ends," "ways," and "means" are tied together in a strategic framework. "A transforming organization concentrates on ends and, in turn must emphasize the ways and means of accomplishing those ends."[14]

Warfare has become infinitely more complex since Clausewitz's time. Despite this increased complexity and greater friction in warfare, military organisations tend to maintain a similar structure and organisational mindset towards fighting. In many cases, the means have changed but the mindset has not.

It is significant to note that in formally adopting capability-based planning and the transformational agenda in defence, both came about in the Quadrennial Defence Review (QDR) of 2001 in the USA. In the course of QDR 2001 the US Department of Defence came to the conclusion that even with limited resources, it had to have effective capabilities across a very broad spectrum. This, in turn, led to a totally different force planning construct which is called the "One-Four-Two-One" strategy. This was different from the two Major Regional Conflicts

(MRC) visualised in QDR 1997 for force planning and capability building purposes.

In conducting QDR 2006, the Department of Defence recognised that it is engaged in a war that is irregular in nature and that the war would be a long one. The enemies in this war are not traditional conventional forces but rather dispersed terrorist networks. This kind of war requires the US military to adopt an unconventional and indirect approach.

Recognising that this is an era of surprise, and uncertainty, with a wide range of asymmetric threats, the QDR 2006 defines two fundamental imperatives for the US Department of Defence:

- Continuing to reorient the department's capabilities and forces to be more agile in the time of war, to prepare for wider asymmetric challenges and hedge against uncertainty over the next 20 years.
- Implementing enterprise-wide changes to ensure that organisational structures, processes and procedures effectively support its strategic direction.[15]

As would be seen, the emphasis is no longer on achieving some particular technological capabilities, but reorientation of capabilities towards greater agility in meeting the asymmetric challenges. Further, making organisational structures and procedures more responsive to strategic challenges is the biggest transformational challenge.

QDR 2006 accepts that the Department of Defence must adapt a model of continuous change and reassessment if it has to defeat highly adaptive adversaries. It provides new direction for accelerating the transformation of the department to focus more on the needs of combatant commanders and to develop portfolios of joint capabilities rather than what is termed as "individual stove-piped programmes." The focus of capability-based planning is invariably on operational needs. That is why the perceived needs of commanders come first and have highest priority in procurement planning.

Thus, capability-based planning and transformation of the armed forces go together, and both get the right direction through periodic defence reviews which help in developing a framework tying together "ends," "means" and "ways." It is the strategy which would determine the capabilities that are needed to be developed. Therefore, we need a well articulated defence strategy, specifying the kinds of contingencies we should be prepared for, which can be used for capability-based planning.

Transformation and Modernisation

In some writings, a distinction is made between modernisation and transformation. While discussing funding of modernisation, this is treated as what are called "legacy systems" and funding of transformation involves investment in innovative systems. This distinction is not valid, as modernisation can also incorporate transformational technologies. Both modernisation and transformation comprise an on-going process. But the emphasis in modernisation is on procurement of technologically advanced equipment, while transformation is an all-embracing concept involving, among others, changes in doctrines, operational concepts, and institutional and organisational changes with the focus on strategic requirements.

Cebrowski, in trying to bring harmonisation between modernisation and transformation stated, "One lens that might prove helpful in understanding transformation is that of a commercial corporate strategy of innovation... Any good corporate innovation strategy. .... has three distinct parts."[16] These are: (i) Focus on Core Missions; (ii) A Series of Small Exploratory Jumps; and (iii) Placing a Few Big Bets.

Regarding the focus on "Core Missions," taking the analogy of a corporate strategy, Cebrowski clarified, "This is the bread and butter of any organization and the main point of any corporate effort. This is where modernization, recapitalization, and taking care of capital plant occur. This is basic stuff. This the realm of evolutionary changes where an organization simply tries to get better at what it is already doing. It should be emphasized that transformation and modernization are not in competition. They are different things and any organization must undertake both processes to be successful."

"Small Exploratory Jumps," take place when an organisation pushes out of the boundaries of a core competency and tries to create something new. Changes in this category are within the existing paradigm.

Cebrowski gives the example of the US Navy pursuing unmanned underwater vehicles for shallow mine-hunting and anti-submarine warfare. Those missions are already core competencies for the navy. But in so far as using this technology in new ways that makes it possible to do something that the navy could not do before, it is transformational.

Placing a “Few Big Bets” involves big jumps. These are the things which will change a military Service, change the Department of Defence. The global positioning system satellites are a prime example. Their advent changed the military, changed the department and changed civil society. Yet another example is putting nuclear ballistic missiles to sea in submarines.

In our approach to modernisation, however, a distinction need to be made among “core missions,” “small jumps” and “big strides.” For “core missions” as per normal business practice, the modernisation process should go on by replacement of equipment and systems which have outlived their utility, and the capital budget of a Service should take care of it. For “small jumps” experimentation would be required to be undertaken and the Services should make a separate allocation for research, development and other measures, and the Services can be stake-holders in Defence Research and Development Organisation (DRDO) projects.

For “big strides,” there have to be inter-agency and inter-departmental efforts. These would require long-term plans for developing each of these capabilities, which should be funded separately by the government as these cannot be fitted in any Service’s budget. C4ISR is such a capability. It is such an important capability that by itself it can transform the entire war-fighting capability. One can have an independent ten-year plan for developing this capability. There should be assured funding for developing this capability, with an inter-agency independent steering committee.

By conceding, however, that transformation and modernisation are different things and both are to be carried out, Cebrowski left the debate inconclusive. Can it happen, for example, that the modernisation process and the transformation process are working at cross-purposes? Is it possible that the modernisation process, by emphasising the need for procurement of “legacy systems” (though of higher capability) in terms of platforms, etc. reinforces the mindset which the transformational process was supposed to change? Can we conceive of a modernisation process, which by its design, brings about transformation of the armed forces? These are basic questions which need to be debated. Particularly, as in our case, defence planning aims at modernisation basically through procurement of equipment and systems.

New Approach to Defence Modernisation and Procurement Required

Transformation of the armed forces cannot come about without adopting a new procurement procedure with renewed emphasis on *research and development,* as also *concept development* and *experimentation*, as the key elements in the procurement procedure. This is because innovation and experimentation are the key requirements of the transformation process.

Modernisation should, first of all, be redefined as modernisation of military capability not just procurement of modern equipment. And it should be that capability which is dictated by strategic needs, as determined by a well-articulated defence policy. This will have its impact on the defence planning itself which needs to be streamlined for determining procurement needs. A streamlined framework has been developed by Glenn A. Kent, and David E. Thaler, which focusses on streamlining the part of the process, often referred to as "up-front" planning.[17]

Referring to the procurement procedure in US defence, "up-front' planning is akin to Phase 0, which begins at Milestone 0, when an authority mandates a particular military mission which deserves increased emphasis. It ends at Milestone I when a decision is made to develop and procure new systems that will equip force elements to enhance military capability. The existing process, apart from being time-consuming, suffers from various "disruptive instabilities" because of lack of communication between disparate elements of the Department of Defence.

To correct the problems, the proposed framework emphasises the need to recognise *concept development* as a separate and distinct phase. The following are the main deficiencies in the existing procedure of up-front planning:

I. Concept development is not defined as an explicit and separable activity.
II. The distinctions between concept demonstrations and technological demonstrations are blurred.
III. The current process does not promote purposeful interaction among scientists, development planners, acquisition personnel and others.

In the proposed system, the forum for concept development is called the "Concept Action Group" (CAG) that would be run by senior officers from appropriate major commands. "The CAG would be the forum for causing purposeful interaction among disparate disciplines. It would serve as the engine for accomplishing the daunting task of matching mission needs to technology opportunities."[18] Concept development efforts should involve (i) formulating, defining and testing alternative operational concepts; (ii) defining and pursuing concept demonstrations for promising concepts; and (iii) defining the functional characteristics of new and existing systems, for implementing selected concepts. These efforts are required to be funded, for which a separate budget should be earmarked from the procurement budget.

The purpose of science and technology (S&T) efforts should be to forge a path from basic scientific research to mature technology aggregates. The Defence Advanced Research Project Agency (DARPA) and the national, service and industrial laboratories should conduct these efforts. "S&T" efforts should begin with basic research; the results of basic research help identify opportunities for new technologies. The most promising new technologies are matured as technology aggregates.[19] The following points from the proposed framework are emphasised:

Concept development (phase 0) is separable from science and technology, on the one hand, and system development and acquisition, on the other.

Concept demonstrations are different in nature and output from technology demonstrations, on the one hand, and engineering/ manufacturing demonstrations, on the other. Concept Action Groups (CAGs) should serve as vehicles for purposeful interaction between disparate communities.

Fig. 1 portrays the activities and inter-relationships of S&T, the concept development and acquisition.[20]

Fig 1

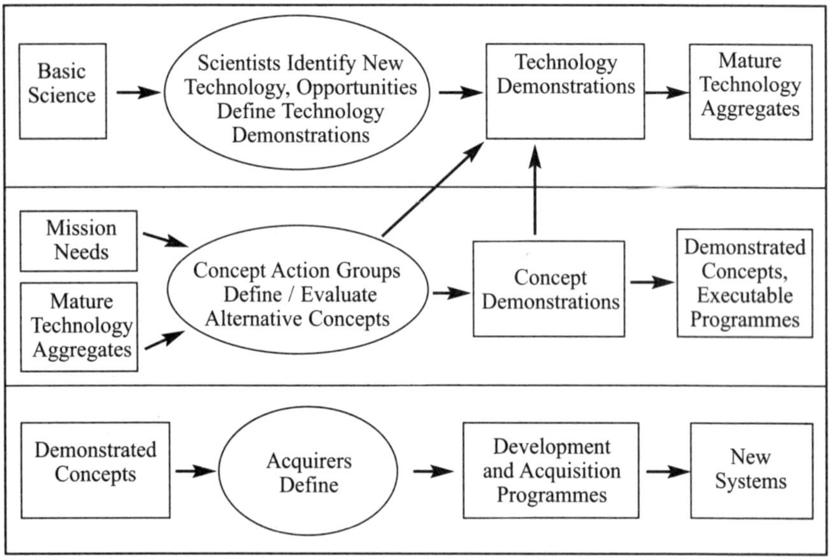

These ideas were taken further in a later work(2003) prepared by Glenn A. Kent and David A. Ochmanek, for the US Air Force, which can directly be placed in the context of transformation of the armed forces. It also helps in bringing together the concept of transformation and modernisation of the armed forces through capability building.

First and foremost, modernisation should be conceived as "modernizing operational capabilities." Explaining this, the authors state, "The words 'modernising operational capabilities' were chosen with care. We could have used the words 'modernizing forces'—but that would suggest that the 'forces' (types of units) remain the same, that we are simply modernizing existing types of platforms or units. More often than not, quantum jumps in operational capabilities have been achieved in the past when new types of forces were conceived."[21]

The authors, therefore, chose to talk in terms of development of the capabilities of the air force when developing a framework for the modernisation of the US Air Force. In this context, they make two more points, right at the beginning, which are important, as it helps to put the whole issue in proper perspective. To quote, "Modernizing the operational capabilities provided by the Air Force is a journey, not a one-time event. Modernizing yields 'transformation' and a revolution in military affairs (RMA) when the capabilities of the force are dramatically superior to (or different from) those that have come before."[22] That means that so long as we conceive of modernisation, as modernising the operational capabilities, it would automatically lead to transformation and no special purpose is served, at least conceptually, by using the term "transformation" of the armed forces.

In this context, the other point made is equally significant from the Service point of view.

They state, "Discussions of whether the Air Force is (is not) transforming are of little purpose. The Air Force modernizes (as in the past) as opportunities appear. The Air Force has been on the journey, seizing opportunities to meet the challenges, for many years, and it shows."[23]

That is, opportunities as they arise, are required to be seized by the Service concerned to modernise the operational capabilities, which will not come about just because the policy-makers have decided to bring in "transformation" of the armed forces. But the emphasis should be on modernising the operational capabilities, and not simply modernisation of existing platforms. There is a reason for repeating the point. They state, "There is another reason to talk in terms of capabilities. The Air Force provides capabilities to combat commanders and achieve these capabilities according to a concept of employment (CONEMP) defined by the Air Force. *If a service thinks of itself as simply 'providing forces' to combatant commanders, it diminishes its role in the development of operational art within its medium."*[24] (italics) added

So the journey of modernisation can serve the purpose of transforming the forces if it is properly conceived, and an institutional framework is provided "that promotes innovation and timely progress."

Modernisation and Promoting Innovation

This calls for a look into the procurement procedure. Kent and Ochmanek criticised the procedure incorporated in this regard in the US Department of Defence Directive No. 5000.1 in the Defence Acquisition System (October 2000), particularly the activity called "concept and technology development," for which a formal procedure is laid down. This step incorporates two major efforts, namely, concept exploration and technology development. They make a very significant point, "This effort to systematize and centralize control over thinking about innovation runs counter to experience and common sense, both of which suggest that good ideas must bubble up from people engaged in trying to solve concrete problems."[25] They also criticise the "requirements generation system." The initial capabilities document (ICD) in practice has become a definition of characteristics of the system which is to provide some operational capability.

Constructions such as "there is an operational requirement for this system" or worse, "there is a requirement that a particular system attain this level of performance" are specifically rejected by the authors. "The term 'operational requirement' should refer to the need for an operational *capability*. The term should not be used to refer to specific system or type of system."[26]

The model that is recommended is to promote timely innovation in modernising operational capabilities. The following characteristics of the model are worth mentioning:

- The model is "actor oriented" as against "document oriented." It defines the role of various actors in fostering and promoting modernisation.
- The model's actors address matters that are focussed at the operational and tactical levels, as distinct from a focus at the campaign level (a level higher).
- The model promotes enduring activities associated with exploration and development of new concepts at three levels: (1) new concepts of systems and platforms; (2) new concepts for accomplishing military tasks; and (3) new concepts for acquiring operational objectives.

- By deriving operational challenges, objectives and tasks from potential joint-Service campaigns, the model promotes a joint perspective.

At the campaign level, the combatant commander defines the campaign operation plan or campaign strategy to achieve the desired effects. At the operation level, the subordinate commanders define the "*concept of employment*" (CONEMP) to achieve each of the operational objectives. At the tactical level, the combatants define the *concept of execution* (CONEX) to accomplish each of the stated military tasks.

The top half of the model of Kent and Ochmanek indicating the process, is depicted in Fig 2 to give an idea of the actors in the concept development stage in the process of modernisation.

Fig 2: A Framework for Modernisation

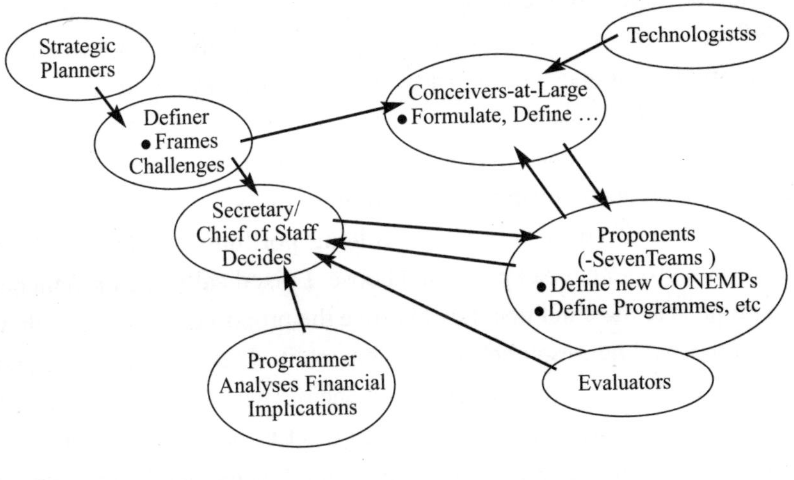

(The top half of the model of Kent and Ochmanek is retained in its entirety as it is the main focus of attention, the bottom half is truncated a bit compared to the original, with some players being left out, as it is not an area of concern for transformation purposes – author.)

The statements of strategic planners, being framed at the strategic level of generality, are not always directly useful in defining the types of operational capability the air force intends to provide. For that reason, the model features a "definer" within the air force who defines what these statements mean in terms of operational capabilities to be provided by the air force. The output of the definer is a set of challenges, which when approved by the chief of staff of the Service, task the air force to develop operational capabilities appropriate to meet each challenge.

The next principal actors in the process are the "proponents." Their primary function is to develop in response to the operational challenges, new concepts of employment that will enable the USAF forces operating in conjunction with the forces of the other Services, to achieve important operational objectives in the face of enemy resistance. The primary input to each team of proponents is one of the chief challenges. Each team is challenged to promote new CONEX and define new CONEMPS so that the air force can provide improved capabilities to fulfill this operational requirement, especially in the future.

Another input to the proponents, generally in the form of new CONEXs, stems from conceivers-at-large. The conceivers, in turn , have two primary inputs: (1) a knowledge of existing and emerging technologies; and (2) statement of proponents as to the military tasks that merit the greatest emphasis. With these two inputs, the conceivers define the concept for accomplishing stated military tasks.

The output of conceivers is an evolving portfolio of CONEX from which each proponent can pick and choose. Episodically, the proponents then propose to the chief that they approve the proposed concept and they seek authority and resources to implement it. The chief of staff and secretary of the air force are then to decide whether to approve the concept as proposed or amended. If they elect to proceed, they propose to the secretary of defence and his principal advisors that the concept be implemented and that resources be allocated to develop the hardware, facilities, and other assets required to make the concept a reality

Among the advisors to the defence secretary and evaluators are the financial manager and the programmer who "will determine the financial implications after estimating full costs of adapting anew CONEMP and the resources required on a year to year basis. They determine if the concept would fit into the overall Air Force budget – again, year-by-year."[27] They have to be proactive in attaining resources for implementation of new concepts. As the authors put it, "They should also act as entrepreneurs and attempt to be creative in financing the proposed concept. They can, for example, suggest possible areas for reduction in other items in the Air Force program."[28]

The important point to notice is that most of these processes are at a conceptual plane. Unless there is conceptual clarity about the operational capabilities to be achieved through modernisation, it cannot be the vehicle for bringing about transformation of the armed forces. To reiterate, it is not just modernisation that we need, it is modernising the operational capabilities that we need. Exploration and development of new concepts are required as part of the modernisation process, not only for systems and platforms, but also for accomplishing military tasks and achieving operational objectives and these have to be made part of the decision-making process for new procurements. Only then will the modernisation process yield both RMA and "transformation" of the armed forces.

A Budgeting Process to Advance Transformation

The key tool available to the defence minister in giving guidance to the Services on the priorities to be reflected in their programmes under PPBS is the Defence Planning Guidance (DPG) – in our system it is called the *raksha mantri's* (RM's) guidance. In response to the directive, statements of proposed programmes and activities of the Services are submitted in the form of the Programme Objective Memorandum (POM). It has seldom worked in a proper way. As Stuart E. Johnson puts it, "The DPG is usually too late and mostly too broad to provide a framework for service programmers or a metric against which service POM can be evaluated."[29]

Another problem is that the attention of the senior leaders does not focus on the front end of the PPBS process, that is, in the planning phase. More attention get focussed on the back end of the process concerned with submission of the budget to the Office of Management and Budget (OMB). As Johnson suggests, "One way to shift leadership attention toward the front end of the process is for a few small teams of half a dozen of decision-makers to meet early in the planning phase to enrich their input to the planning of the PPBS. Each group could develop one or two transformational issues that could become an integral part of the DPG. Groups should meet for a limited time, which encourages focus on high-impact transformational initiatives and avoids entanglements with details better handled by staff."[29A] The key would be to ensure that each issue is high leverage and expressed in output terms.

The Future Year's Defence Programme (FYDP) was originally conceived in the 1960s in US defence to give the secretary of defence an insight into how money was allocated in major programme areas across military departments. Ten Major Force Programmes (MFPs) were defined that expressed the principal missions the military needed to perform. This allowed the secretary to see how the objectives of each mission area were being funded, to identify duplication in effort among the Services and enable the secretary to make strategic choices. But the structure of the FYDP has not kept pace with the change in the security environment. In 1986, MFP11 – special operations forces – was added at the direction of Congress as part of the Goldwater-Nichols Act. Other than that, the structure has changed little. Changes in the categories can be made to make the FYDP more amenable to focussing Service programmes on transformational initiatives. The obvious candidate for an MFP would be C4ISR programmes. Joint expeditionary forces, special operation forces, missile defence could be others. War-fighting functions could be segregated from general support functions to provide insight into the cost of support functions which have a tendency to grow disproportionately.[30]

Some programming must be done jointly. The obvious first step would be have an integrated, joint programme submission in the area of C4ISR programmes. An interoperable C4ISR suite is critical to seamless operation of forces for information dominance over the enemy.

We have not adopted PPBS. But the above brings out how resource allocation decisions and processes are required to be structured to bring in transformation, which remains valid whether we adopt PPBS or programme budgeting or continue with our present system. For this is the rational method of resource allocation in defence. The decision-making process has to undergo a basic change as indicated above, if we want to bring in transformation.

Essential Elements in Transformation Strategy

As per the Office of Force Transformation of US Defence (set up in 2001, whose first head was Admiral Cebrowski). "The overall strategy of transformation consists of three parts: transforming culture; transforming processes: and transforming capabilities through force or military transformation."[31] It identified four Military Transformation Pillars:

- Strengthening joint operations.
- Exploiting intelligence advantages.
- Concept development and experimentation.
- Developing transformational capabilities.

As would be seen, only one of the four pillars calls for funding. Additional funding is not the most important requirement for embarking on a transformation process. What would be essentially required is reallocation of resources.

This would also be evident from the effect of transformational culture on force structure. In the transformation process, as in the US Army, the emphasis has gone from divisions as viable units in the force structure to independent brigades, for better manoeuvrability. The same feature is seen in the modernisation of the Chinese defence forces (PLA – People's Liberation Army). The other is the emphasis on the role of special operations forces. By the time of Operation Iraqi Freedom, the special operations forces had emerged as pillars of strategy in the US armed forces. As Stephen Cimbala says, "Their performance there was followed by the DoD announcement that US Special Operations Command (SOCOM) would have its own planning structure like other unified and special commands. It would no longer be a mere supplier of forces but now could plan its own missions."[32]

The emphasis on special forces is also observed in the modernisation of the PLA of China. For attaining specific objectives as also meeting asymmetric challenges, more and more attention has to be given to the raising of special forces.

Joint operational concepts, joint capability-building and joint training are the most important ingredients of the transformation process. Since this is the biggest challenge for ushering in a transformation culture, we have to deliberate upon, and bring about, the necessary institutional changes. This underlines the need for a Chief of Defence Staff (CDS) with the mandate of the kind as given to the chairman, Joint Chiefs of Staff in the Goldwater-Nichols Act, 1986, of the US, without which the transformation process would have never taken off there. This was the most significant contribution of the US Congress to the defence transformation process. Our law-makers should also give attention to this very important aspect of defence management.

Transformation and Revolution in Military Affairs (RMA)

Since 1997, the US DoD has placed a great deal of emphasis on transforming the force. The emphasis first appeared in the Quadrennial Defence Review (QDR) of 1997. It committed the DoD to "harnessing new technologies to give US forces greater capabilities through advanced concepts, doctrine, and organizations" and linked the RMA to the ongoing transformation of US military capabilities. The QDR of 2001 also linked exploiting the RMA to transforming the country's military forces. It stated that "transforming defence" is at the heart of America's strategic approach to achieving its defence policy goals.

The conceptual basis for the US force transformation is found in Joint Vision 2010, which was released in 1996. It was a landmark document. Without mentioning the term "revolution in military affairs," Joint Vision 2010 discussed technological advances in sensor, command and control, precision force, and stealth capabilities as also doctrinal changes towards increased jointness, littoral warfare and rapidly mobile lethal ground forces. It discussed organisational changes towards smaller units, decentralised command and control, etc. Joint Vision 2020, released in May 2000, carried forward the ideas expressed in Joint Vision 2010. *In contrast to the more technological focus of Joint Vision 2010, however,*

Joint Vision 2020 emphasised the need to broaden the focus beyond technology and capture the importance of conceptual innovation as well. The document stressed that for achieving full-spectrum dominance, even more important than technology is the development of doctrine, organisations, training and education, and the need for leaders to take advantage of the technology. This is a significant shift in emphasis. The new vision offered a second look at the RMA. Joint Vision 2010 states that new sensor technology will make the battle space more transparent. By contrast, Joint Vision 2020 emphasises the opposite nuance. “We must remember that information superiority neither equates to perfect information nor does it mean the elimination of the fog of war. Information systems, processes, and operations add their own sources of friction and fog to the operational environment.”[33]

Whereas Joint Vision 2010 stressed the merits of information superiority during a military operation, Joint Vision 2020 notes that such superiority is only useful when it is translated into superior knowledge and superior decision-making. So the role of leadership is actually enhanced under a transformed military which can be provided by the CDS.

Vision documents are necessary for developing the required strategy. A vision document which provides a basis for defence policy can emanate when there is a CDS.

US Air Force Transformation

The philosophy of transformation of the US Air Force is contained in the following statement “What we require is a capability mix consistent with pre-defined operational concepts and effects-driven methodology. Future programs must be conceived with this mix in mind. Systems or capabilities based on arguments that do not consider the emerging joint character or asymmetric nature of warfare will find themselves obsolete, irrelevant, and candidates for elimination.”[34]

They have defined the transformation as follows: “A process by which the military achieves and maintains advantage through changes in operational concepts, organization, and/or technologies that significantly improve its war-fighting capabilities or ability to meet the demands of a changing security environment."[35]

The major emphasis is on organizational and operational concepts. It states, "Transformation is more than new hardware. Equally important, if less glamorous, are the organizational concepts that capitalize on the technological advances and allow the US military to truly transform. In addition, the process of transformation begin and ends with people.[36] It also indicated that the Air Force Council had embraced a new vision and construct to *transform human capital management.*

It was announced that all air force operational, programming, and budget decisions would be driven by predefined capability. To make this essential shift, the air force has developed six new concepts (CONOPS) of warfare. It is stated, "The Air Force is transforming around these CONOPS. In addition to serving as the roadmap for operators, the CONOPS construct will form the basis for resource allocation, future system acquisitions, and POM submissions in order to find capabilities-based solutions to war-fighting requirements."[37]

It is apparent, since the main emphasis is on developing operational concepts dictated by change in the security environment and in setting up the required organisation, it would be rather premature to discuss about the financial implications of transformation, before the operational concepts are developed. As the US Air Force Transformation Flight Plan stresses, "Transformation demands innovative thinking and a process that can identify examine, and turn bright ideas into reality – whether the idea is a new technology, concept, or a novel way to organize."[38]

It mentions that the key components of the innovation in US Air Force include: *innovation panel, science and technology (S&T) development, air force battle labs, advance technology demonstrations, advanced concept technology demonstrations, agile acquisition, experimentation, war gaming, modelling and simulation, and training transformation.*

No wonder, as one eminent defence analyst has observed, under the Bush Administration, "the Pentagon's research, development, testing, and evaluation (RDT&E) has actually increased faster than the procurement account in recent years."[39] As per this approach, military transformation basically requires innovative thinking, evolving of relevant war-fighting concepts, technological experimentation, war-gaming, etc, and the issue of "financing the transformation process" would certainly not be in the priority list. Just pumping in more and more money in defence will not bring about transformation, for it basically calls for a cultural change.

Though not in the priority list, finance would pose a problem for acquiring high performance weapon systems and other systems which are expected to play a key role in bringing about transformation. These include high performance stealthy aircraft, unmanned combat aerial vehicles, advanced C4I, miniaturised munitions, etc. For example, because of the budgetary constraints, critics of the plans of the US Air Force to acquire F-22s and JSFs argue that these aircraft are modernisation programmes, and that the air force's requirement for new fighters would be adequately satisfied in the near term by upgrading and procuring F-15s and F-16s. "They argue that the effectiveness of today's fighter and attack aircraft can be maintained through upgrades to their radars, command and control systems, and weapons. Future adversaries, they argue, will increasingly employ mobile cruise, ballistic and surface-to-air missiles... this will jeopardize the forward operating bases… By cancelling or truncating the F-22 and JSF, critics argue, the Air Force can free substantial funds that can be used to more aggressively pursue programs such as space-based assets, directed energy weapons, UCAVs, long range bombers. Such programs are more likely to overcome tomorrow's anti-access threats, and offer more transformation potential."[40]

The point is, there is always competition for resources between one programme and another which are funded by a Service's share of the capital budget. The Service has to decide what its allocation should be to maximise the transformation potential. Upgrades of existing platforms is today a cost-effective option to free resources for other priority programmes which may give a better push towards the transformation process.

How Much of the Forces Needs to be Transformed – and How Quickly?

While considering the financial implications of transformation of the forces, apart from deciding upon the package that will go into transformation, one of the important issues would be to decide how much of the forces needs transforming and how quickly. "Most of the discussion deals with what to transform, but one must also consider how much of the force needs transforming and how quickly."[41] Thus, the basic questions about how much of the force needs to transform, in what way, and how fast, depend on the strategy we want to adopt in fighting our potential enemies and the capabilities we want to have. Without having answers to these strategic questions, transformation cannot be planned nor can the financial implications be discussed.

Financing the RMA and Transformation: The Quadrennial Defence Review (QDR), 1997 Approach

Before going further, let us take a look at how the QDR 1997 wanted to implement the RMA. While it adopted the rhetoric of the RMA movement espousing information superiority, dominant manoeuvre, precision engagement and focussed logistics, it also indicated its explicit decision not to pursue these goals too fast. It adopted a cautious approach. It did not increase the total amount of resources devoted to the acquisition accounts—the sum total of procurement with research, development, testing and evaluation.

For purposes of fiscal planning, the QDR projected a stable annual defence budget of roughly $250 billion per year in constant FY1997 dollars. It was felt that if there was no marked deterioration in world events, "the nation is unlikely to support significantly more resources for national defence."[42] It noted that funding for modernisation has been insufficient in the past, with the procurement budget stalled near the $40 billion level. Even though QDR 1997 planned an increase in the procurement budget to $60 billion by 2001, on the basis of assessment of existing trends and assumptions, it estimated that the procurement plan was likely to stall in the range of $45- $50 billion.[43]

The broad direction of the path adopted by the QDR was to focus on balancing near-term and longer-term risks. Following this path required reducing active military personnel, reserve component personnel and civilian personnel by significant numbers. These force reductions were expected to allow increases in the level of investment, with about $60 billion per year applied to procurement which would help in the defence transformation process.

The need for transformation was further encouraged by the National Defence Panel (NDP) which was commissioned by the US Congress to review the new strategy indicated in the QDR 1997.

It is necessary to appreciate the fact that basic changes like "RMA" and "transformation," which have many dimensions and may involve restructuring of forces, cannot be initiated without such a comprehensive defence review based on periodic in-depth deliberations, as in the QDR. Such reviews should be made mandatory and should be an integral part of defence planning and budgeting – in fact, should provide the basis for these as also for defence acquisition.

Further, the operation and maintenance expenditure as also increase in personnel cost impinge on the procurement budget. Unless specific and determined steps are taken to contain and bring down the personnel cost and maintenance expenditure, as a percentage of each Service's budget, it would be impossible to increase the procurement budget to a level which would be conducive to bring in RMA and transformation of the military.

Funding the Transformation and RMA: The NDP Approach

Both the QDR 1997 and NDP advised caution in the process of transformation. Accordingly, the investment requirement for carrying out the transformation process in the short and medium term was comparatively modest. The report was entitled, significantly, "Transforming Defence, National Security in the 21st Century."

The issue of funding the transformation was addressed by the NDP. The procurement goal could not be met in the past, because increases in operations and maintenance (O&M) expenses, coupled with inability to increase the defence budget had "crowded out" procurement spending. This trend, as per the NDP assessment, was likely to continue.

The panel estimated that an annual budget wedge of $5 to 10 billion would be required to support the transformation strategy. This money will fund such initiatives as intelligence, space, urban warfare, joint experimentation, and information operations, the report stated. *Prima facie*, this is not lot of funds, as it represents about 3-4 per cent of the annual defence budget.[44]

In the absence of additional funding, the panel contended that the transformation could be funded by the infrastructure and acquisition reform, reducing the operational tempo associated with non-fighting activities, cancelling acquisition programmes, or reducing force structure and end strength. There will be no easy answers, and difficult choices must be made, the report stated.[45]

One of the reasons for a comparatively modest assessment of funding for transformation in the medium term was that the NDP was placing much greater emphasis than the QDR on the need to prepare for the putative challenges of the post-2015 world.[46] It laid great stress on diplomacy and cooperation as a part of the security dialogue. It was not very supportive of the existing two-war strategy, and felt that it was a device for preserving the existing force structure. It is worthwhile to look at what the NDP says about better resource management in support activities, where generally the money is. It states: "The Department should shift its strategy for reforming the defence support infrastructure to a bottom-up approach that empowers managers at all levels with greater capability and authority to make common sense decisions for the benefit of the Department." [47]

Points for Us

The following are the five basic principles, which were identified as the key elements in the report, which are applicable in our case also if transformation is the goal:

- **Cost Visibility/Accuracy.** Accurate cost information is a prerequisite for improved resource allocation decisions. The department should develop financial systems that help managers to identify inefficient practices and target areas for process improvement.

- **Positive Incentives.** The DoD must establish credible mechanisms to ensure that at least a portion of savings achieved through streamlining efforts is retained by the local organisation for its own use.
- **Choice and Competition.** Choice and competition motivate individuals and organisations to seek innovative approaches to meeting customer needs. Increasing the role of competitive forces in the delivery of support services should be essential to achieving lower costs and improved service quality.
- **Resource Flexibility.** Under the current budget rules, defence managers have little flexibility to shift resources to common sense trade-offs or respond to unanticipated requirements. Greater flexibility in resource management would encourage innovation and process improvement throughout the department.
- **Civil/Military Integration.** Defence personnel should be integrated into their local communities, using commercial services to the maximum.

For generating funds for transformation, we have to seriously look into streamlining the support infrastructure, where generally the money is. In this regard, the approach of QDR 1997 and the NDP report 1997 were similar. As per the written statement of Dr. Warner, assistant secretary of defence, in his testimony to the US Congress (House National Security Committee), "The path ultimately chosen in the QDR required modest reductions in today's force structure – concentrated on the 'tail' rather than the 'teeth' of forces – along with a commitment to fundamentally reengineer the Department's infrastructure and support activities to fund badly needed increases in a focused, executable modernization program and in broader transformation efforts."[48]

Comments by the chairman of the Joint Chiefs of Staff contained in his independent assessment of the QDR 1997 as mandated by law, to the secretary of defence also endorsed the above "strategy" to bring in transformation. To quote, "We need to get every dollar we can by reducing our infrastructure… Ultimately, we must commit ourselves to a major reengineering of our infrastructure. Without that reengineering, the patterns of the last four years are likely to continue – investment programs will be cut and the force of the future will be sold to pay current operations and support bills. In short, *we will not be able to realize the promise inherent in the Revolution in Military Affairs unless we embrace the revolution in business affairs*."[49]

The revolution in business affairs would also call for accurate costing of activities. To quote the NDP, "The Panel recommends that the Department accelerate the deployment of financial management systems in defence support organizations with strong activity-based costing capabilities. Such systems enable managers to understand true costs, identify inefficient practices, target areas of process improvement"[50]

In other words, transforming the financial management system, with an accent on activity-based costing should be an integral part of the defence transformation process to bring in economy and efficiency in resource management.

Reallocation of Resources

This is a recurring theme, with the defence analysts looking for funds for transforming the defence in an information age. For example, Jacques Gansler, the eminent defence analyst, writing about the new challenges in 2003, claimed that future adversaries will use the asymmetrical approaches, focussed on areas the nation is potentially weak in, which cannot be contained by conventional forces. In response, the military will need to shift resources, training, organisations, and equipment to non-traditional areas. These areas include special operations forces, urban warfare, cyber warfare defence, ballistic missile defence and 'brilliant' systems for carrying out intelligence, surveillance, reconnaissance, communications, and control activities, as well as precision strikes on adversary activities. In view of the scarcity of resources, what is required is a shift in resources from traditional areas to non-traditional areas or reallocation of resources. "Needless to say, such shifts, particularly of resources and organizations, tend to be countercultural and fiercely resisted by the entrenched institutions in the military, the defence industry, and

Congress. Perhaps most difficult, advancing the revolution in military affairs will require reallocating resources and modernizing traditional military organizations. The commanders who have come of age with the 'platform-centric' model in which ships, planes and tanks are critical elements; the industry that builds this equipment; the members of Congress who support the business as usual — none of these elements is likely to enthusiastically support the necessary shift to the new and increasingly information-based weaponry needed to deter or defeat future adversaries." This is the negative side of the story. But there is another side. "The good news is that sufficient resources to pay for such changes can be generated out of current defence budgets."[51]

The most important way of finding funds for transforming by following the RMA route is cutting duplication of the support function among the armed Services. These include logistics, communications, medical services, and intelligence currently provided within each military Service and various defence agencies.

RMA in Asia

Systems integration skills are the most demanding aspect of RMA. The qualities of creativity, innovation, and independence of thinking require a lot of encouragement, and these will provide the basic challenge.

Paul Dibb, in a seminal article on RMA in the Asian region, has indicated the challenges posed by RMA for this region. They are:

- The development of a joint force doctrine is required for the organisational changes associated with RMA "By and large, most countries in the region have given insufficient attention to the changes in military culture and organization that are required to maximize the use of RMA." [52] Separate single-Service cultures are the norm in the region. "No appropriate set of joint-service operational concepts exists or is practised in most countries."[53]
- Integrated logistic support and maintenance is part of the overall infrastructure required for joint force operations.
- The systems integration challenge is a formidable one. This is the most crucial skill for ushering in RMA.[54]

What is significant to note in the above list is that financing the RMA for undertaking the transformation process has not been indicated as one of the problem areas. In fact, from what we have described above, financing the transformation process, if a proper phased programme is developed, may not be a problem.

By the late Nineties, analysts noted three variants of a regional RMA within Asia:[55]

- The Australian model, primarily focussed upon building wide area surveillance, information and command links to become a regional military integrator within the region, able to work with the United States and with Australia's adjacent allies
- The Japanese model drew upon its technological relationship with the United States and its military relationship with the US Navy to put in place a naval RMA to adjacent military technology areas.
- The South Korean model had been based on the effort of large industrial combines to work with the United States and Europe to forge global partnerships that would allow Korean firms to become partners in the development of their own military platforms.

Chinese military and civilian officials have affirmed the importance of a "revolution in military affairs" to China's modernisation. The December 2004 White Paper for Defence describes the process of modernisation of defence in China in the context of global trends in military transformation. The general assessment in the West is that "China's indigenous military and civilian technology sectors are insufficiently advanced to spur a dramatic reappraisal of People's Liberation Army doctrine and organization."[56] RMA advocates within China commonly observe that Chinese military technology is flagging relative to cutting edge technology. That China must import most of its technologically advanced military equipment demonstrates that its indigenous technology lags behind. Recent acquisitions made by China have enabled it to develop some "pockets of excellence" which do not necessarily lead to RMA. All the same, there is no doubt that major steps towards force modernisation and RMA have been taken.

From the Chinese experience, one learns that for a developing country, RMA should come through the efforts at modernisation of the armed forces. And for generating funds for modernisation, apart from increase in defence budgets, it is necessary to streamline the force structure. The PLA has undergone two large reductions in force in the past decade, starting with three million people in 1995, and losing 500,000 people from 1997 to 2000 and another 200,000 from 2003 to 2005. Chinese sources noted that by the end of 2005, the PLA was likely to have 2.3 million people on its active duty roster.[57] The PLA has adopted the term "revolution in military affairs (RMA) with Chinese characteristics" to describe how it will build a smaller, more technologically advanced force through "mechanization and informalization."[58] The conduct of joint operations is an important element of all levels of professional education. The Chinese have also the streamlined the logistic system.

These lessons are important. If India has to transform the forces, it has to be part of the modernisation efforts, with focus on RMA technologies. The forces have to be streamlined, particularly in the support areas, to generate funds for modernisation. Periodic comprehensive defence reviews would be the key tool to bring in transformation in defence. The result, of the reviews should be published in a White Paper on Defence.

The Chinese experience also underlines the point that advance in military science and technology is the key to RMA, as experimentation and innovation provide it the needed impetus. As indigenous abilities in critical technologies having military application may be limited, collaborative efforts would be required.

The recently promulgated policy of "offsets" in defence procurement should be directed towards obtaining critical technologies which would help in ushering in RMA.

In this way, the defence procurement process itself can help in financing the transformation, by getting the critical technologies and also generating collaborative research and development in cutting-edge technology. An Indian strategy and a model for ushering in RMA is urgently called for.

Some words of caution, however, are in order. It is well to remember that setting in military operations will determine the advantage provided by access to new technology. There is also the question of opportunities provided by the prevailing political conditions to use these technologies. The Gulf War (1991) which dramatically demonstrated possibilities of RMA, could take place because of the end of the Cold War. It appeared to validate a particular line of technological and doctrinal development. As Lawrence Freedman almost prophetically put it, "Whether or not this presaged a revolution in military affairs depended on whether future patterns of conflict offer similar opportunities."[59] He observed that the apparent Western advantages in conventional military strength must be "qualified by reference to opportunities available to a determined and intelligent opponent to take advantage of local conditions," and it may be difficult for an "expeditionary force" to succeed.[60] Even with RMA, it is not easy to obtain "dominant situational awareness" which will enable one to make an attack with confidence.[61]

Secondly, the impression should not be carried that emerging technologies have made the conventional force structure and legacy systems obsolete. Drawing defence planning lessons from the war in Iraq, the eminent strategic analyst Macubin T. Owens, comments, "A transformed military is a valid objective, but the war in Iraq illustrates the limits of transformation."[62] He further observes, "There is no question that the effectiveness and efficacy of US forces have been enhanced by precision strike weapons and networking, but the idea that technology can banish friction, chance, and uncertainty from war has been shown to be overly optimistic."[63]

That means that for defence planning purposes, financing for conventional forces and the legacy system cannot be curtailed. There can be streamlining by economising on support infrastructure to generate some funds for transformation. But transformation would not be cheap. Additional funds would be required, which calls for better long-term planning, linking planning with budgeting through the programming route. Again, this should be treated, as far as we are concerned, as part of the transformation process.

These conditions notwithstanding, in today's world, where potential adversaries are adopting RMA with enthusiasm, adoption of RMA and transformation of the armed forces as a process is necessary. Modernisation of the armed forces has to adopt the transformational route. There is no alternative to it.

Notes

1. Department of Defence, "Elements of Defense Transformation," http://www/oft.osd.mil/library_files/document_383-Elements of Transformation_LR.pdf. 2004.
2. Executive Summary, "Defence Transformation in Asia-Pacific Region. Meeting the Challenge," March 30-April 1, 2004 http://www.apcss.org/core')/ Confèrenee/CR-ES/ Defênse Trans. doc.
3. Vice Admiral (Retd.) Arthur K. Cebrowski, "What is Transformation ?" http://www.oft.osd.mil/what_ is _transformation.cfm.
4. Walter P. Fairbanks, "Implementing the Transformation Vision," September 30, 2006, http:// www.trackpads.com/magazine/publish/printer_1738.shtml).
5. Douglas Berenson and Kerala T. Cowart, "QDR 2006: Transformation Via Process Reform," *DFI Quarterly International*, Spring 2006, p.12.
6. Berebson and Cowart, Ibid., p.13.
7. Quoted by Thomas G. Mahnken, "Transforming the US Armed Forces, Rhetoric or Reality?" *Naval War College Review*, vol. 54, no. 3, Summer 2001.
8. Mahnken, Ibid., p.216.
9. Mahnken, Ibid., p.225.
10. Mahnken, Ibid.
11. Stuart E. Johnson, "A New PPBS Process to Advance Transformation," *Defence Horizons*, no 32, September 2003, a publication of the Centre for Technology and National Security Policy, National Defence University of USA.
12. Johnson, Ibid
13. Ryan Henry, "Defence Transformation and the Quadrennial Defense Review," *Parameters*, Winter 2005-06.
14. Col. Jack D. Kem (Retd.) "Military Transformation, Ends, Ways and Means," *Air and Space Power Journal*, Fall 2006, p.88.
15. Quadrennial Defence Review Report, US Department of Defence http://www.global security. org/military/ library/policy/dod/qdr-2006-report.htm)

16. Cebrowski, n.3.
17. Glenn A. Kent and David E. Thaler, "A New Concept for Streamlining Up-Front Planning," RAND, 1992.
18. Kent and Thaler, Ibid., p.11.
19. Kent and Thaler, Ibid., p.7.
20. Kent and Thaler, Ibid., p.7.
21. Glenn A. Kent and David A. Ochmanek, *A Framework for Modernization Within the United States Air Force* (RAND, 2003), p.1.
22. Kent and Ochmanek, Ibid.
23. Kent and Ochmanek, Ibid., p.13.
24. Kent and Ochmanek, Ibid.
25. Kent and Ochmanek, Ibid., p.2.
26. Kent and Ochmanek, Ibid., p.10.
27. Kent and Ochmanek, Ibid., p.16.
28. Kent and Ochmanek, Ibid., p.17.
29. Stuart E. Johnson, "A New PPBS Process to Advance Transformation." *Defence Horizon* (Centre for Technology and National Security Policy, National Defence University), September, 2003.

29A. Johnson, Ibid.

30. Johnson, Ibid.
31. n.1, p.6.
32. Stephen Cimbala, "Transformation in Concept and Policy," *Joint Forces Quarterly,* June 27, 2005.
33. Quoted by Elinor C. Sloan, *The Revolution in Military Affairs, Implications for Canada and NA TO* (McGill-Queen's University Press, 2002).
34. The US Air Force Transformation Flight Plan, November 2003. http.//www.dtie.mil?jointvision/af _trans flight plan.pdf
35. Ibid.
36. Ibid.
37. Executive Summary, The US Air Force Transformation Flight Plan 2003, n. 34.
38. Ibid.
39. Michael 0'Hanlon, *Defence Strategy (For the Post-Saddam Era)* (Manas Publications in collaboration with Brookings Institution Press), p.75.
40. "Air Force Transformation," CRS Report for Congress, updated January 18,

2006, http://www.Fas.org/spg/crs/natssec/RS 20859 pdf.

41. Thomas 1. Searle, "The Air Force of the Future," *Air Space Power Journal*, Summer 2004.

42. QDR 1997, Section iv, http: /www.defenselink.mil/puhs/qdr/sec4.html

43. Ibid., http://www.defenselink.mail/pubs/qdr/sec4.html

44. Report of the NDP, December 1997, section on "A Transformation Strategy," http://www.fas.org/man/docs/ndp

45. Ibid.

46. Carl Conetta, "Future Tense: An Assessment of the Report of the National Defence Pane," http://www.comw.org/qdr/ndppda 1.htm.

47. NDP report, hitp: www.fas.org/man/docs/ndp/front.him

48. Written statement of Dr. Edward L. Warner, assistant secretary of defence for strategy and requirements, testimony to the House National Security Committee, Military Personnel Subcommittee, January 29, 1998, on the QDR 1997. http://www.globalsecurity.org/military/library/congress/1998_hr/01-29-98warner.htm.

49. Comments by the Chairman of the Joint Chiefs of Staff on the QDR 1997, http://www.fas.org/man/docs/qdr/sec10.hmtl.

50. The NDP report http://www.fas.org/man/doc.sindp/part 05.htm

51. Jacques S. Gansler, "Next Steps in Defence Restructuring," *Issues in Science and Technology*, Summer 2003 http://www.issues.org/19.4/gansler.html.

52. Paul Dibb, "The Revolution in Military Affairs and Asian Security," paper presented at the Annual Conference on Security Challenges in the Rising Asia-Pacific, Singapore, September 1997.

53. Dibb, Ibid.

54. Dibb, Ibid.

55. Source: Robbin F. Laird and Hogler H. Mey, "The Revolution in Military Affairs: Allied Perspectives," *McNair Paper*, 60, April 1999.

56. Jason Kelly, "A Chinese Revolution in Military Affairs?," *Yale Journal of International Affairs*, Winter-Spring 2006.

57. Kelly, Ibid., p.60.

58. Lt. Col. Dennis J. Blasko, (Retd), "China's National Defence in 2004," *Military Review*, September-October 2005. "Revolution in Military Affairs," quoted by Lt. Col. Blasco mentioned above.

59. Lawrence Freedman, "The Revolution in Strategic Affairs," *Adelphi Paper* 318, p.32.

60. Freedman, Ibid., p.45.

61. Freedman, Ibid., p.47.

62. Macubin T. Owens, "Transforming Transformation: Defence–Planning Lessons from Iraq," Editorial, National Review Online, Ashbrook Centre, April 2003, http://www.ashbrook.org/publicat/oped/owens/03/transform.html

63. Owens, Ibid.

6

National and Defence Budgeting in India

V.N. Srinivas

Introduction

Defence spending forms one of the largest components of Central Government Expenditure (CGE) in India. The defence budgeting procedures and practices are part of, and conform to, the larger national budgeting system. For a better perspective and understanding of the defence budgeting procedures, it becomes important to examine the national budgeting system itself, including the institutional mechanisms and the constitutional provisions governing the overarching budgetary system.

The financial administration of the Government of India, like other bureaucratic procedures, is a colonial legacy and has evolved over a period of a century and a half. However, the present day financial structures and processes have their roots in the Government of India Act, 1935, wherein major reforms were introduced, including the sharing of revenue resources between the central and provincial governments. The constitutional provisions are the basis of government financial administration and, therefore, any study on the budgeting system must commence with the understanding of these statutory provisions.

Government Financial Administration and Constitutional Provisions

Articles 112 to 117 of the Indian Constitution contain the provisions related to financial matters. Article 112 prescribes that the "annual financial statement" for every financial year must be laid before both Houses of the

Parliament. The annual financial statement reflects the estimated government receipts and expenditure for a particular financial year. The statement will also reflect separately the "charged expenditure" and other expenditure from the Consolidated Fund of India. A distinction is also made between the expenditure on revenue account from other expenditure. The Article also contains the list of expenditure to be treated as "charged" expenditure. Article 113 prescribes that the estimated expenditure from the Consolidated Fund of India is subject to a vote of approval by the Parliament, except for the charged expenditure which is not subject to such vote of approval. However, discussion by the members of the Parliament on all items of expenditure, including the charged expenditure, is permissible. The House of the People shall have power to assent or refuse to assent to any demand, or to assent to any demand subject to a reduction of the amount specified in the financial statement. It is interesting to see that the term "budget" is not found anywhere in the Constitution. Instead, the term "annual financial statement" is used for estimated receipts and expenditure of the Union of India. Article 114 prescribes the procedure for passing the Appropriation Bill by the Parliament and that no money shall be withdrawn from the Consolidated Fund of India except under appropriation made by law, passed in accordance with the provisions of the Article. Article 115 provides that any supplementary, additional or excess grants could only be undertaken with the approval of Parliament. Article 116 contains provisions related to the powers of the Parliament with respect to "Vote on Account" (i.e. to make any grant in advance in respect of estimated expenditure for a part of any financial year pending the completion of the voting and passing of such grant), "Votes on Credit" (i.e. to make a grant for meeting an unexpected demand upon the resources of India, when on account of the magnitude or the indefinite character of the service, the demand cannot be stated with the details ordinarily given in an annual financial statement or to make an exceptional grant which forms no part of the current service of any financial year). Articles 202 to 206 contain provisions related to financial matters related to state legislatures. These provisions are similar to the provisions contained in Articles 112 to 117, as applicable to the budgetary procedure of the central government.

The above constitutional provisions clearly define the enormous (albeit formal) powers vested with the Parliament (and state legislatures in respect of states, as the case may be) in so far as the government budget is concerned. It is noteworthy that no item of expenditure or grant can be incurred without prior approval of the Parliament. Similarly, no revenue through taxation can be raised without sanction by the Parliament. It is important to note that whilst the Parliament has enormous powers with regard to approval of the budget, the actual control over such powers is in effect exercised by the executive, i.e. the Union Council of Ministers.

The review and approval of the budget proposals by the Parliament is carried out in four stages i.e. (i) general discussion on the budget; (ii) discussion and voting on the demand for grants, (iii) passing of the Appropriation Bill and (iv) passing of the Finance Bill. The occasion of the general discussion on the budget in the Parliament is meant to provide an opportunity to the members to discuss the financial and other policies of the government. During this stage, the members are free to discuss the budget as a whole or any questions or principles involved therein. The second stage in the legislative approval of the budget commences with the start of the debate on "demand for grants." At this stage, the members may resort to cut motions such as disapproval or policy cut, economy or token cut. After the demands for grants are approved by the Lok Sabha, a Bill is introduced to provide for the appropriation of moneys required to meet the grants. The provision in the Appropriation Bill is not to exceed in any case, the amount as previously asked for by the government while presenting the demands for grants. The passing of the Appropriation Bill completes the authorisation by the Parliament for incurring expenditure by the government. The Parliament then sets to approve the Finance Bill which contains the proposals of the government for raising the required revenue. A general discussion on the Bill takes place, which is followed by a clause by clause discussion. This forms the fourth stage in the approval of the budget by the Parliament. The budget is said to be passed with the passing of the Finance Bill.[1]

The Constitution of India provides for the creation of three separate funds at both the union and state levels. These are as follows:[2]

(a) **Consolidated Fund.** All revenues received by the government, all loans raised by the government by issue of treasury bills, loans, advances and all moneys received by the government in repayment of loans, form one "Consolidated Fund."

(b) **Contingency Fund.** The Contingency Fund is in the nature of an imprest, into which are paid from time to time such sums of money as may be determined by law. The fund is placed at the disposal of the president of India or the governor of the state, as the case may be, to enable advances to be made for the purpose of meeting unforeseen expenditure pending authorisation of such expenditure by the Parliament or the state legislature.

(c) **Public Account.** All other moneys not forming part of the Consolidated Fund received by or on behalf of the government are credited to the Public Account.

The demarcation of moneys by the union or a state government into three separate funds is based on a rational basis. All the moneys, whether received by way of tax or non-tax revenues, or from any other source where the ownership of the moneys vests with the government, form part of the Consolidated Fund. Moneys received by or on behalf of the government where the government acts as a trustee form part of the Public Account. The nature of the Contingency Fund is self-evident. No moneys can be withdrawn from the Consolidated Fund for incurring any expenditure without prior approval of the Parliament or the state legislature through a process of legal appropriation. Therefore, unforeseen expenditures, or expenditure in excess of approved appropriations, are met from the Contingency Fund.[3]

Centrality of Finance Ministry

In the financial administration, policy formulation, coordination and control of finances of the Government of India, the Ministry of Finance (MoF) plays a crucial role. The centralisation of powers in the MoF was criticised in the past by a number of committees. As a result of the pressing demands for reforms in the system of financial control, greater powers were delegated to the administrative ministries. A scheme of significance was introduced from August 1950 whereby the MoF delegated considerably larger powers to the administrative ministries. This was followed by other delegation schemes introduced in 1962, 1968, 1975 and 1979, which vested the administrative ministries with enhanced financial powers.[4] For speedy and effective discharge of their functions in financial matters which include planning, programming, budgeting, internal control, monitoring and evaluation, an integrated financial advisor (IFA) is attached to each administrative ministry. The IFA acts as both internal and external financial advisor. He functions as an internal financial advisor in the exercise of powers delegated to the administrative ministries under the rules concerning delegation of financial powers, and acts as an external financial advisor on behalf of the MoF in respect of matters outside the delegated financial powers of the administrative ministry.[5] The MoF also carries out a careful scrutiny of budget proposals put forward by the administrative ministries. The administrative ministries generally have a tendency to overestimate their requirement and seek allotment of funds accordingly. This is a practice that has its origins during the British time and is echoed in the present day system of financial control, through lump-sum cuts by the MoF while scrutinising the budget estimates prepared by the administrative ministries.[6] The cuts are imposed by the MoF, since it is in a position to see the bigger picture and has overall control of the funds. Such cuts are imposed not only at the stage of scrutiny of the budget proposals but also at the stage of finalising the Revised Estimates (RE), owing to various reasons such as the need to reduce fiscal deficit, inter-adjustment of funds among the administrative ministries, and so on. Thus, the MoF plays a key role in the budget formulation of the central government. The crucial role played by the MoF in allotment of funds under the defence budget will be discussed separately, while examining the defence budgeting system.

Control of Public Expenditure

Since the Parliament is vested with the responsibility of voting and approving the budget, it will also ensure that government expenditure is incurred in accordance with the provisions laid down in the Constitution. This exercise is undertaken by scrutinising the appropriation accounts prepared by each administrative ministry to show utilisation of funds, as earlier voted by the Parliament. Besides scrutiny of appropriations, the efficiency of public expenditure through judicious utilisation of funds is also paramount. Towards this end, two parliamentary committees viz. the Public Accounts Committee (PAC) and the Estimates Committee carry out the scrutiny of public expenditure and submit their reports to the Parliament for examination. The role of these committees is discussed in brief, as follows:[7]

(a) **Public Accounts Committee.** This committee is constituted every year, consisting of 15 members from the Lok Sabha and 7 members from the Rajya Sabha. The committee does not deal with the policy aspects of government expenditure. However, it examines the Appropriation Accounts and the Report of the Comptroller and Auditor General (C&AG) for any lapses on the part of the executive and follows them up with further investigations, if need be. It also examines the income and expenditure accounts of autonomous bodies, public corporations, trading and manufacturing schemes with the objective of legality, authorisation, propriety, etc. However, public undertakings are out of its purview. It may also be noted that the task of the PAC, though very helpful, is in the nature of a *post-mortem examination*. It cannot anticipate possible acts of mismanagement and suggest preventive measures.

(b) **Estimates Committee.** The task of the Estimates Committee is to maintain overall supervision of the financial affairs of the executive so as to indicate possible economies in expenditure without loss of efficiency. Consistent with the policy underlying the estimates, it recommends possible reforms and improvement in efficiency. It also suggests alternative policies for enhancing efficiency and the forms in which estimates should be presented to the Parliament. Public undertakings do not fall under its purview, for which a separate Committee on Public Undertakings exists.

Yet another institutional mechanism for exercise of control over public expenditure is in the form of the C&AG of India. A constitutional appointment, the office of the C&AG came into being through an Act of Parliament in 1971. The provisions related to the appointment, duties and powers of the C&AG and his audit reports are contained in Articles 148-151 of the Constitution. The mission of the C&AG is "to enhance accountability of the executive to the Parliament and State Legislatures by carrying out audits in the public sector and providing accounting services in the states in accordance with the Constitution of India and laws as well as best international practices."[8]

Budgeting System: A Historical Perspective

The budgeting system in the government, at the centre as well as the states, follows what is commonly known as line-item of budgeting. Line-item of budgeting typically categorises the expenditure based on its generic nature such as salaries, travel expenses, expenditure on transportation, and so on. The main drawback of the line-item system of budgeting is that it does not clearly reflect the objectives and purposes of expenditure. Though a number of budgetary reforms were initiated over a period since independence to overcome its limitations, the line-item budgeting system continues to be followed even now in government budgeting and accounting.

Performance-Based Budgeting

Realising the need for changing over to a better budgeting system that would help in effective decision-making, the Estimates Committee of Parliament in 1954 made a recommendation for the introduction of performance budgeting in the Government of India. Such a system of budgeting had already been adopted by the federal government of the USA on the recommendations made in 1949 by the Hoover Commission. The experiment of the operation of performance budgeting in the USA had been successful and encouraging.[9] In 1965, the United Nations published a *Manual for Programme and Performance Budgeting* and suggested that the developing countries could adopt this technique with the view to obtaining a better return on resources.[10] In 1966, a high powered Administrative Reforms Commission (ARC) was set up under the chairmanship of Shri Morarji Desai (who later became prime minister). During its tenure of five years (1966-70), this committee submitted 20 reports on various aspects of public administration. The committee, in its report titled "Finance, Accounts and Audit" recommended to the government that, starting with the 1969-70 budget, performance budgeting should be introduced in all departments and organisations of the government which were in direct charge of developmental programmes. Performance budgeting, according to the ARC, seeks to achieve the following objectives:[11]

(a) To present more clearly the purposes and objectives for which the funds are sought and to bring out the programmes and accomplishments in financial and physical terms;
(b) To help a better understanding and better review of the budget by the legislature;
(c) To improve the formulation of the budget and to facilitate the process of decision-making at all levels of the government;
(d) To enhance the accountability of the management and, at the same time, provide an additional tool to management control of financial operations; and
(e) To render performance audit more purposeful and effective.

Changes in Accounting Classification

In order to facilitate the implementation of performance budgeting, the accounting classification in the government was revised and restructured in April 1974 to bring it in line with performance budgeting. This classification was further revised and restructured in April 1987 to accommodate new developments and to take account of the changed importance assumed by some of the expenditures.[12] Under the revised system adopted in 1987, a four-digit Arabic numeral code was assigned to the major heads, followed by a two-digit code for the relevant sub-major heads, and further followed by a three-digit code for the minor heads. The codification pattern for the major heads was designed in such a way that the last three digits (out of the four digits) represent the same function in the four sections, viz, Receipt Heads (Revenue Section), Expenditure Heads (Revenue Section). Expenditure Heads (Capital Section) and "Loans and Advances," except in a few cases where more than one function was grouped together (as sub-major heads) under a single major head.[13] The accounting classification is illustrated as follows, citing the codes as applicable to Ministry of Defence (Table 1):

Table 1

FUNCTION	Major Head Code in the Section for			
	Revenue Receipt Head	Revenue Expenditure Head	Capital Expenditure Head	Loans and Advances
Defence				
(a) Army	0076	2076	4076/01	-
(b) Navy	0077	2077	4076/02	-
(c) Air Force	0078	2078	4076/03	-

Zero-Based Budgeting

Yet another technique adapted by the Government of India towards reforming the budgetary system is the concept of zero-based budgeting (ZBB). ZBB requires that organisations, while preparing their budgets, should not take the earlier year's expenditure for granted and, therefore, should start on a clean slate each year. It implies that while framing its budget for the ensuing year, an organisation should start from ground zero instead of treating the current budget as the starting point or the base. It means that a complete reexamination of ongoing programmes and activities should be carried out to assess their continued utility instead of following the incremental approach to budgeting.[14] Following a considerable period of investigation and examination, zero-based budgeting was adopted in India in 1986 as a technique for determining expenditure budgets. Accordingly, the Ministry of Finance instructed all the administrative ministries to review their respective programmes and activities in order to prepare expenditure budget estimates, based on the principle of zero-based budgeting. Performance-based budgeting and ZBB were seen as complementary to each other as the goal of both systems is similar i.e. an objective analysis of expenditure, including its cost-benefit analysis. However, ZBB did not require any structural or accounting classification changes for its implementation unlike performance-based budgeting which saw changes in the government accounting classification.

In the overall analysis, it can be concluded that the traditional and time tested line-item of budgeting system has not been replaced, although a number of steps were initiated in improving the overall budgetary system. As a result, various techniques such as performance-based budgeting and zero-based budgeting have become tools for improving and enhancing the efficacy of the traditional budgeting system rather than completely replacing it.

Budgetary Reforms: Recent Attempts

After the introduction of performance budgeting in 1970 in select ministries and zero-based budgeting in 1986, no further attempts were made towards budgetary reforms for a long time. However, public expenditure management has undergone sweeping changes in other countries such as the UK, Australia and USA in the last two decades or so. The primary focus of these revolutionary changes has been on "efficiency" in utilisation of public resources, measurable targets and outputs, and accountability for expenditure management. A need has, therefore, been felt in India too for quite some time now to introduce similar reforms. The nature of some of these reforms is as follows.

Accrual-Based Accounting

The government accounting system as it exists today is a colonial legacy which has stood the test of time for more than a century and half. The present system is a cash-based one, wherein the focus is on inputs and expenditure management. The current system does not take into account the performance parameters of these inputs. In the absence of performance criteria, it becomes difficult to fix responsibility or accountability in achieving the desired objectives. On the contrary, if a system could be introduced that focusses on the outputs and outcomes, assigning responsibility and identifying accountability become easier. One of the ways of achieving this objective is to switch over to the accrual-based accounting system as practised in the commercial sector. Commenting on the cash-based system of accounting, the Twelfth Finance Commission has noted that "the cash-based system of accounting lays emphasis on transactions vis-à-vis the budget. It does not record and report complete financial information required for management of resources. It does not provide a full picture of the government's financial position at any given point and the changes that take place over time as a result of government policy. ….Another major limitation is its inability to record the full cost of providing services by the government's departments or commitments made by the government regarding payment in future years."[15] These limitations can be overcome in the accrual-based accounting system, in which the cost of resources consumed in an accounting period is taken into consideration, whether actual cash outflow takes place or not within that accounting period. Citing the advantages of the accrual-based accounting system, the report mentions that "compared to the cash-based system, the system of accrual accounting recognises financial flows at the time economic value is created, transformed, exchanged, transferred or extinguished, whether or not cash is exchanged at that time. It is different from the cash-based system in that it records flow of resources. Expenses are recorded when the resources (labour, goods and services and capital) are consumed, and income when it is earned, i.e. when the goods are sold or the services rendered."[16]

Fiscal Responsibility and Budget Management Act (FRBMA), 2003

The growing fiscal deficit has been a cause of concern for the government for many years now. In order to bring down the revenue and fiscal deficits, the government passed the FRBM Act in 2003. This Act will provide a legal and institutional framework to bring down the fiscal deficit, contain the growth of public debt and stabilise debt as a proportion of gross domestic product (GDP) over the medium term. It binds future governments to a pre-specified path of fiscal consolidation.[17] In terms of the Act, the centre's revenue deficit was required to be eliminated by March 31, 2008. The rules under the Act further require the central government to reduce the revenue deficit by an amount equivalent to 0.5 per cent or more of the GDP at the end of each year beginning with 2004-05. The fiscal deficit is to be reduced by 0.3 per cent or more of the GDP at the end of each financial year, beginning with 2004-05, so that it is brought down to 3 per cent of the GDP in 2008.[18] In view of the growing concern for reducing the fiscal deficit and to achieve the targets set out in the Act, the government will be hard pressed to reduce its expenditure. Since defence expenditure forms a considerable proportion of the Central Government Expenditure, this sector may be hard pressed and liberal annual budgetary allocations of up to 3 per cent of the GDP (as advocated by a few defence analysts) are unlikely in the near future.

Outcome Budget

Outcome budgeting is yet another effort in the direction of budgetary reforms (after experimenting with performance budgeting and zero-based budgeting in the 1970s and 1980s respectively) to fix quantifiable targets for achieving efficiency of financial outlays. For long, a need has been felt to address certain weaknesses that have crept into the performance budgeting framework such as lack of the clear one-to-one relationship between the financial and performance budgets and inadequate target setting for the ensuing financial year. Besides, there is a growing concern to track not just the more readily measurable intermediate physical "outputs" but the "outcomes" which are the end objectives of state intervention.[19] Towards this end, while presenting the union budget for 2005-06 in the Parliament, Finance Minister P. Chidambaram remarked, "I must caution that outlays do not necessarily mean outcomes. The people of the country are concerned with the outcomes." He further added, "During the course of the year, together with the Planning Commission, we shall put in place a mechanism to measure the development outcomes of all major programmes. We shall ensure that programmes and schemes are not allowed to continue indefinitely from one Plan period to another without an independent and in-depth evaluation."[20] In accordance with the assurance given by the finance minister, a compilation of outcomes/outputs identified by various ministries/departments were brought out by the Ministry of Finance in August 2005, in a document titled "Outcome Budget: 2005-06." This exercise was taken up only for "plan expenditure" to begin with. It was assured that from the subsequent year onwards, similar outcome budgets will be prepared also for non-plan expenditure (including the defence budget which forms part of non-plan expenditure). "The outcome budget would be a pre-expenditure instrument to help realise the ministries' vision through clearly defined outputs/outcomes, as a supplement to the current system built around post-expenditure scrutiny. It will also further strengthen the citizen's right to information, by putting crucial data and information on expected outcomes in the public domain, public scrutiny of which will help ensure value for money."[21] It will take a few years to determine whether the outcome budgets have achieved the intended purpose. The outcome budgeting in the case of defence budgeting has, however, yet to be introduced, most probably owing to the practical difficulties in assigning outcomes in the defence sector.

Government Accounting Standards Advisory Board (GASAB)

The disadvantages of the cash-based accounting system and the need for switching over to the accrual-based accounting system were touched upon earlier in brief. The distinction between the public and private sector accounting methods which existed hitherto is fast disappearing, with the public sector opting for the commercial pattern of accounting. Many governments have either already switched over to such type of accounting or are in the process of doing so. The resource-based accounting (RAB) adopted by the UK with effect from 2000 is an example. The Australian government has also been experimenting with accrual-based accounting in recent years. However, such a changeover to newer accounting methods requires structural changes. Towards this end, the C&AG appointed a Government Accounting Standards and Advisory Board (GASAB) in August 2002. "The principle objective of setting up GASAB was to formulate accounting standards for the Union and State governments to improve the usefulness of financial reporting to the various stakeholders from a viewpoint of understandability, reliability, relevance, consistency and comparability across different arms/units of the government. GASAB has representation from four major accounting departments of the government – the Indian Audit and Accounting Department, the Indian Civil Accounts Department, the Indian Defence Accounts Department and the Indian Railways Accounts Department."[22] These accounting standards are currently in the draft formulation stage.

Defence Budgeting

The importance of the defence budget can be gauged from the fact that on an average, it accounted for around 15 per cent of the Central Government Expenditure (CGE) in recent years. In absolute terms, the defence budget went up from Rs 7,987 crore in 1985-86 to Rs 96,000 crore in 2007-08. This amount does not include expenditure on defence pensions, which roughly accounts for another 15 per cent of the defence budget on an average. Considering that such a huge amount of public resources are diverted for defence, it is essential to examine the operative mechanism for defence budgeting in India, the various pros and cons of such mechanism and to see whether the existing system has scope for improvement. First of all, it must be understood that the general operative mechanism of defence budgeting is as applicable to the overall national budgeting system, as explained above, in terms of accounting classification, the applicability of various legislative procedures and processes, etc. Within the overall context of this commonality, the peculiarities, as applicable to defence budgeting, are examined as follows.

Categories of Expenditure and the Budgeting Process

The defence expenditure is determined based on the projections made by the Ministry of Defence to the Ministry of Finance during the months of October –November wherein, the Revised Estimates (RE) of the current financial year and the Budget Estimates (BE) for the ensuing financial year are prepared. Prior to formulation of the RE and BE figures, extensive consultations are held between the representatives of Service Headquarters (HQ) and the finance wing of the Ministry of Defence i.e. MoD (Fin). The budget is divided into two broad categories of expenditure i.e. revenue expenditure and capital expenditure. The former denotes the running expenditure of the Services such as pay and allowances, stores, transportation, works, training and other miscellaneous expenditure. The capital expenditure denotes expenditure on "creation of assets," and has a direct bearing on force modernisation. The expenditure on aircraft, ships, tanks, infrastructural facilities such as buildings and other construction works are covered under this category. The financial planning directorates of the Service HQ are vested with the responsibility of finalising the budgetary figures for the ensuing financial year, based on the inputs from various specialist directorates within the Service HQ. It has already been brought out earlier that the national budgeting system runs on a cash basis and any unspent amount is "surrendered" at the end of the financial year, since the current system does not follow a roll-on method of carrying forward the unspent amounts. In the case of defence, a majority of the schemes, particularly those belonging to the category of capital expenditure, take several years to fructify. This is due to the complexities involved in the defence hardware procurement such as the Request for Proposal (RFP), negotiations, technical evaluations, contracting and factory-cum-user trials among others. The actual receipt of equipment itself may be spread over several years in most of the cases. For example, in the case of import of aircraft or ships, the equipment may arrive in batches spread over several years. Consequently, the payment against such imports too tends to take place over several years. Normally, a small percentage of the overall cost is paid as advance to the vendors on signing of the contract, while the remaining amount is paid in instalments till the final consignment is received. This gives rise to the term "committed liability" while preparing the budget estimates. Every year, a major chunk of the budget, particularly under capital expenditure, is categorised as committed liabilities i.e. to meet the obligations entered into during the preceding years. The outflow on account of fresh schemes, the payment for which is likely to take place in the ensuing financial year is categorised as "new schemes."

In the context of budgetary management, it is important to understand the relative equation between committed liabilities and new schemes. Firstly, a large proportion of capital expenditure is budgeted to meet the committed or obligatory expenditure in respect of the ongoing schemes, almost to the tune of 75 per cent or more of the overall budget. The remaining amount is catered to meet the outflow of expenditure on account of the new schemes. Secondly, there is always a possibility of the expected payment not taking place under both these categories for various reasons. In the case of committed liabilities the reasons for failure of payment outflow could be various slippages such as: vendor not meeting the deadlines for delivery, any modifications sought from the vendor half way through the delivery process, and contractual slippages by either party, etc. In the case of new schemes, the reasons could be: schemes that were expected to be approved during the current financial year not being approved till the end, delay in processing of the case file either at the Service HQ or MoD, delay in approval by the Cabinet Committee on Security (CCS), and schemes being relegated for the time being for a host of other compulsions. Non-outflow of funds owing to any of these reasons results in surrender of funds. To avoid such surrender of funds, various measures are taken. Some of these are: parking of funds with defence public sector undertakings in the form of advance payments in respect of contracts awarded to them; inclusion of new schemes (which were not included in the Budgeted Estimates earlier) but which can be approved quickly within a short span at the end of the financial year and are likely to materialise immediately with the resultant outflow of funds.

Structure of the Defence Budget

The defence budget derives its structure from the national budgeting and accounting classification system. The defence budget is covered under major heads, minor heads, sub-heads and code-heads. The major head (MH 4076) pertaining to the capital budget is common for the three Services, defence research and development (R&D) organisations and the ordnance factories, while each Service, defence R&D organisation and ordnance factory has a separate major head for revenue expenditure. The most important criticism of the current structure is that it is input oriented which only facilitates expenditure management. Another basic criticism is that the objects of expenditure in the system do not indicate any programmes. It is true that the existing system does not follow any programme-based budgeting as such, despite the desire to have such a system in place. For example, recommendations to follow programme-based budgeting were made in 2001 by the high powered Group of Ministers (GoM) that looked into various aspects of national security. At the same time, it must be pointed out that the current budgetary classification does indicate programmes, albeit in a broad framework and rather vague form. For example, take the case of minor heads under major head 4076 (Capital Budget), viz: "Aircraft and Aero-engines," "Construction Works," "Naval Fleet," "Naval Dockyards/Projects" and "Heavy and Medium Vehicles." What are these classified heads, if not programmes? These are indeed programmes. What is the purpose behind laying down programmes, to begin with? The purpose of programming is to aid better decision-making, by converting and expressing these programmes in monetary or budgetary terms. Therefore, the existing budgetary system does follow a kind of programming budget, a very vague one at best. What one finds in the Defence Services Estimates (DSE), an annual Government of India publication, is only a broad set of programmes (major heads and minor heads). The detailed breakdown of these heads is always available to defence managers in the Service HQ and MoD (concerned directorates), (in the form of code heads/case files pertaining to each and every category of expenditure), constantly aiding decision-making in the day-to-day working, even though such detailed information is not made available openly. What is absent are recognisable "outputs" of these programmes. With a little more refinement of the existing system, it is possible to undertake an exercise of assigning outputs, just as some of the Western countries have attempted in the recent past. Having said so, it must be conceded that mere redesigning the pattern of accounting classification cannot result in programme-based budgeting. Plans and programmes are essentially managerial decisions, which are subsequently converted into budgets. Therefore, any attempt to introduce budgetary reforms *must be* preceded by management reforms. For these management reforms to be effective, it is essential that they originate from the topmost echelon of the organisation.

A Critical Assessment of Defence Budgeting

Since vast and precious national resources are diverted towards security of the nation at a time when there is intense competition for these resources from other vital sectors such as health, education, infrastructure and other developmental programmes, it is important to know whether these precious resources are being put to the best use, in terms of efficiency and effectiveness vis-à-vis the national security objectives. This section examines the effectiveness of India's defence budgeting system within the overall parameters of the national budgeting system, the dimensions of frequent criticism of defence budgeting by analysts, and the pros and cons of the existing budgeting system.

Congruence Between Defence Plans and Budget

A budget is nothing but a plan expressed in financial terms. Ideally, therefore, there must be a perfect congruence between plans and financial outlays. On the other hand, if there exists a mismatch between plans and budgets, it only indicates that there is something amiss and that there is a dichotomy between the planned objectives and what is actually achieved on the ground. In this context, a brief examination of the defence planning system will be useful. Firstly, there are in place what are known as the Services' Long-Term Perspective Plans (LTPPs). The range of these plans is 15 years. A 15-year period is taken into consideration for drawing up plans because foreseeing the future beyond this period would be unrealistic. Ideally, the LTPPs are expected to take into consideration all macro level aspects concerning national security, including political, economic, military and technological factors. They are also expected to address crucial issues concerning the Services such as manpower related issues, equipment acquisition issues, force levels, and so on. "The Perspective Plan, properly drawn up, can show future alternatives with regard to the structures and content of the defence forces. As there are alternatives from which decision-makers have to choose at various decision points in the future, freedom of action and possibility of avoiding early commitments should be the central points of the defence Perspective Plan."[23] The LTPPs prepared by the army, navy and air force become the guiding documents for the preparation of the Five-Year Defence Plan (FYDP). One noticeable difference between the LTPP and FYDP is that the latter is approved by the government, while the LTPP is the internal plan document of the Service and is not approved by the government. In addition to the FYDP, there is the Annual Acquisition Plan (AAP). The AAP consists of new schemes to be taken up for approval during the ensuing financial year. It is prepared by the Services and finalised by the Headquarters Integrated Defence Staff (HQ IDS), before being approved by the Defence Acquisition Council, chaired by the defence minister. The AAP is the most realistic of all plans since predicting a short-term period of one year is easier than foreseeing a five-year or fifteen-year period.

The general criticism of the LTPPs is that these are prepared by the Services individually and, therefore, lack the much desired integrated planning. After the establishment of HQ IDS, however, such an integrated approach is being pursued in earnest. In fact, the term now used is "Long-Term Integrated Perspective Plans" (LTIPPs). These plans are not approved by the government, thereby, diluting their effectiveness. LTPPs also do not conceive frameworks for alternative force structures under different budgetary constraints. Further, the concept of Perspective Plan was ushered into Indian defence without introducing programme planning and budgeting.[24] By now, it is well known that the Five-Year Defence Plans are either not approved by the government and if they are approved, it is only at the fag end of the plan period, thereby, lowering their effectiveness. This aspect has been criticised repeatedly by the Standing Committee on Defence (SCOD) in their various reports. However, it must be added that just because there is repeated delay in approving the FYDPs does not mean that these have completely lost their utility. The FYDP is still the principle guiding document for the inclusion of schemes in the AAP, the funding requirement of which is included in the Budgeted Estimates. However, many a time, owing to a variety of reasons, new schemes are added in the AAP which have earlier not figured in the FYDP. Such inclusion of schemes in the AAP has been construed as giving place to ad-hoc practices. However, this criticism too is not completely tenable, since many changes tend to take place during the intervening period of finalising the FYDP and formulation of the AAP. It is the AAPs which are more realistic and usually one finds a near harmony between the AAP and the Budgeted Estimates. Therefore, it can be concluded that congruence between plans and financial outlays varies with the type of plan that is being referred to. An ideal harmony is desirable between the FYDPs and the annual budgets. But in real life, particularly in a bureaucratic set-up, ideal situations do not exist, be it in the advanced countries such as the US and the UK or the developing countries such as India. The problem acquires a different dimension in the Indian context where there is absence of roll-on budgets and lack of assured funding for the schemes drawn up in the FYDPs. In the absence of the desirable harmony between the plans and budgets, the existing system may not be perfect or ideal, but it is still serving the purpose of meeting the national security objectives within the constraints, as explained above.

Inter-Service Prioritisation

Inter-Service prioritisation is an important area which requires examination while discussing the defence budgetary allocation. First of all, currently there are no set norms or principles existing either in the

MoD or in the HQ IDS for inter-Service prioritisation of allocation of resources. Since there is no scope for roll-on budgets in the current system, the allocation of budgetary resources is taken up only at the RE-BE stage. There is no pre-laid fixed percentage of allocation to each Service. The army, being the largest Service and manpower intensive, gets the largest share, followed by the air force and navy. The air force and navy are capital intensive and, therefore, during the years in which force modernisation is given a boost (as was the case in the last five years so, wherein the capital budget of the air force and navy went up substantially), the share of the Services tends to fluctuate. Non-adherence to any set norms for inter-Service prioritisation was acceptable earlier in the absence of any agency which could undertake this task. But now that the IDS is in place (though the Chief of Defence Staff (CDS) is yet to be appointed), it must undertake the responsibility for this task, in that, it must evaluate the budgetary plans, including the acquisition plans of the Services carefully, before the process of resource allocation commences. Ideally, such an exercise should be undertaken while evaluating the Services' FYDP. At the same time, HQ IDS must indicate the likely budgetary allocations for the Services (even approximations will do) that will give some idea to the Services on the likely availability of budgetary allocations over the next five years. On the issue of prioritisation, the 2001 Report of the Group of Ministers on reforming the national security system stated, "There is also a need for rigorous prioritisation and the order of charge on the budget being established with reference to the plan objectives. The monitoring of inter-Service and intra-Service prioritisation of capital schemes by the VCDS/CDS needs to be institutionalised for ensuring time-bound action and the best value for money."[25] Despite such an important recommendation, there does not appear to be any norm in place for inter-Service prioritisation of budgetary allocations. The current basis for allocation for each Service is on a "need" basis which, in a way, results in fulfilling the requirements of all the Services by rotational and fluctuating budgetary allotments. This is evident from the fluctuating ratio of allocation among the Services, as can be seen from the comparison of data of several years put together.

Perennial Surrender of Funds

Constant surrender of budgeted funds is yet another drawback associated with defence budgeting. There are various reasons assigned for such surrenders such as bureaucratic apathy, delays in timely processing of acquisition cases in both the Service HQs and MoD, cuts by the MoF at the fag end of the year to reduce the fiscal deficit and non-payment of budgeted funds owing to default on the part of vendors, etc. Though surrender of funds has been commented upon adversely by the Standing Committee on Defence and Public Accounts Committee repeatedly in their reports, no serious action has been initiated to plug the loopholes in the system and establish the accountability of those responsible for such surrenders. What has ultimately been affected by such repeated surrender of funds year after year is the force modernisation of the Services. Of course, the payment for the approved schemes will eventually take place in the subsequent years if not during the current year in which they are budgeted for. But the force modernisation is set back by several years in the bargain and new schemes have to wait in the queue, until the liabilities on account of existing committed expenditure are redeemed. It is not that steps were not initiated earlier to address this problem. Based on the GoM recommendations, a number of measures were initiated to strengthen the defence procurement system in recent years. The Defence Acquisition Council (DAC) was set up and a comprehensive Defence Procurement Procedure (DPP) was promulgated. These measures were supposed to arrest the perennial problem of surrender of funds. Despite such major structural changes, funds continued to be surrendered year after year for one reason or the other.

Budgetary Reforms in Defence

Significant budgetary/expenditure reforms took place in the defence sectors in the past two to three decades or so in the USA, UK and Australia among other countries. These countries had realised the drawbacks of the "input" oriented budgets and tried to overcome the shortcomings by undertaking budgetary reforms in the defence sector. Robert McNamara, US secretary of state for defence, set a revolutionary trend with the introduction of the Planning, Programming and Budgeting System (PPBS) in 1961. The strength of the PPBS in decision-making can be seen from the fact that the concept has not been abandoned even after four and a half decades, though it has undergone significant changes during this period. In the UK too, budgetary reforms were introduced in various forms. The latest series of reforms were introduced in 1999, titled "Resource Accounting and Budgeting" (RAB), wherein the emphasis is on outputs rather than inputs, aiding performance measurement of a given resource more accurately.

What about the Indian experience with defence budgetary reforms? As already brought out earlier, the realisation of incorporating budgetary reforms in the government sector dawned upon the Indian planners early enough i.e. way back in the late 1960s. The Administrative Reforms Commission (ARC), with considerable wisdom, recommended the introduction of performance budgeting in the government. However, while these ideals were lofty, something seems to have gone amiss in the implementation stage and giving a shape to the wisdom of ARC. Firstly, performance budgeting was introduced in only select ministries/departments. The Ministry of Defence was not one of them. Secondly, what seems to have been done in the name of performance budgeting was only an accounting reclassification exercise in 1974. There is nothing wrong with such accounting reclassification *per se*, as long as such exercises lead to improved clarity and better analysis and decision-making. As A.K. Ghosh, a former financial advisor of the defence Services comments, "….thus, a dichotomy in the classification of accounts between defence and civil departments arose. While in the departments other than defence, the minor heads in classification of accounts were to represent programmes, in defence, minor heads were to represent the object of expenditure, like pay and allowances, TA, stores, etc. The accounting frameworks in many departments outside defence were designed to usher in performance budgeting. But the Department of Defence turned its back on performance budgeting." He further adds, "So this vital link in the chain of budgetary reforms got broken in the case of defence budgeting in India because of the inadequate perceptions of the policy-makers in the mid-

Seventies regarding the goals of budgetary control and management in defence."[26] The next exercise in reforms process, undertaken in 1987, was also an accounting reclassification exercise and cannot be strictly labelled as a step in the direction of budgetary reforms.

The next major call for budgetary reforms came when the GoM submitted its report in 2001 on reforming the national security system. The report noted and recommended, "A need has been felt for a review of the form and content of the Defence Services Estimates and the expansion of budgetary classification to promote programme-based budgeting, while ensuring compliance with security requirements. As such, a Study Group, headed by a senior official from the Finance Division and including representatives from Service Headquarters and the Controllor General of Defence Accounts (CGDA), should be constituted to make recommendations on budgetary reforms."[27] Based on this recommendation, a study group on budgetary reforms, headed by an additional secretary in the MoD, was set up in 2001. The committee submitted its report in 2002. Based on the report of this committee, the Defence Services Estimates (DSE) which was hitherto being compiled in a single volume, is now published in two volumes. While the information contained in volume 1 has always been in the public domain, the information in volume 2 (though not classified) is restricted for the internal use of the Services, MoD and CGDA. The ostensible purpose of volume 2 was to introduce programme-based budgeting as envisaged in the GoM report. However, what has happened on the ground is a mere expansion of existing minor heads and code heads into additional detailed heads. Thus, the effort to introduce programme-based budgeting in the defence Services does not appear to have made much headway.

Conclusion

The financial administration and budgeting system in India is governed by the constitutional provisions. The Ministry of Finance plays a pivotal role in the formulation of budgetary policies as well as allocation of resources to other administrative ministries. The budgeting system as prevalent in the Ministry of Defence is part of the overall national budgeting system and, therefore, cannot be examined in isolation. Various attempts have been made to bring in budgetary reforms in the country from time to time. But very little substantial changes have been witnessed on the ground. The few reforms which have been attempted over a period in the form of accounting reclassification changes can only be termed as cosmetic. Essentially, the budgeting system remains what it had been for more than a century. While sweeping budgetary reforms have been introduced in a few other countries, India's track record on this score can only be termed as slow. The defence sector on which mammoth public resources are spent year after year has also not witnessed noticeable budgetary reforms such as programme-based budgeting, so that these precious resources are utilised most judiciously and efficiently. However, it would be incorrect to argue that the existing system is inefficient. Whatever budgetary practices and procedures are currently in place have served the nation well in the past and will continue to do so in the future. But taking a critical look at the existing organisational systems and practices from time to time is essential, so as to infuse better organisational practices. Management of organisations, be it in the private sector or the public sector is all about introducing dynamic changes from time to time so that the resources are put to the best use. What is desirable is that these management changes are introduced in the government sector at a much faster pace than hitherto.

For defence budgeting to be effective, the process of planning which precedes the exercise of budgeting must be strengthened. The process of planning, however, is a managerial responsibility and if the planning process is to be made more effective, such an exercise must originate from the topmost level in the organisation. Presently, the defence planning process is predominantly confined to Service HQs, with limited involvement of the MoD. In certain other democracies, such as the US, UK and Australia, the planning process commences in the MoD. In our case, the plan document must originate from the *raksha mantri* and further linkages of plans with the process of budgets must also commence at his level so as to have a stamp of authority and approval. In the final analysis, the entire system of defence planning and budgeting needs a review to reap the benefits of optimum efficiency of resources utilised.

(The views expressed in the paper are the author's own and not those of any organisation) .

Notes

1. Dr. K.L. Handa, "The Budgetary System in India," www.cgda.nic.in
2. L.T. Kulasingham and A.C. Tiwari, "Financial Accountability and Management in Government," Chapter IV, a Research Project of the Asian Organisation of Supreme Audit Institutions, 1992 www.asosai.org
3. Kulasingham and Tiwari, Ibid.
4. Handa, n.1.
5. Kulasingham and Tiwari, n.2.
6. Handa, n.1.
7. H.L. Bhatia, *Public Finance* (New Delhi: Vikas Publishing House Pvt Ltd, 25th edn), 2006, p.500.
8. www.cag.gov.in
9. K.L. Handa, *Expenditure Control and Zero Based Budgeting* (New Delhi: Indian Institute of Finance), 1991, p.10.
10. Handa, n.2.
11. Handa, n.9, p.11.
12. Handa, Ibid.
13. S.P. Ganguly, *Fundamentals of Government Budgeting in India* (New Delhi: Concept Publishing Co., 2000, 3rd edn), p.23.
14. Handa, n.9, p.19.
15. Report by the 12th Finance Commission, Government of India, November 2004, p. 253.
16. Ibid., p. 254.
17. www.indiainfoline.com
18. Handa, n.9, p.91.
19. Comment on "Outcome Budget," *Economic Survey of India 2005-06* (Ministry of Finance, Government of India).
20. www.thehindu.com/2005/09/26
21. Foreword by Finance Minister P. Chidambaram, in the Ministry of Finance document titled *Outcome Budget: 2005-06*, August 2005.
22. www.thehindubusinessline.com/2004/12/23

23. A.K. Ghosh, *Defence Budgeting and Planning in India* (New Delhi: USI, 2006), p. 279.
24. Ghosh, Ibid., p. 283.
25. GoM Report on Reforming the National Security System, 2001, Government of India, p. 108.
26. Ghosh, n.23, p.129.
27. Ghosh, Ibid., p. 109.

7

Directed Energy Weapons: An Insight into the Weapons of the Future

Sanjay Poduval

> The most effective way to cope with change is to help create it.
>
> \- L.W. Lynett.

> O divine art of subtlety and secrecy! Through you we learn to be invisible, through you inaudible and hence we can hold the enemy's fate in our hand
>
> \- Sun Tzu

Introduction

The war between Israel and Hizbollah in the summer of 2006 took much of the world by surprise. Israel won the battle but lost the war. This was largely because it was neither a conventional war nor was it fought in the conventional manner by the militants.[1] In the short course of the conflict, Hizbollah fired some 4,228 rockets at an average of about 120 rockets a day (92 per cent of these were Katyusha rockets), paralysing northern Israel. The Israelis fared relatively well in every aspect, but their counter to the rockets and missiles was ineffective. The Israeli Defence Force (IDF) was at times reduced to providing warning of incoming fire to the vulnerable civilian population.[2]

The loss of this war was the price Israel had to pay for the lack of an effective anti-rocket defence. This might not have been the case if Israel had not backed away from funding the development of the mobile version of the tactical high energy laser (THEL) in 2004. The THEL, in field trials between 1996 and 2004, had shot down many different types of rockets, mortar rounds and artillery shells in flight. Thus, in 2006, when even a prototype may only not have saved lives and property in northern Israel but also demonstrated to the world the immense capability of the weapon, nothing was available. The shattered lives and buildings in Israel once again underlined the need for an effective, affordable defence against indirect fire and a host of other weapons—a defence made feasible by high-energy laser technologies and high power microwaves in the future.

Aim

The aim of this paper is to enable us to understand the potential of the directed energy weapons (DEWs) which are a new class of weapons, never fielded before. In the process, the paper will also discuss what these weapons are, their unique characteristics and limitations, the potential applications, the role they could play in transformation of military tactics, the power levels that have been achieved so far and the current developments in the field of high energy weapon systems.

The Beginning of Directed Energy Weapons (DEWs)

Both the Allies and the Axis powers conducted basic research and studies into primitive directed energy weapons before World War II. However, British scientists calculated that the electronic systems of the time could not generate the power necessary for a "death ray," and research was redirected into early radar detection systems.[3]

During the Cold War, the US and the Soviet Union studied the possibility of creating particle beam weapons, which fire streams of electrons, protons, neutrons, or even neutral hydrogen atoms. The kinetic energy imparted by a particle stream destroys the target by heating the target's atoms to the point that the material literally explodes. These weapons were considered for both land and space-based systems. However, because beam strength degrades rapidly as the particles react with the atoms in the atmosphere, it requires an enormous power plant to generate a weapons-grade beam. Therefore, the countries abandoned particle-beam weapon research as impracticable.

Simultaneously research on the effects of high altitude electromagnetic pulse (HEMP) was also underway. Its effects first became clear in 1962 during the high altitude nuclear test (codenamed Starfish Prime) conducted by the US over the Pacific Ocean, when radio stations and equipment were disrupted 800 miles away throughout Hawaii. It is widely believed that the erstwhile Soviet Union was aware of these effects much earlier.

The invention of lasers in 1960 opened an entirely new avenue of directed energy research. Lasers produce narrow, single-frequency (i.e. single-colour), coherent beams of light that are much more powerful than ordinary light sources. Lasers are the most mature of the DEW technologies because they are extensively researched.

What are Directed Energy Weapons?

Since the invention of gunpowder, a weapon's effectiveness has no longer depended on the wielder's strength, but on the chemical energy of the propellant or explosive. While centuries of technological advances have improved the power of these materials, the basic operating principle ultimately remains the same. Modern battlefield weapons are descendents of the musket and cannon but with greater range, accuracy and more power packed in them. Another revolution in weaponry is currently underway, with DEW on the cusp of entering the domain of chemical-powered weapons on the battlefield. DEWs use the electromagnetic spectrum (light and radio energy) to attack and destroy targets at the speed of light. After decades of research and development, DEWs are becoming an operational reality. Such weapons generate streams of electromagnetic energy that can be precisely aimed over long distances to disable or destroy targets.

DEWs include high power microwaves (HPMs), high energy laser and particle beam technologies. Research is currently on in the field of high energy lasers and high power microwaves. Therefore, this paper will focus on these two aspects of DEWs.

High Altitude Electromagnetic Pulse (HEMP)

HEMP is a subset of HPMs, which operates in the Mega Hertz (MHz) to the low Giga Hertz (GHz) regions. It is produced when a nuclear weapon is detonated high above the earth's surface, creating gamma-radiation that interacts with the atmosphere to create an intense electromagnetic energy field, in the range up to a few MHz that is harmless to plants and animals as it radiates outward, but which can overload computer circuitry, with effects similar to, but causing damage much more swiftly than, a lightning strike[4]. The HEMP effect can span thousands of miles, depending on altitude, design and power of the nuclear burst. The effect similar to HEMP can also be produced by non-nuclear sources in the same frequency band by explosively pumped flux compression generators (EPFCG) which comprise the most mature technology applicable to E-bomb designs. An FCG is capable of producing energies in a relatively compact package with peak power levels of the order of 10^{12} watt (W). It consists of an explosive train packed inside a cylinder[5] to detonate the main explosive. Energy from this explosion is used to generate the high energy electromagnetic (EM) pulse. The explosion destroys the device but produces an ultra short, intense microwave burst and depending on factors such as burst height, microwave frequency, and shielding of target electronics, such an E-bomb could effectively destroy electronic systems operating in its frequency range up to several hundred metres[6]. These devices are portable, can be carried by aircraft and detonated over an area of interest[7].The equipment most susceptible to EMP effect are digital signal processors, electronic flight controls, telecommunication sets, receivers of EW equipment, satellites, HF, VHF, UHF, low band communication equipment, etc.

High Power Microwaves (HPMs)

The FCG are not only limited to the low GHz region but also make the focussing of energy difficult. An HPM device, also sometimes referred to as a high power radio frequency (HPRF) device, overcomes both these problems because its output power can be more tightly focussed and it operates in the same frequency band as the conventional electromagnetic systems of today and, therefore, it too lies in the same frequency range, which ranges from approximately one GHz to about 20 GHz. These weapons work by generating an intense blast of electromagnetic energy[8] (in the mega watt range) which can disable, destroy or permanently burn out equipment and yet not harm the people caught in the blast or leave any trace of where it came from. There are basically two methods by which electromagnetic energy is coupled into targets:

(a) **Front Door Coupling.** In this method of coupling, the electromagnetic signals enter and propagate into a target through its primary sensing circuitry and paths designed to carry signals into the system. Pathways can be antennas, domes, or other sensor "windows". An example would be the propagation of a signal into the enemy's radar through its receiver circuitry.

(b) **Back Door Coupling.** In this method, electromagnetic signals enter and propagate into the target through circuitry and paths not intended for signal entry. Pathways can be cracks, seams, ventilation holes, slots, gaps or seals.

The power levels that have now been achieved lie in the giga watt (GW) ranges. If we consider a 10 GW weapon detonated at a distance of 30 km, the power density at the victim radar receiver would be about 176 watt/sq m. The typical receiver sensitivities (sensitivity of a receiver is defined as minimum signal strength that a receiver can detect) as of today are -70 dbm to -90 dbm which is equivalent to 10^{-10} watt to 10^{-12} watt. The difference in power is obvious and would be more than sufficient to destroy the receiver electronics through the front door. These would, of course, be more lethal at closer ranges but with a smaller footprint.

HPMs can penetrate more readily into equipment as compared to low frequency weapons because of their ability to couple easily through the back door i.e. through poorly shielded wires, gaps between panels, ventilation holes, slots, etc and, in many instances, bypass protection devices. This is because under these conditions, the aperture behaves like a slot antenna which allows the radiation to form a standing wave pattern thus, exposing the components to potentially high electromagnetic fields, especially those components placed at the current maxima. Therefore, the higher the density of components in a system, the greater is the damage. The components most likely to be affected are the high density dynamic random access memories, microprocessors, metal oxide semiconductor field effect transistors (MOSFET) and other components which operate between 5V and 65V supplies.

Like explosive warheads, the electromagnetic weapons coupled with a microwave generator can be delivered over an area of interest by cruise missiles, unmanned aerial vehicles (UAVs), conventional aircraft or global positioning system (GPS) guided glide bombs[9] (*this will be the mode of delivery of these weapons in the near future*). The choice of the platform will determine the destructive capability of the weapon. For example an electromagnetic warhead was fitted in an AGM–68 air launched cruise missile. This restricted the weight of the weapon to about 340 kg. A limit in such applications is the need to carry an electrical energy storage device to provide the trigger current to the FCG. A more capable warhead can be carried by a conventional aircraft because the trigger current required by the FCG can be supplied by the aircraft itself. An E-bomb delivered in this manner offers a much better ratio of electromagnetic device mass to total bomb mass, as most of the bomb mass is now dedicated to generating the high frequency radiation.

High Energy Lasers

These are powerful bursts of coherent light (single phase and single frequency) that are focussed and aimed with mirrors in a very narrow beam to quickly pierce or overheat a wide range of targets like missiles, rockets, aircraft, artillery shells, etc. The electromagnetic spectrum occupied by these weapons lies in the range from the infrared i.e. wavelength (λ) = 40 micro metres (frequency = 7,500 GHz) to the ultraviolet i.e. λ = 0.3 micro metres (frequency = 1 lakh GHz). Laser light can be produced by a number of different methods, ranging from rods of chemically doped glass to energetic chemical reactions to semiconductors. The power output necessary for a weapons-grade laser ranges from 10 kilo watts (KW) to 1 mega watt (MW). When such a laser beam strikes a target, the energy from the photons in the beam heats the target to the point of combustion and destroys the target mid-flight. The laser systems being developed for either space-based or surfaced-based weapons are free electron laser, hydrogen fluoride (HF), deuterium fluoride (DF) chemical oxygen iodine laser (COIL) and solid state lasers (SSL).

Free-Electron Laser. One of the most promising laser devices is the free-electron laser. This laser produces laser beams that can be tuned up and down the electromagnetic spectrum from microwaves to ultraviolet light. This is the only laser which can generate light in different wavelengths. Power up to 20KW has been achieved.

Hydrogen Fluoride Laser. This laser operates in the wavelength between 2.7 and 2.9 microns. The wavelength in this region is susceptible to absorption by the atmosphere, therefore, it is best suited for combat as part of the space-based laser programme. The Ballistic Missile Defence Organisation has already demonstrated a hydrogen fluoride laser with mega watt power in a simulated space environment. This laser system is also being developed for the boost phase intercept of ballistic missiles.

Deuterium Fluoride Laser. Deuterium is the isotope of hydrogen and, therefore, has more mass than hydrogen atoms which results in a longer wavelength of about 3.5 to 3.7 microns, and can transmit better through the atmosphere. The deuterium fluoride-based mid-infrared advanced chemical laser (MIRACL) that can produce more than one MW of power was used in tests to shoot down Katyusha rockets at the White Sands Missile Range in 1996 in New Mexico.

Chemical Oxygen Iodine Laser (COIL). This is another type of chemical laser which has a wavelength of about 1.315 microns, smaller than either of the two previously mentioned lasers that might be used in ballistic missile defence. This smaller wavelength means that smaller optics could be used to develop a space-based lasing system. Right now, this is the most promising of the spaced-based lasers in development.

Solid State Laser (SSL). These lasers promise to be small and compact and will be electrically operated unlike the chemical lasers discussed above. The electrical power required for their operation can be derived from the aircraft electrical system itself. Therefore, these weapons have the potential of generating energy as long as the aircraft engine runs if some method to dissipate the heat generated is found. At present, ammonia gas is used to dissipate the heat. Lockheed Martin and Raytheon are collaborating on developing a powerful 100 KW infrared laser for use on the F-35 joint strike fighter. This laser could be used to destroy communication lines, power grids, or fuel dumps.

Unique Features of Directed Energy Weapons

Directed energy weapons have several unique features which conventional weapons do not possess. The combined features of DEWs and conventional munitions can be synergistically used to combat a wide range of threats. Some of the important features of DEWs are discussed below.

- **Highly Agile Speed-of-Light Delivery.** The first and most obvious point is that the beams generated by DEWs reach targets at the speed of light — about 300,000 km per second i.e. about 160,000 times faster than the muzzle velocity of a bullet. Therefore, a weapon using directed energy as its destructive mechanism can traverse great distances almost instantaneously. Thus, the challenge of tracking and intercepting a target is greatly simplified, and the target's capacity to evade harm is greatly diminished.
- **Immune to Gravity.** A key feature of DEWs is that their beams are not affected by gravity or atmospheric drag (although the bending of light by gravitational fields has significance for cosmologists, within the limited domain in which human warfare unfolds, energy beams are essentially immune to gravity because they have no mass). This lack of mass also frees them from the kinematical and aerodynamic constraints to which more traditional weapons are subject. The complex calculations required to determine ballistic trajectories and other flight characteristics of conventional munitions are irrelevant in using directed energy devices.
- **Precision.** An important aspect of laser weapons is that they are extremely precise. Once cued by radar or other sensors, laser weapons use a low powered beam to acquire and track targets. This beam is focussed on the most vulnerable point on the target with great precision before the co-aligned high power laser is

engaged to deliver the destructive punch. This unprecedented precision makes it possible to accomplish surgical strikes with no collateral damage or fratricidal effects.

- **Graded Effect.** The effects of DEWs can be tailored to achieve a range of results, lethal or non-lethal, destructive or disruptive. This is achieved primarily by adjusting the amount of energy that is deposited on targets or the wavelengths at which the energy is delivered. For example, radio frequency (RF) weapons can generate waves at particular frequencies and power levels to accomplish the temporary upset of certain types of electronic devices while leaving other types unscathed. Graded[10] effect is, thus, possible with DEWs.
- **Cost-Effective.** Directed energy weapons cost relatively little to intercept targets compared with conventional munitions. Although the beam-generating system may be expensive to build and maintain, the price of engagements is minimal because the system expends only energy. In the case of missile defence, interceptor rockets costing millions of dollars can be replaced with DEWs costing only a few thousand dollars per shot to achieve equivalent or superior probability of kill, offsetting the tremendous cost imbalance that favours the attacker today. For example, a THEL shot is estimated to cost about $8,000. In comparison, firing a PATRIOT (PAC-3) missile costs $3.8 million[11].
- **Multiple Target Engagements and Rapid Retargeting.** Directed energy weapons have the capacity for repetitive engagements over protracted periods, constrained only by the availability of power and the need to vent the side-products of beam generation (heat, chemicals, etc.). Moreover, DEWs have few moving mechanical parts and shifting from one target to another involves repositioning of antennas or repointing or refocussing of mirrors, hence, they are well suited for multiple target engagements.
- **Diverse.** Directed energy weapons could be based on a variety of platforms, since they come in a wide range of power levels which largely determines the size. For terminal or point defence, comparatively small systems can quickly kill very short-range targets

by focussing the laser's tremendous power precisely on a target's most vulnerable point. Larger systems could generate even high power levels, focussed in a beam about the diameter of a basketball. Such a weapon can kill a target moving at one thousand miles per hour at a distance of up to several hundred miles, within a few seconds of acquiring the target.

- **Deep Magazines.** Conventional weapons, especially those firing precision-guided munitions, are typically constrained in the number of engagements that can accomplished because they carry only a limited supply of ‘rounds’. Even when the rounds are cheap expendables, number, space and weight limitations place a ceiling on the number of engagements that can take place without replenishment. Directed energy weapons are not entirely free of such considerations, but they do have the potential for deeper magazines arising from the low cost and high energy potential of their power sources which means that they can emit energy as long as there is sufficient power. The implication is that a majority of DEWs may not be “single use” assets because they do not emit expendables in the traditional form of conventional bombs and bullets. Therefore, the number of shots they can fire will be limited only by the amount of fuel available and they will have to shut down to recharge batteries or eliminate heat. Microwave weapons using FCGs are single use weapons.
- **Lower Logistical Support Requirements.** Unlike guns that must be re-supplied with ammunition or missiles that must be replaced once expended, microwave and laser weapons require only additional chemical fuel or fuel to generate electricity needed for power. Hence, the logistics support associated with these weapons systems i.e. the ground crew, supply, maintenance and repair will be significantly less than that required for a conventional weapon system. However, for microwave weapons powered by EPFCG, the logistics will be equivalent to that for conventional munitions.
- **Versatile.** A final unique characteristic of DEWs is their versatility in also serving as sensing devices. Lasers can be used not only to

attack targets, but also to detect, image, track and illuminate ('acquire') them. High power microwaves operate in the same wavelengths as radars, giving them similar tracking potential in some applications. Thus, the distinction between weapons and sensors that prevails in traditional warfare begins to disappear in considering the military impact of directed energy.

Besides the above, they also eliminate the Dead Zones[12] as required by missiles. However, not all of the unique characteristics of directed energy weapons are positive qualities. Radio frequency (RF) beams can be readily diverted by conductive material between their source and intended targets. Laser beams dissipate through interaction with water vapour, dust and atmospheric turbulence. And the highest-frequency, shortest wavelength forms of electromagnetic energy are difficult to generate and condition into directed beams.

Comparison of High Power Microwaves and High Energy Lasers

These two forms of directed energy provide complementary capabilities in the development of weapon systems. Lasers are precise; however, their precision requires complex pointing and tracking systems. By contrast, RF systems offer area coverage with less stringent demands for target tracking; however, the penalty is reduction in the ability to discriminate between friend and foe. While a narrow laser beam has the potential to deliver greater energy at point targets over long distances, such systems can be severely degraded by weather and atmospheric conditions. On the other hand, while RF systems are limited to substantially shorter ranges even under the best conditions, they have the distinct advantage of suffering only modest attenuation due to weather and atmospherics and, therefore, have the potential to provide an all weather capability. The fundamental differences between lasers and RF systems are tabulated in Table 1[13].

Table1: Comparison of High Power Microwaves and High Energy Laser Technologies

High Power Microwaves	High Energy Lasers
Generally affects targets from the inside out. Mechanism is electronic destruction or disruption.	Generally affects targets from the outside in. Mechanism is typically structural destruction.
Wavelengths from 0.1 cm to 3.0 m. Invisible	Wavelengths from 0.3 microns to 40 microns. Ultraviolet to infrared (visiblc/invisible).
Relatively weather insensitive. Clouds and dust are not major factors. Potential for all weather capability.	Environmentally sensitive to clouds, dust, and molecular absorption.
Monolith and/or phased emitters.	Generally monolith. Phased arrays under development
Generally large apertures, metal antennas, ground planes. Relatively durable.	Modest apertures, glass mirrors, coatings and cleaner transmitters needed. Optical surfaces more susceptible to damage.
Relatively large beamwidths (minimum on the order of 1 degree in laboratory tests). Typically flood the target with radiation. Possibility for illumination of multiple targets simultaneously.	Extremely narrow beams. Uses small laser spot to surgically attack individual targets. Requires precise target tracking. Limited to engaging one target at a time.
Both approaches share the following characteristics: Destructive power travels at the speed of light. Capable of graduated effects from degrade, disrupt, damage and destroy.	

Transformation in the Conduct of Wars

A transformation occurs when a nation's military seizes an opportunity to transform its strategy, military doctrine, training, education, technology, organisation, equipment, operations, and tactics to achieve decisive military results in fundamentally new ways.

Directed energy weapons are a new type of weapon system which has never been fielded so far. These weapons, with their unique features discussed above will change the character of warfare, both offensively and defensively. These weapons will bring in changes in all aspects of warfare and will require a new set of ideas, procedures for operation, maintenance and safety. In short, these weapons will be instrumental in evolving new strategies and tactics which will effect changes in the present doctrines. The transformation will occur due to the potential applications of these weapons.

Potential Applications of Microwave Weapons

The significance of microwave weapons is that they provide a range of strategic and operational capabilities in both offensive and defensive operations. The discussion in this section focusses on a few of the operations that could be performed by microwave weapons.

- **Suppression of Enemy Air Defences.** If friendly forces are to gain air superiority and supremacy, aircraft must be able to fly into enemy territory and attack targets without being stopped by enemy aircraft or missiles. To ensure air supremacy, one of the first missions to be completed is the suppression of the enemy's air defence systems, which includes the suppression of communication systems, surveillance radars and missile control, guidance and intercept functions; for example, in the first hour of Operation Iraqi Freedom, 500 high speed anti-radiation missiles (HARMs) were fired to shut down the entire air defence (AD) network of Iraq.

  The conventional strategy is to attack and destroy an enemy's air defence system with a combination of both precision-guided and 'dumb' conventional munitions. Since the explosive kill and damage radius of a 1,000-pound munition is on the order of 35 metres, the effects of explosive blast and fragmentation will have only minimal effects on equipment located beyond that distance. One way for the enemy to ensure that its air defence system will survive is to physically separate the individual systems by ensuring that the tracking radar is located some distance from the targeting radar. In this case, it will be necessary for friendly forces to attack the entire air defence system with multiple munitions if they want to ensure that it is destroyed. However, a reasonable estimate is that a single high power microwave weapon, depending on its range and power and also the shielding of the targeted system, could destroy the entire air defence system. This is because the footprint of the microwave system is expected to be at least 100 times greater than that of a conventional munition[14].

In this case, there are several microwave weapons options that could accomplish this mission, including microwave precision-guided munitions, microwave unmanned combat air vehicles (UCAVs), or microwave self-protection pods on the attacking fighter aircraft[15]. The concept for the employment of a microwave precision-guided munition would be the same as that of a conventional munition. It would have the same blast and fragmentation pattern as a conventional munition, and, thus, operate as a "single shot" device (use of a microwave generator coupled with an EPFCG). However, for the microwave munition, the primary kill mechanism is microwave energy rather than an explosion.

- **Disrupting Enemy C3I.** With net-centric operations playing a very important role in modern warfare, command, control, communication and information (C3I) form a vital link between victory and defeat. The objective of C3I warfare is to give friendly forces the capability to limit the enemy's ability to control and direct its military forces; the reality of modern warfare is that military commanders rely heavily on telephones, satellite communications, etc. for communicating with their units. A microwave munition would present an extremely effective weapon for use against these enemy systems.
- **Close Air Support.** The purpose of close air support is to assist friendly ground forces by using direct fire by conventional munitions and large calibre aircraft guns (20 or 30 millimetre guns) against enemy tanks, artillery and forces. The use of HPMs will disrupt radio and satellite communications, artillery and guidance and control functions and effectively prevent the enemy from using its weapons.
- **Space Control.** For the purposes of space control, microwaves could be used as defensive or offensive weapons. In that capacity, they could protect friendly satellites from guided kinetic-kill weapons as well as attack satellites that provide information, directly or indirectly, to enemy forces.[16] One advantage of microwave weapons is that these do not produce debris, whereas all other proposed weapons will cause physical disintegration of the satellite.

- **Active Denial System.** The active denial system (ADS) is a non-lethal anti-personnel DEW that uses millimetre wavelength beams to create a painful sensation in an individual without causing actual injury. It is relatively close to deployment. The system generates a focussed beam of energy at the frequency of 95 GHz. This millimetre waveband energy penetrates the human skin to a very shallow depth (1/64th of an inch), heating the tissue below, and produces a burning sensation without actually damaging the tissue. This sensation increases in intensity until the affected individual moves out of the beam envelope or the radiations are shut off. The pain, therefore, forces the personnel to flee the area without causing any physical injuries. This type of weapon shows great potential as a riot-control device or area-denial system[17]. The United States Navy is also developing this system as an anti-terrorist weapon to be used on the high seas[18]. A demonstration system was tested at Kirtland Air Force Base in 2000. A year later, testing showed that the ADS could produce effects at ranges beyond current small-arms range. A prototype ADS system mounted on a Humvee went into testing in August 2005[19].

Potential Applications of Laser Weapons

Defensive Operations. Lasers can provide air, land, sea and space platforms the ability to defend themselves, other platforms and geographic areas. They can defend against missiles, aircraft, bombs, artillery shells or rockets by destroying or neutralising these threats before they reach their intended targets.

One of the first emerging missions for laser weapons would be aircraft self-defence. Heat seeking surface-to-air-missiles (SAMs) are demonstrating an increased capability to overcome passive counter-measures such as chaff and flares. The laser weapons could be employed in the future on tactical aircraft and will be triggered by the aircraft's own missile warning system. These could also be used for self-protection of commercial aircraft if the requirement so arises.

Laser defences could provide an on-board active defence capability for aircraft that could defeat or destroy incoming missiles or aircraft within their range. This greatly increases the survivability and simultaneously reduces the requirement of air defence cover of many non-stealthy, subsonic, vulnerable platforms like the joint surveillance and target attack radar system (JSTARS), airborne warning and control system (AWACS), etc.

Ground-based laser defences can defeat most indirect fire threats (rockets, artillery and mortars), significantly increasing ground force survivability and freedom of manoeuvre.

For naval forces, lasers could provide an effective shield against an adversary's ballistic or cruise missile attacks. Their inherent flexibility makes them attractive candidates for other missions, including the neutralisation of small fast patrol boats, sensor blinding and other anti-surveillance measures[20].

For missile defence, lasers can provide point defence of a specific target or area defence against theatre ballistic and cruise missiles. Air-borne and space-based lasers may also provide active defence over large areas and could engage targets, primarily ballistic missiles, much earlier in their trajectories than surface based defences. At present, lasers are the only weapon system to show promise for boost phase interception of ballistic missiles. Laser weapons can also help to provide a more affordable and, thus, more widely-spread, terminal point defence against theatre ballistic missiles.

The same characteristics that make laser weapons effective for these military active defence missions could also allow them to defend critical infrastructure or government facilities against aircraft and direct and indirect fire ground weapons.

Offensive Operations. Lasers can provide the capability to achieve highly precise lethal or non-lethal effects against a range of suitable targets, mostly as a complementary capability for chemical and kinetic weapons.

The application of lasers has the greatest potential to change the conduct of warfare over a long term in space. The current generation air-borne laser (ABL) is said to have the capability to degrade or damage low earth orbiting satellite, but a high confidence would require the present system to be at least twice as powerful.

US experiments have already demonstrated that satellites hundreds of kilometres up are vulnerable to high energy lasers. The importance of this capability has not been lost on countries like China, which are pursuing a robust high energy laser capability.

Offensive applications of lasers will most likely be dedicated to those missions where laser weapons characteristics (e.g. precision, speed and number of engagements) are more important than pure destructive power. The same laser weapons that provide an active defence capability for aircraft can also be used against ground targets, providing a significant air-to-ground capability.

Limitations of Directed Energy Weapons

Directed energy weapons clearly offer some novel and potentially very important military capabilities that could serve as the basis for entirely new missions and operational concepts. However, DEWs are not the proverbial "silver bullets," therefore, like other weapons, they too have their limitations which could impact operational utility and pose some serious problems under real world conditions. For lasers, the principal limitations are atmospheric effects, mechanical scanning, and the maximum power that can be delivered. The absorption and scattering effects will preclude lasers from becoming true all-weather weapons in the near term, even if the transmissivity window in the one-micron region could be exploited. Moreover, any sensor limited to a single relatively narrow band is vulnerable to counter-measures.

Radio frequency directed energy weapons face a number of physical limitations. As transmitted power is increased, high-power microwave weapons confront the problem of air breakdown[21]. Current research efforts are devoted to identifying waveforms that permit the maximum transfer of energy without reaching the breakdown threshold. Propagation losses can limit the effective range of RF systems, since even a focussed beam spreads dramatically as the range to the target increases. Some of the limitations of these weapons are discussed below.

- **Battle Damage Assessment.** Damage assessment has always been critically important because it determines whether more missions are required to accomplish the task. Unlike conventional weapons which physically destroy the targets, microwave weapons do not leave any smoking holes on the ground. The effects on targets are, thus, difficult to assess externally because, for example, the absence of electronic emission from a bunker may be a sign that the facility was neutralised or, conversely that the target is playing possum.

- **Shielding.** The effectiveness of DEWs is reduced by screening or shielding or use of ablative materials that cannot be readily burned through. Shielding can work, but it is difficult to fully shield either platforms or facilities. It is very expensive to provide such protection and, therefore, it is likely that only a small number of platforms will have even modest hardening. A fixed facility such as a command bunker could be built inside a metal grid, a sort of Faraday cage, in order to be secure against electromagnetic energy. But this is costly. By shutting itself off from the external world, a command centre effectively places itself out of action. Or the command centre could stock spare electronic devices such as radios and computers in the event of an HPM attack, but it is unlikely that even the best-equipped facility could withstand more than one such event. It would be extremely difficult to effectively shield aircraft, helicopters or tactical missiles.
- **Fibre Optic Lines.** Deployment of fibre optic communications networks also can reduce the effects of HPM weapons. But unless the facilities at either end of a fibre optic cable are also hardened, it may make little difference in terms of the overall vulnerability of the network to attack.
- **Atmospheric Attenuation and Turbulence.** Laser beams have to propagate through the atmosphere, therefore, they are affected by air-borne particles (dust, smoke), water vapour or atmospheric turbulence that absorb, bend or scatter laser energy. Modern laser systems employ adaptive optics[22] to compensate for the problem of beam attenuation caused by atmospheric turbulence. This, however, is not a major problem for HPMs.
- **Line-of-Sight Dependence.** Directed energy weapons require the target to be in the direct line-of-sight for it to be engaged.

- **Target Suitability.** The relatively low power levels of lasers compared to chemical weapons means that laser weapons will probably lack the 'punch' of larger non-laser chemical or kinetic weapons for some time. They are best suited for targets that must be engaged very quickly and precisely, such as rockets, missiles or artillery rounds in flight, or those which can be destroyed or disabled by focussing energy accurately on vulnerable areas. Their effects are minimal on hardened structures like bunkers or even buildings. Against armoured vehicles, they are effective only in disabling vulnerable components such as antennas, sensors and external fuel stores.
- **Eye Safety Issues.** Eye safety is a major concern in the use of laser weapons. While some chemical lasers operate at eye-safe wavelengths, high-power solid state lasers currently do not, because any laser energy that is not absorbed by the target is either scattered or reflected; this non-absorbed energy poses an eye safety risk to personnel without laser eye protection, and to civilians in the target's vicinity.
- **Chemical Fuels and Exhaust.** Chemical lasers require chemical fuels and generate exhaust when they fire. Some fuels, like the highly corrosive fuel of the air-borne laser's chemical oxygen iodine laser (COIL), require multiple safety systems. Others, like the deuterium fluoride reactants used by THEL, are relatively safe.

Current State of DEW Technology

A lot of progress has been made towards the weaponisation of microwaves and lasers. There are a number of programmes which are being actively pursued by China, Israel Russia and the US, to name a few. Though the US is in the forefront of these technologies, countries like China and Russia have not lost sight of these weapons and are investing a lot in this field. Israel too has its own programme but it is also presently being aided by the US. Recently, countries like North Korea, Japan, and the UK have also initiated research and development (R&D) programmes.

In the following sections we shall see the current state of development of the microwaves and laser weapon systems.

High Power Microwave Technology Programme

A lot of technological advancements have been made in antenna design, beam focussing, pulsed power sources and microwave sources that operate at different frequencies and transmit at these high power levels.

Solid state switching technologies and phased array techniques have made it possible to design conformal antennas and have also made it possible to steer the beams and focus them into very narrow beamwidths of one degree. This has been made possible by the impulse antenna radiating technology[23]. These antennas are still in research stages and till such time they mature, FCGs coupled with microwave sources will be used.

A wide range of FCGs as power sources have been built and tested in the US and Russia. The FCGs at present are capable of producing mega joules of energy lasting for about 100 micro seconds. The peak power levels that have been achieved so far are in the order of 1,000 GW[24]. FCGs have been developed for different power levels to suit a wide range of applications.

Research is also underway in the development of microwave generators. The important ones among these are the spark gap devices, backward wave oscillators, virtual cathode oscillators (vircators), klystrons and magnetrons. The most promising among these are the vircators. This is because they have a tuneable cavity enabling generation of microwave frequencies over a wide band. The power levels that have been achieved so far are in the range of 170 KW to 40 GW in the frequency band of 1 to 20 GHz.

Steady progress has been made in size reduction and increase in power of these weapons. Microwave weapons have been developed which radiate one GW of power for a few nanoseconds and weigh less than 45 pounds, another microwave source radiates 20 GW of power for a few nanoseconds and weighs about 400 pounds. To comprehend these power levels, the power generated by the Bhakra Nangal Dam is approximately 3,000 MW or 3 GW per day.

Kirtland Air Force Base in Albuquerque, North Mexico, is supposed to be the epicentre of the Pentagon's research on pulsed power electromagnetic weapons. It is here that the multi-mega watt HPM "Shiva Star" is housed behind metre thick walls. It has the capability to produce 120 thousand volts and 10 million amps for one milli second. This is equivalent a power of a 1,000 GW. Besides developing the high power systems, extensive research is also being undertaken to understand the effect of HPMs on the avionics and flight control systems of different platforms.

Research is also on in China for the development of an HPM warhead, which is likely to be operational by 2015, and HPM sources[25]. Extensive studies are also being carried out to study the effect on electronics due to HPMs with the aim of developing impregnable shields.

Russian scientists at the Physico-Technical Institute in St. Petersburg have achieved many firsts in HPM generation; for example, they have developed a multiwave Cerenkov generator with a peak output power of 15 GW. Their successes are based on their impressive capability in pulsed power technology which has yielded high-current generators of tera watt peak power. They have transformed the energy of these currents into microwave radiation using tubes of both conventional and novel designs exploiting HPMs. The recent development of high-current mini-accelerators has moved HPM generation out of the laboratory and enabled the development of deployable military systems with peak powers in the giga watt range. As a result, they now see development of a DEW-based radar system as one of the most promising directions in radar systems[26]. They are also in an advanced stage in the development of impulse radiating antenna.

High Power Laser Weapons Programme

Of the present DEW systems, lasers are the most widely researched and developed. The hydrogen fluoride (HF) laser, deuterium fluoride (DF) laser, chemical oxygen iodine laser (COIL), free electron laser and solid state laser are being widely researched.

The Tactical High Energy Laser (THEL). This system, based on the DF laser illuminator, can engage up to 60 nearly-simultaneous threats at a range of up to 5 km, while maintaining a near-100 per cent rate of success[27]. This system is located at the US Army Missile Range at White Sands, New Mexico, and has been successfully tested against short-range Katyusha rockets. The THEL is also being modified into a deployable combat system called high energy laser – rockets, artillery and missiles (HELRAM), which can be used against multiple types of threats as the name suggests.

Mobile Tactical High Energy Laser (MTHEL). The MTHEL system grew out of the larger stationary tactical high-energy laser programme in 1996. This is a joint US-Israeli system aimed at providing battlefield missile defence via focussed, high-powered laser beams. It was designed to use existing laser fire C3I technology to produce an effective low cost defence against short and medium range artillery, rocket and ballistic missile threats. The stationary MTHEL test bed has destroyed 28 Katyusha rockets and five artillery shells in single and multiple engagement tests since testing began in 2000. The Pentagon and the Israeli Ministry of Defence have spent nearly $300 million on MTHEL since development began ten years ago. Once fielded, MTHEL is expected to cost approximately $3,000 per use – slightly less than a single Mk84 2,000 lb 'dumb' bomb[28]. Although the system is not likely to meet its original target of initial operational capability this year, MTHEL could be deployed and operational by 2010, assuming that no significant delays or difficulties are encountered in future testing.

Air-borne Laser (ABL). This programme is integrating a multi-megawatt chemical laser with a modified Boeing 747-400 so that theatre ballistic missiles can be intercepted in their boost phase. The basic operational concept of ABL[29] is to fly at 40,000 feet and intercept boosting missiles after they have exited cloud cover, but before they can escape enemy air space or release warheads and penetration aids. In a tiered defensive architecture, ABL would substantially thin out attacking missiles near their source, leaving a less challenging threat for defenders to address during the later mid-course and terminal phases of trajectory. This type of laser system is not likely to be fielded before 2012.

Besides the US and Israel, China too has a robust laser programme. China's DEW related R&D[30] and application programmes are massive and sophisticated by any international standards and some estimates suggest that approximately 10,000 personnel, including 3,000 engineers, are involved with China's laser programme alone (40 per cent of these are for defence applications alone).

The National Engineering Research Centre for Solid State Lasers, Beijing, is conducting R&D on solid state lasers. The SSL Shenguang -2 reportedly has a power output of a tera watt. The establishment has also developed a tuneable titanium-sapphire ruby laser with a power output of 650 MW. They are also in the process of developing high-energy lasers to be used as ground based anti-satellite (ASAT) weapons (this currently has a capability to damage, under specific conditions, optical sensors of satellites).

The DEW programmes of China have also been aided by the erstwhile Soviet Union's scientific and technology community absorbed by China. Recent reports attributed to the US Defence Intelligence Agency also indicate that Israeli Aircraft Industries may have transferred key high-energy laser technologies to China.

DEW in the Indian Context

The Bhabha Atomic Research Centre (BARC) developed the kilo-ampere linear injector (KALI) microwave in the year 1999 which had the potential to generate 40 GW of power for 100 ns in the low microwave region but the system was bulky (26 tons) and had to be reduced in size before it could be used for military purposes[31]. Though this was not done, the system, however, provided vital inputs for hardening of electronic equipment against EMP due to a nuclear burst.

The Laser Science and Technology Centre (LASTEC), Metcalfe, New Delhi, has been entrusted with the task of development of high power lasers for defence applications. Their mission is to carry out research in the field of lasers photonics and opto-electronics and to develop and deliver DEW systems for the Services. They are also working on development of adaptive optics which plays a vital role in focussing laser beams through turbulent atmosphere.

There is also a lot of research going on at Indian Institutes of Technology (IITs) in the field of high power microwaves and lasers, though not specifically for military purposes[32] but this knowhow can always be absorbed by the defence industry. As can be seen, the progress in this field is slow and it will take some time before these weapons surface on Indian soil.

The slow progress notwithstanding, HPMs could have a major role to play in close air support and battlefield interdiction by effectively cutting off communication between command centres and troops by disabling electronics. A microwave weapon or a microwave UCAV could be used to attack and disable enemy airfields by damaging and destroying electronics in air borne aircraft, aircraft on the ground, air traffic control equipment, communications facilities, radars, and ground defence systems. The rising trend of the proliferation of ballistic missiles in our neighbourhood will most likely pave the way for the use of high power lasers against these missiles in the future. The ballistic missiles, if launched from Pakistan, would give us a reaction time of about 5-10 minutes at the most. Air-borne lasers would be ideally suited for interception of these threats in their boost phase itself because of the speed at which they reach the targets. This, of course, would require an elaborate network for detection, identification, tracking and communication, but it will still be worth the effort considering the population and the cities that will be protected.

China, with its latest ASAT test, has conveyed a message to the world that, in any future conflicts with it, no country will be able to use its satellites (at least the low earth satellites) for military purposes. A very prudent answer to this would be to develop our own capability to destroy satellites but without causing any debris in space. DEWs could be the answer because of their inherent capability of destroying the electronics, sensors, solar power panels, etc of the satellites and not the satellite structure.

Another area where DEWs can play an important role is at sea, particularly against cruise missiles as a hard kill option. This is because since these high speed sea skimming missiles offer very little reaction time, high power lasers can be used to destroy them before they reach their destination.

Use of microwave weapons by anti-national elements is a real possibility since a low power HPM device is easy to build[33] and the cost of such a device would be about $400[34]. According to Carlo Kopp, an Australian-based expert on high-tech warfare, the threat of E-bomb proliferation is very real; terrorists could use a less expensive, low-tech approach to create the same destructive power. It is, thus, important for us to study how these weapons are going to affect our electronics[35] and provide proper protection and hardening techniques to critical equipment at the design stage itself.

Conclusion

Directed energy weapons have come of age and will revolutionise the way wars are fought in the future. Within the next few years, the first weapon systems built with directed energy as their kill mechanism will be deployed. Just as digital technology is greatly increasing the pace and precision of information flow, DEWs will enhance the discrimination and speed at which targets are engaged.

Considerable progress has been made in high power beam generation and control of DEWs. These weapons possess certain unique features which make them particularly suitable against guided missiles, cruise missiles, UAVs, and fast moving ballistic targets. The air-borne laser currently holds the promise for an effective boost phase intercept of ballistic missiles.

The first and possibly the most significant impact of directed energy weapons will be defensive in character. Tactical lasers for the first time will provide a means of active defence against short range rockets, artillery shells and mortars. They have the potential to protect civil airliners against man-portable surface-to-air missiles.

High power microwaves operate like steerable radio transmitters, generating intense bursts of electromagnetic energy to disable or destroy electronic systems. HPMs offer the prospect for the first effective means of conducting non-lethal engagements at medium ranges. HPMs could be particularly useful in destroying critical targets that are buried and located in populated areas without causing collateral damage.

Recent analyses have indicated that the volume, weight, power, and cooling requirements of these technologies may limit air-borne and space-based applications for the foreseeable future. Cost is a constraint at present. In the long-term, however, cost does not appear to be an insurmountable obstacle. The continuing commercial demand for improvement in manufacturing of electronic components is likely to reduce the cost of components. While it is unrealistic to expect that the trend towards lower unit costs over the last decade will continue unabated, the demands placed upon the commercial electronics market should further reduce costs.

The characteristics, capabilities and limitations of the use of directed energy weapons must be clearly understood for them to be effectively employed. They have to be properly integrated with the present systems and platforms and used synergistically with the existing weapon systems to unleash the promise they hold.

Notes

1. Jasjit Singh, "Interpreting the Lebanon War of 2006," *Air Power*, vol. 1, no.2, Winter 2006, p.33.
2. Alon Ben-David, "Israel Revises Plan for Anti-Rocket Laser System," *Jane's Defence Weekly,* September 6, 2006. http://www.janes.com/defence/land_forces/news/jdw/jdw060901_1_n.shtml.
3. David E. Fisher, *A Race on the Edge of Time: Radar—The Decisive Weapon of WWII* (New York: McGraw-Hill, 1988), pp. 15–31.
4. A nuclear explosion produces gamma rays, which interact with air molecules in a process called the Compton Effect. Electrons are scattered at high energies which ionizes the atmosphere, generating a powerful electrical field. This EMP effect is strongest at altitudes above 30,000m, and lasts so briefly that current cannot start flowing through a human body to cause harm to people. http://www.physics.northwestern.edu/classes/2001Fall/Phyx135-2/19/emp.html.
5. A flux compression generator consists of explosives packed inside a cylinder, all of which is contained within a cylindrical copper coil structure. The explosive is detonated from rear to front, causing the tube to flare in a wave that touches the copper coil, which produces a moving short circuit. This compresses the magnetic field and creates an electromagnetic pulse that is emitted from the front end. http://www.physics.northwestern.edu/classes/2001Fall/Phyx135-2/19/emp.htm.

6. GlobalSecurity.org, "High Power Microwave (HPM)/E-Bomb," at http://www.globalsecurity.org/military/systems/munitions/hpm.htm, March 15, 2006.
7. Carlo Kopp, "The Electromagnetic Bomb—A Weapon of Electrical Mass Destruction," at http://www.globalsecurity.org/military/library/report/1996/apjemp.htm, January 16, 2007.
8. US Air Force Research Laboratory, "High-Power Microwaves," Factsheet, September 2002, at http://www.de.afrl.af.mil/Factsheets/HPM.swf , September 15, 2006.
9. Kopp, n.7.
10. Alane Kochems and Andrew Gudgel, *The Viability of Directed-Energy Weapons* (The Heritage Foundation).
11. Sandra Erwin, "Directed Energy Weapons Promise Low Cost per Kill," *National Defence Magazine*, September 2001, at www.nationaldefensemagazine.org/article.cfm?Id=591.
12. The Dead Zone is the zone in which the missile is in its unguided phase of its flight before it is finally acquired by the radar system for guidance. Therefore, in this zone, the missile is least effective.
13. William J. McCarthy (USN), "Directed Energy and Fleet Defence Implications for Naval Warfare," http://research.maxwell.af.mil/papers/ay2000/csat/csat10.pdf
14. Eileen M. Walling (UASF), "High Power Microwaves Strategic and Operational Implications for Warfare," http://www.au.af.mil/au/awc/awcgate/cst/csat11.pdf
15. Kopp, n.7.
16. Direct information includes GPS coordinates, information concerning reconnaissance/surveillance activities, communications, and weather forecasting, among others. Indirect information involves radio and television broadcasts because these could provide knowledge of intelligence value to the enemy.
17. Alane Kochems and Andrew Gudgel, "The Viability of Directed-Energy Weapons," http://www.heritage.org/Research/NationalSecurity/bg1931.cfm
18. "Tuning Up The Heat: High-Power Microwave Weapons," *Jane's Navy International*, vol. 112, issue 2, March 2007, p. 39.
19. http://www.irconnect.com/noc/press/pages/news_releases.mhtml?d=89438
20. McCarthy (USN), n. 13.
21. Air breakdown occurs because the air in the vicinity of the HPM turns into a plasma state and this ionised region begins to absorb the energy from the radiations.
22. Several extraneous factors can interfere with beam propagation through the atmosphere, including scattering, thermal blooming (heat-induced spreading),

and defocussing due to turbulence. In addition, performance factors intrinsic to the laser device itself can diminish the energy of the beam at its point of destination. Adaptive optics measures these sources of distortion and deforms the beam at its point of origin so that it achieves maximum lethality after encountering such influences. In other words, the beam is actually more lethal when it reaches the target than when it began.

23. United States Air Force Fact Sheet "High Power Microwaves," http://www.de.afrl.af.mil/Factsheets/HPM.pdf
24. Kopp, n.7.
25. Source Jane's Defence at http://www.aeronautics.ru/archive/ research literature/ aviation_articles/Jancs/topics/plasma_stealth/Directed%20Energy%20Weapons %20and%20Sensors.pdf
26. Sylvian Gauthier, "High Power Microwaves Development in Russia," http://adsabs.harvard.edu/abs/1995hpm.....1Q....G
27. Israel High-Tech & Investment Report June 2004, "*US-Israeli Laser Destroys Medium-Range Missile in Flight*," http://www.ishitech.co.il/0604ar3.htm.
28. Ibid.
29. Dr Loren Thomson and Dr Daniel Goure, "Directed Energy Weapons," http://lexingtoninstitute.org/docs/321.pdf.
30. Source Jane's Defence at http://www.aeronautics.ru/archive/research_literature/ aviation_articles/Janes/topics/plasma_stealth/Directed%20Energy%20Weapon s%20and%20Sensors.pdf
31. "India Said to be Building Microwave Beam Weapon," http://www.rense.com/ politics4/ beamweapon.htm
32. India Daily "Advanced Weapon Systems Using Lethal Short-Pulse Terahertz Radiation From High-Intensity-Laser-Produced Plasmas," http://www.india daily.com/editorial/1803.asp
33. Clay Wilson, "High Altitude Electromagnetic Pulse (HEMP) and High Power Microwave (HPM) Devices: Threat Assessments," http://www.fas.org/ man/crs/RL32544.pdf
34. Jim Wilson, "Electromagnetic Pulse Risks and Terrorism," http://www.united statesaction.com/emp-terror.htm
35. The components of the electronics of the present generation have shown a trend towards operating at substantially lower currents and voltages, making them vulnerable to even low power HPMs.

8

Air Power in Small Wars: Fighting Insurgents and Terrorists

Arjun Subramaniam and
R. Bhasin
Alex Merz
S.K. Nair
P. Navad
S.K. Paul
Sarabjit Singh
K. Sundarmani

Part I

> This is another type of war, new in its intensity, ancient in its origin — war by guerrillas, subversives, insurgents, assassins, war by ambush instead of by combat; by infiltration, instead of aggression, seeking victory by eroding and exhausting the enemy instead of engaging him. It is a form of warfare uniquely adapted to what has been strangely called "wars of liberation," to undermine the efforts of new and poor countries to maintain the freedom that they have finally achieved. It preys on economic unrest and ethnic conflicts. It requires in those situations where we must counter it … a whole new kind of strategy, a wholly different kind of force, and, therefore, a new and wholly different kind of military training.[1]
>
> —President John F. Kennedy, 1962

Background

The world is today faced with a continually evolving landscape of small conflicts, driven by a host of issues spawned by globalisation. Groups increasingly compete for resources and recognition, even while there is increasing pressure to avoid conflict. Additionally, even small conflicts can have a broad impact on an interconnected world. Whereas earlier, a small war was very much localised in its effect, now a seemingly insignificant insurgency can disrupt economies and political systems on the opposite side of the planet. Thus, while major warfare seems to be becoming more and more rare, small wars, with limited objectives and scope, are becoming more significant, if not more numerous. It only makes sense that one of the central enabling technologies of globalisation — powered flight — is also central to the effective prosecution of the small war. The unique capabilities of air power lend themselves readily to many of the requirements levied by small wars. However, a great capability misused is often more destructive than helpful, and the same holds true of air power. Air power employed foolishly in a small war is just as likely to contribute to the defeat of the nation that wields it. To evolve a doctrinal framework for employment of air power in small wars, it would be important to wade through some definitions and theories of small wars, look at a model that describes the fundamental elements of a small war, and a delineation of the characteristics of air power that fit into the model. An analysis of several significant small wars from the past will attempt to draw lessons from the application of air power in these wars. Technology and lessons learnt will form the last part of the article that will also attempt to draw a template for the Indian context.

Definitions, Theory and Doctrine

Small wars are operations undertaken either at home or abroad by national military forces at the direction of their government, in conjunction with political, social, and economic efforts, to defeat violent efforts by non-state actors to destabilise established civil authority within a given region, territory, or country.

This definition is an expanded version of the one first presented by the US Marine Corps (USMC) in its *Small Wars Manual,*[2] and encompasses other more commonly discussed concepts such as low-intensity conflict, counter insurgency, counter-terror, guerrilla warfare and civil war. As such, it lends itself well to the the types of conflicts India is likely to face in the next few decades. Several other common terms closely related to small wars bear definition here.

Terrorism

Terrorism is defined in a variety of ways, depending on the focus of the agency giving the definition. Here, the Indian Ministry of Defence (MoD) definition will be used: "The wanton killing of persons or involvement in violence or in the disruption of services or means of communications essential to the community or in damaging property with a view to putting the public or any section of the public in fear; or affecting adversely the harmony between different religious, racial, language groups or overawing the sovereignty and integrity of a nation."[3]

Insurgency

The Indian MoD expands the definition used by the US and North Atlantic Treaty Organisation (NATO)[4] to the following: "Armed rebellion by a section of population against the legally constituted government, with the support or sympathy of the local population, obtained voluntarily or by coercion. It covers the full spectrum of conflict from subversion to full-scale guerrilla war, including the emergence of guerrilla bands into regular units."[5] The Indian definition again will be used here.

Low Intensity Conflict (LIC)

The Indian MoD describes low intensity conflict (LIC) as follows: "LIC encompasses a variety of violent and low-level conflict situations. In most cases, such conflicts fall under the category of 'politico-military confrontation' between contending states or groups. Such conflicts are at a much lower scale than conventional war but are above the routine and peaceful competitions among states. One of the parties to the conflict may not be a state, as in an insurgency situation. It frequently involves protracted struggle of competing principles and ideologies. LIC ranges from high grade internal struggle situations to extensive employment of the armed forces in counter-insurgency operations. It is waged by a combination of means, employing political, economic, informational and military instruments. It includes terrorism but excludes purely criminal acts."[6]

Small Wars Theory

Although the working definition presented above for small wars effectively bounds the discussion, it is inadequate to fully describe the dynamic of the small war. Small wars are, at their very root, a contest for authority over a civil population. Fig. 1 depicts this contest, whose three primary participants are the established government, the civil population in question, and the non-state actor who seeks to take the government's place. Authority can be exercised over a population by force, by permission, or by some combination of the two. But in no case can authority be executed without a certain amount of legitimacy. The legitimacy of a government is the degree to which its population recognises the government's right to rule or exercise control. Thus, the contest for authority is a contest for the greatest relative legitimacy with a given population. This can be achieved by increasing one's own legitimacy, reducing the legitimacy of the established government or, most often, by doing both. Authority may be exercised for a variety of motives. Most often, it is to promote the welfare of the population, enrich those in top positions, or promote the ideals of those in authority.

However, it can also be exercised for more sinister reasons, such as extermination or ethnic cleansing. Examples of this latter case can be seen in Bosnia-Herzegovina, Rwanda and Uganda, Sudan and in the Israeli-Hizbollah conflict.

Legitimacy in Small Wars

Legitimacy with a population is primarily built on four elements. The first is the perceived ability of the government to control the population. The second is the government's ability to provide security to the population from perceived threats. The third element of legitimacy is the government's perceived ability to maintain an environment wherein the population can provide for itself physically and financially. The fourth element is identification, or the degree to which the population feels the government has the same ideals, history, culture, religion, ethnicity, language, and so on.

Implications for Small Wars

Since the primary participants in a small war do not include two recognised governments, a small war does not legally fall under the Geneva Convention for war. At the same time, the impact of human rights and security on legitimacy results in human rights and terrorism emerging as a huge pivot point for small wars. Therefore, most governments seek to respect the principles of the Geneva Convention, even though they don't legally apply. Additionally, in most cases, non-state actors are not initially able to engage the forces of established government head-to-head and destroy them, demonstrating their superiority in the first two elements of legitimacy (control and security). Nor are they in a position to convince the population that they can provide the best economic environment. Thus, they generally start at the economic, ideological and cultural seams of a population, and at the seams of government control, incrementally undermining government legitimacy, while building up their own. Hence, we commonly see increased criminal activity to undermine the popular sense of government control. We see terrorist acts to undermine the popular sense of security. We see attacks on the economic infrastructure to reduce prosperity and attack the popular sense of economic security. And we see attempts to polarise the population along ideological lines to fracture the population into segments within which the non-state actors can compete more effectively for legitimacy. In addition, for the reasons discussed above, the contest for greatest relative legitimacy is a complex equation of continuously changing factors which contestants must balance over time to succeed. Very rarely are small wars decided in a few months. Most often, these conflicts take years, or even decades, as we have seen in Malaya,

Fig 1[7]

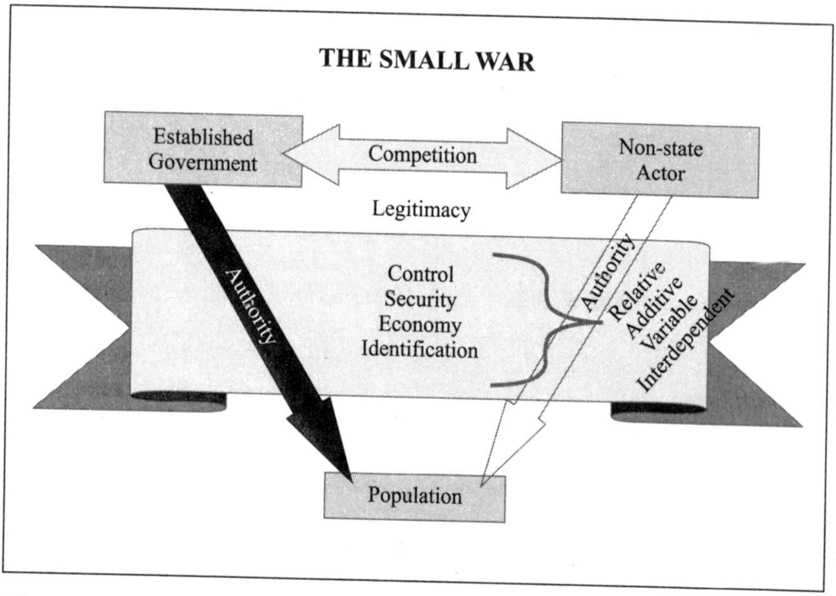

Vietnam, Peru, Northern Ireland … and the list goes on. Third party involvement in a small war can have a significant impact on the outcome of the conflict as it provides additional resources, international recognition and an additional way to pressure opponents and decrease their effectiveness. Third parties may be governments, non-governmental organisations (NGOs) or individuals with personal influence. Their motives for involvement are nearly infinitely varied. And they can prolong a contest for legitimacy, change the outcome or even become contestants themselves. Therefore, contestants in small wars frequently also compete to shape third party involvement, since it may well determine their success in gaining legitimacy with the population in question.

Doctrine

Even though small wars, to tackle insurgent or LIC situations, have become increasingly common in the last 50 years, none of the air forces of the world have evolved a comprehensive doctrine for them. At best, in their doctrines, there is a brief mention of the possible roles for air power in such situations. This includes the doctrines of the US Air Force, the

British Royal Air Force, and the Indian Air Power Doctrine 2000. As a result, air forces are seldom optimally organised or equipped to tackle such situations. To evolve a comprehensive doctrine for small wars, it is important that one understand the small war itself. For the established power, or the state, to tackle this problem of legitimate control over the population, undertaking combat operations against the non-state actor is only one of the aspects. To tackle the issue in its entirety, besides combat operations, other parallel lines of operation (LOOs) are required, such as providing good governance, essential services and economic opportunities. These LOOs, whatever they be, must be mutually supporting, not contradictory, in order to successfully achieve legitimacy. This is the concept of "Full Spectrum Operations"[8] which must be followed in any small war scenario. Aerospace power usually, but not always, falls into the domain of combat operations, as a LOO. To evolve an aerospace doctrine for small wars, which ensures combat operations are mutually supporting to other LOOs, it is essential to understand two further aspects. Firstly, the basic characteristics of aerospace power itself, i.e. flexibility, mobility, responsiveness, shock effect, concentration and offensive action,[9] with which every air warrior is familiar. Secondly, it is important to understand the basic feeders or inputs that enable a non-state actor to sustain operations. These basic feeders are people, material supplies and information.[10] Therefore, to be used effectively in a small war, aerospace power must focus its inherent characteristics specifically to meet the requirements of legitimate control while interdicting the basic feeders themselves. To give an example, the characteristic of offensive action can be directly translated to carrying out punitive strikes on non-state actors like insurgents. However, to ensure that this action does not adversely affect government legitimacy, the punitive strikes need to be surgically precise ones, with least collateral damage. On the flip side, no aerial weapon has been developed with such a precise yield as to target a single person, without harming anyone else in the immediate vicinity. Therefore, it may be wiser to seek an alternative method to strike in such cases. One alternative could be to insert air-mobile quick reaction special forces to engage the target quickly, utilising the strengths of aerospace power, but in a different way. Likewise, we must analyse and adapt each of the characteristics of aerospace power along with the traditional roles of air power in small wars. When one talks about flexibility, it includes both the ability to adapt quickly to changed circumstances, and the ability to use combat power in ways suited to the situation. It also means that the same weapon platform can be used for a variety of missions. The dynamic requirements of fighting small wars make this characteristic of air power particularly pertinent, if employed effectively. To adapt this characteristic for use in small wars, one must identify where flexibility is needed most. In addition, it may be necessary to consider what organisational structures, command and control mechanisms and doctrine are necessary to take full advantage of aerospace flexibility. The unique ability of aircraft to manoeuvre freely and swiftly in three dimensions gives aerospace power the speed and range to apply military power and other forms of support wherever needed, over a very large area. Aircraft have very important applications in the rapid movement, support and resupply of forces, with the emphasis being on "rapid." To adapt this characteristic for use in small wars, the obvious question is: where would mobility be most beneficial in a small war scenario and how could it provide a measure of terrain-immunity to combat forces? The previous three characteristics of aerospace power naturally combine to make it also one of the most responsive elements of military power. This responsiveness means it can be used to apply combat power quickly to where it is needed most. But it also means it can provide other assistance quickly when and where required. Thus, it expands the 'presence' of the established government in a small war. As with the other characteristics of aerospace power, one must consider what aspects of responsiveness are needed in the small war scenario, and how air power can be applied to meet them. An important characteristic of aerospace power, when used offensively, is shock effect. It is an effect that goes beyond surprise and can cause confusion and psychological disorientation. It is brought about by the aircraft's ability to deliver with little or no warning and with telling effect. While this characteristic is great for conventional conflicts, one must carefully consider whether shock effect is always desirable in the case of a small war. If the answer to this question is "No!" then one needs to further consider how to control the shock effect. While tailoring the characteristics of aerospace power to contribute effectively in small wars, key operational requirements must not be neglected. Without factoring these in, smooth conduct of combat operations may not be possible. These requirements are reliable intelligence through various intelligence, surveillance, reconnaissance (ISR) assets, secure and compatible communication systems between all the fielded forces and parallel LOOs, and joint planning and cohesiveness between the fielded forces and other agencies. Another important aspect is the threat scenario for aerial assets in a small war. In the case of non-state actors, the main threat is likely to be from MANPADS and small arms. Aircraft must have sufficient defensive systems or must minimise the threat through appropriate tactics, techniques and procedures (TTPs).

Case Studies

To trace the evolution of the use of air power in small wars of different kinds, it is important to cover the full spectrum of these wars ranging from classical guerrilla warfare in Vietnam, the Indian Peace-Keeping Force (IPKF) intervention in Sri Lanka and the Chechen conflict, to the urban scenarios of Lebanon and Iraq. These wars, along with the technologies that were used, would provide a bird's eye view of whether air power is an effective instrument in helping resolve these unusual conflicts; or is it, instead, an impediment to speedy conflict resolution.

Vietnam

The Vietnam War began in 1960, when the Communist National Liberation Front (NLF) began an insurgency to remove the South Vietnam government. The NLF, sponsored by North Vietnam, with strong support from Communist China and the Soviet Union, sought to unite the South with the North under Communist rule. The US, fearing the spread of Communism in Southeast Asia, backed the South Vietnam government. However, the conflict escalated, and by 1964, after the North Vietnamese attacked US ships in the Gulf of Tonkin, the US

Congress authorised President Johnson to take all necessary measures to protect American interests in Vietnam. Thereafter, US forces were actively involved in combat operations, increasing from 16,000 to 500,000 troops in the country by 1968. After the Tet Offensive in January 1968, in which the NLF and North Vietnamese forces combined in a conventional assault on the South, the US gradually constructed and implemented a withdrawal plan. By the time they left in 1973, the US had lost nearly 60,000 troops. North Vietnam invaded the South two years later and united Vietnam under Communist rule in 1975. It is quite understandable if there is doubt as to whether the war in Vietnam could be considered a "small war." However, the point that needs to be kept in mind is that, in spite of the massive quantities of effort, the focus of the war was within South Vietnam where the nature of conflict was that of an insurgency against the established government. War against North Vietnam was restricted to air strikes with the purpose of preventing the North from shoring up the NLF insurgents. Even when North Vietnamese regulars directly took part in the conflict, the war was never taken to the North. Hence, even though the war itself was by no means small, it could be considered to be a small war in the manner it unfolded.

The overall US strategy was to support the South Vietnam government and destroy the NLF, while interdicting North Vietnam's support for the NLF. The US focus was, thus, largely on combat operations, leaving other aspects of legitimacy mostly to the Vietnamese. The NLF strategy, on the other hand, was to incrementally undermine the South Vietnam government and US forces, while building popular support for the idea of a unified Communist country. They began by infiltrating the political seams along the edges of the South, and gradually worked their way toward the east, taking over towns, establishing their own government, and launching guerrilla attacks against government and US forces. Both sides essentially succeeded. The US largely destroyed the NLF over the course of the war. However, the government of South Vietnam never gained much legitimacy, and popular sympathy shifted gradually toward the NLF.

Application of Air Power

US aircraft dropped more tons of bombs in Vietnam than in World War II; a total of 7,078,032 tons between 1964 and 1973. However, aircraft also undertook extensive reconnaissance missions, casualty evacuation, troop movement and aerial resupply in addition to strike operations. Throughout the war, B-52s were employed for carpet-bombing of suspected NLF base areas, and for tactical support of ground forces. Fighter aircraft struck targets on both sides of the border. Defoliants were used to eliminate vegetation, making it more difficult for insurgents to hide. Electronic warfare took on much greater proportions, as aircraft fought past the dense Soviet surface-to-air missiles (SAMs) deployed by North Vietnam, and electronic sensors were placed along the Ho Chi Minh trail. Precision-guided munitions (PGMs) were used for the first time, in the Linebacker Operations, greatly improving the effectiveness of air operations. In one of the more infamous events of the war, the South Vietnamese village of Trang Bang, which was occupied by NLF forces, was struck with a napalm bomb. Civilians fled and the pilots turned to attack them, thinking they were also the enemy. This was a defining moment in the indiscriminate use of air power after which the president and the secretary of defence approved every target that would be hit and tightly controlled air strikes against the North. Strikes were calculated to pressure the North to negotiate, without escalating the conflict from an insurgency to open warfare. As a result, over time, the Administration approved a series of air operations of gradually increasing intensity, starting with Flaming Dart I and II, then Rolling Thunder, and finally Linebacker I and II, just before the final agreement that allowed the US to somewhat gracefully leave South Vietnam. Air strikes were targeted against the Ho Chi Minh Trail, used to move men and supplies from the North to the insurgency in the South, and North Vietnamese industry and SAM sites. The Tet Offensive in 1968, though a military debacle for the North, convinced US officials that the war could not be won with air power. Thus, renewed effort was put toward a negotiated agreement with the North to stop the flow of support to the NLF and allow the US to leave, with the South Vietnamese government in place in the South. When talks stalled and infiltration into the South increased, President Nixon used the Linebacker Operations to pressure the North back to the negotiating table.[11] On a final analysis, air power did not achieve any of the objectives set before it. Some blame this on the considerable limitations placed on the military, citing the success of Linebacker I and II vis-à-vis Rolling Thunder. But it is debatable whether the US could have conducted such large-scale operations early in the war without serious escalation. Vietnam clearly illustrated the limitations of non-precision strikes in small war scenarios and highlighted the profitability of air power in innovatively used support missions. In Vietnam, strike missions used without clearly identifying and isolating combatants resulted in many dead civilians, undermining the credibility and legitimacy of the US and South Vietnamese governments. The US kept the war limited to South Vietnam and intentionally kept it a small war. But the US did not very effectively take the next step of building a strategy to win a small war before it was much too late. Hence, all the combat power that it used, despite its ferocity, could not win the war. It is a fact that the US achieved success in most of the military engagements it undertook in Vietnam. But within two years of the US departure from the scene, the Communist North had annexed the South, amply proving that the US did not achieve its original objective and lost the war on that count. The Americans lost the war because they did not fight this war as a small war should be fought; i.e. by focussing on the populace. The war in Vietnam was as much a contest for legitimacy with the people of South Vietnam as it was a struggle to defeat the military forces of the NLF and North Vietnam. The South Vietnamese government, in the course of the conflict, became highly unpopular and support for it steadily eroded. The rural population drifted from being initially neutral toward favouring the Communists as the war progressed. The heavy-handed approach of both the Americans and the Republic of Vietnam Army created a sense of alienation among the population, which increased the relative legitimacy of the Communist forces.

One way in which air power could have been used in South Vietnam, which would have benefited the Americans, was to maintain presence. Militarily, the US forces had been successful against the Communist combatants, but what was left undone was the consolidation of the gains made militarily. This required policing, and for that, ground presence was mandatory. Absence of American forces allowed the insurgents to regroup and work upon the villagers for material support. Air power could have been of immense help in moving men across to maintain the required presence. The British had been able to quell the insurgency in Malaya primarily because they sustained the necessary presence to ensure that the insurgency did not hurt the masses' general social and economic well-being. The same should have been done in South Vietnam. Air power would have been an ideal platform in providing non-linear movement between nodes if the Americans had intended to maintain a presence for administrative and security purposes. In fact, it was the same mobility that helped the American forces on the battlefield. The failure to recognise this requirement is probably why the Americans finally lost the war in spite of having won most of the battles.

IPKF Operations

Following an accord between the Indian and Sri Lankan governments, Indian Peace-Keeping Force (IPKF) operations were undertaken against the Liberation Tigers of Tamil Eelam (LTTE) in Sri Lanka from 1987 to 1990. The accord was originally designed for peace-keeping, with the expectation that the Tamils would lay down arms and the Sri Lankan forces would observe the ceasefire. However, the operations quickly took on the shape of war due to political infighting and instability over various issues. In the ensuing conflict, the original objectives were redefined – the IPKF aimed for forcible disarmament of the militants and the LTTE aimed for all out war against the IPKF. The IPKF was faced with guerrilla tactics and suicide attacks in an unfriendly environment, inhospitable terrain, belligerent locals and apathetic Sri Lankan defence forces. In the course of the war, limited success against the LTTE was obtained at considerable loss to the Indian Army, which later led to the withdrawal of the IPKF in 1990.

Because the IPKF mission was originally a peace-keeping one, the initial task for the air force was only strategic and tactical airlift[12]. These were achieved in the initial phase without any opposition due to the nature of the accord. However, once fighting broke out, air-borne operations and casualty evacuation became the prime roles. Once the rules of engagement were relaxed, helicopter gunships were pressed into action, with Cheetah helicopters as scouts. During the 32 months of operations, some 70,000 sorties were carried out with no loss to enemy action or accident, a matter of great professional satisfaction. The main aircraft types involved in Sri Lanka were the An-32, Mi-8 and Mi-25. Also taking active part in the operation were the Indian Army's Chetaks and Cheetahs; and the Indian Navy's Chetaks and Alizes. The first air action took place on June 4, 1987, when five An-32 transport aircraft, escorted by four Mirage 2000 fighters, air-dropped some 24 tonnes of relief supplies over selected zones in the Jaffna Peninsula. Thereafter, within hours of the signing of the accord on July 29, 1997, some 24 An-12 and An-32 tactical transport aircraft flew into Palaly airfield near Jaffna town in the north of the island. These, with the bulk of two Indian Army battalions, constituted the "peace-keeping force." Operation Pawan was launched in the first week of October to disarm the LTTE forcefully. However, the rules of engagement for the IPKF were strict i.e. use of artillery, heavy weaponry and offensive air support was forbidden, to ensure minimum civilian casualties and damage to property. When peace-keeping changed to combat, the initial offensive by a single Indian brigade followed five different axes leading into Jaffna town. A bold attempt was made to capture the LTTE leadership by inducting para-commandos into the university area by Mi-8 helicopters, but this costly operation was aborted, with heavy casualties amongst the troops and a number of helicopters damaged. The prime operational base for the overstretched IPKF was Palaly airfield, where dozens of Mi-8 and Chetak helicopters and An-32 and HS 748 transport aircraft were based, all of which had to be protected against the LTTE raiders. Additional troops and equipment from various cantonments in India as well as from Trincomalee and Batticaloa in Sri Lanka were flown in using IL-76, AN-12, AN-32, HS 748, and civil Boeing 737 aircraft. Additional Mi-8 helicopter units arrived from air bases in India, plus Cheetah helicopters for reconnaissance and casualty evacuation. The most formidable additions were the Mi-25 helicopter gunships. It is estimated that during the 20 days from October 11 to 31, some 2,200 tactical transport and 800 assault helicopter sorties were carried out to fly in troops, weapons, vehicles, stores and various other equipment, and fly out the mounting casualties to military hospitals. During the second half of October 1987, the Indian Air Force (IAF) carried out more transport and helicopter sorties in support of the ground forces than at any similar period of time in the history of the country's armed forces. The Mi-25 gunships were employed to interdict the movement of militants from the Jaffna peninsula to the neighbouring islands and mainland of Sri Lanka, as the LTTE attempted to bring in reinforcements of personnel and logistics and, later on, to exfiltrate its cadres from Jaffna. Additionally, the Mi-25s were used in the lagoon areas to destroy militant boats and vehicles[13]. The first use of Mi-25s for close air support was on October 29, when Mi-25s attacked LTTE entrenchments 32 km east of Jaffna with rocket and cannon fire. This action enabled army battalions to overwhelm the last resistance and affect a link-up. In another action, Mi-8 helicopters flew para-commandos into areas on the western part of the peninsula and onto islands to engage LTTE strongholds. Mi-25s patrolling the key roads, destroyed a number of LTTE vehicles. It is evident that in the entire IPKF campaign, the army was suitably supported by the air force in all possible roles by the transport aircraft and helicopters. Though the air environment was conducive for all transport operations involving para-drops, air landed operations, special heli-borne operations (SHBO) and casualty evacuation, they were nonetheless fraught with danger from enemy fire below 2,000 feet altitude. In the later part of conflict, suitable reconnaissance sorties were flown, with available intelligence inputs to gather more information on the enemy hideouts before carrying out any of these operations. The Cheetah helicopters were used in the scout role to direct the gunships accurately onto the known hideouts. Interdiction of supply and communication lines was effectively carried out in this manner. The roles of SHBO and casualty evacuation were supported by gunships to minimise the ground threat. Search and strike operations on opportunity targets were carried out frequently in different sectors of the conflict. The army cordons were tightened with patrolling sorties by the gunships, thus, forcing the enemy to operate only by night.

The advantages of air power were exploited in the IPKF operations in conditions of total air superiority. However, the concept of operations was different from classical conventional operations. There was no requirement of counter-air operations and the role of fighters was minimal throughout. At the same time, transport and helicopter operations were operating under severe limitations common to small wars, with a fleeting enemy in hostile surroundings. Challenges involved difficult terrain, unfriendly locals and urban operations, with restrictive rules of engagement that prohibited attacks that might hurt civilians or damage buildings. The mobile and fleeting nature of targets meant ineffective fire unless area targets like enemy camps or headquarters (HQ) were discovered. Meanwhile, there were significant limitations in the ability to gather intelligence, conduct night reconnaissance and night attack, in terms of tactics and equipment. Political constraints early in the war greatly restricted the effective use of air power. The rules of engagement also prevented any forcible disarmament in the initial stages of the accord. The policy was of nil collateral damage and no damage to civil property. The irony was that the enemy was deeply entrenched in the local population and their dwellings. Thick jungles and equally thick urban centres were the prime locations of the enemy. This complicated navigation, reconnaissance, target identification and acquisition. Lack of force landing fields was a major concern for the helicopter operations. Helicopters were compelled to fly low for target acquisition, thus, inviting small arms fire. Consequently, reconnaissance mission altitudes had to be increased, which, in turn, led to decreased mission effectiveness

Accurate intelligence is the key to air-borne assault, SHBO and targeting. The IPKF operations were marred by lack of intelligence on the enemy disposition, due to the huge local support enjoyed by the LTTE. The mistrust between the IPKF and the Sri Lankan forces added to that effect. Even though the LTTE did not have equipment capable of intercepting air-to-air and air-to-ground communication, they always managed to intercept the army's communications, thus, always being informed in advance. This led to many SHBO and gunship missions falling short of achieving their aims. All reconnaissance sorties were visual only, eliminating night reconnaissance efforts. Moving on to aircraft and equipment, helicopters were ill-equipped in navigation and targeting aids. There was no armour protection for the Mi-8 and Cheetah helicopters, nor were they equipped for night operations. Target acquisition was by visual means, undermining the rate of success. There was no provision or thought given to fitment of searchlights onto helicopters, which completely prohibited any night search and patrolling. Finally, there were no precision weapons or any stand-off capability with the helicopters.

Lessons From Operation Pawan

Air operations in Sri Lanka were marred by political restrictions, lack of advanced equipment and inherent limitations owing to terrain, populace and weather. However, the absence of enemy air threat allowed air transport operations to be undertaken with a great degree of success. The limited use of gunships in the interdiction and battlefield air strike (BAS) roles in direct support of ground operations was also successful. A study of the environment and the limitations of air power under which the operations were conducted in Sri Lanka brings out several lessons. Joint planning at all levels of war is imperative. The use of fighter aircraft for photo reconnaissance missions at regular intervals could have resulted in a major show of force in addition to increased intelligence inputs. However, in today's environment, the advent of unmanned aerial vehicles (UAVs), satellite reconnaissance, precision weapons and guidance systems, advanced munitions such as fuel air explosives (FAEs), night attack capabilities, and so on, would definitely add lethal punch to such small wars in the future. A major requirement is that of continuous surveillance over the area of operations. In such conflicts, a dedicated UAV could cover the required area in repeated cycles, giving an updated picture. Night reconnaissance and targeting capability would have restricted the LTTE's freedom of movement around the clock, thus, completely paralysing them.

Known hideouts in thick jungles could have been effectively destroyed with FAEs. Inaccessible targets could have been attacked with precision weapons on confirmed intelligence. Notwithstanding the advantages that modern technology could have provided during the IPKF operations, the ever present limitations of political will would have remained a major factor in air power employment. Further, the kind of terrain, targets and environment prevalent during the IPKF operations illustrate the challenges of small wars. No amount of modernity would suffice to target an enemy that is deeply entrenched within a sympathetic civilian population. The rules of engagement will always seek to limit damage to civilians and property, which are the inherent by-products of the use of air power in such environments.

Afghanistan and Iraq

Operation Enduring Freedom (OEF) and Operation Iraqi Freedom (OIF) were by no means small wars by any definition; they nevertheless evolved into small wars, and a number of operations that were carried out in these campaigns will be applicable in future small wars or low intensity conflict (LIC) situations. Typical examples that can be given are Operation Anaconda in Afghanistan, which was the bombing of caves to flush out terrorists, and the urban close air support (CAS) warfare in Iraq launched to flush out terrorists from cities.

Operation Enduring Freedom

OEF commenced on October 7, 2001, in response to the 9/11 terrorist attack on the Pentagon and the World Trade Centre in the US. The stated Coalition objectives were the destruction of terrorist training camps, the capture of Al Qaeda leaders, including Osama bin Laden, and the removal of the extremist Taliban regime to prevent future use of Afghanistan as a safe haven by terrorists. The backbone of the effort consisted of special operations forces (SOF) employed in the reconnaissance and direct action roles, and coordinating Coalition air strikes in support of the Afghan Northern Alliance ground operations against the Taliban. Within 20 days, the provincial capital of Mazar-e-

Sharif fell; Kabul and Jalalabad followed soon after. An Afghan interim government was in position within 78 days of the start of combat operations. Following combat operations, OEF became a small war, focussed on stabilisation of Afghanistan under a new government.

Enduring Freedom opened with a short sharp air campaign to establish air superiority, followed by air strikes to aid attacks by Northern Alliance forces on strong points of the Taliban. Since there were few high value targets, there was little reason to conduct a traditional strategic air campaign. Joint operations were woven around information technology, which supported rapid communication across thousands of miles between the forces of multiple countries. Imagery from commercial and military satellites and surveillance and reconnaissance aircraft strongly aided operations.UAVs were used in both reconnaissance and strike roles as the Predator and Global Hawks came into their own. Battlefield imagery picked up by these UAVs was beamed to the satellites orbiting overhead. This information was then relayed back to command nodes, including the Central Command (CENTCOM), enabling top situational awareness at all the locations. Predators also downlinked the streaming video directly to AC-130 gunships, which then engaged targets on the ground. For the operations, the Pentagon bought commercial satellite communication bandwidth. These commercial orbiters complemented ultra high frequency and super high frequency tactical military satellite systems. The global broadcast system (GBS) distributed high bandwidth products from the continental US to low levels of command. The Secure Internet Protocol Router Network (SIPRNET), an encrypted global area network, served as a major conduit of sensitive data. The result was enhanced situational awareness. This, combined with the ubiquity of PGMs, changed the traditional roles of the war-fighter and weapons platform. A striking example is the B-52, which, when provided with real-time target data and PGMs, was used as a battlefield loiter weapon platform with almost omnipresent capability.

Operation Anaconda, in which the United States Air Force (USAF) tried to flush out the terrorists from the caves in eastern Afghanistan, represents a use of air power in a small war scenario. On March 2, 2002, the Coalition kicked off the biggest ground offensive of the war, codenamed "Anaconda". Anaconda was to be a raid on a concentration of Al Qaeda and Taliban forces that had retreated to the Shah-i-Kot Valley in eastern Afghanistan. The Combined Air Operations Centre (CAOC) funnelled fighters and bombers into a tiny air space about nine miles by nine miles. Immediate close air support (CAS) supplied consistent support, even at night. The intensity and precision of the air strikes topped anything seen bcfore, even in Desert Storm. Strategic bombers were the mainstay due to their long loiter times and large payloads. At night, gunships under SOF control illuminated Al Qaeda positions and drilled them with precision heavy artillery.

Stability Operations

With the declaration of the conclusion of major combat operations, the 'small war' phase of OEF began. Air power continued to play a central role as the Coalition worked to stabilise the country and establish a new government. Reconnaissance and strike aircraft continued to loiter overhead, providing continuous 'presence'. Helicopters provided rapid transport for quick reaction and security forces. In one case, an airfield was scratched out of the high desert near the Pakistan border, disrupting insurgent operations throughout the area. Transport aircraft facilitated the delivery of humanitarian supplies and resources for rebuilding the Afghan infrastructure. Operations are ongoing to the present, and air power continues to play a central role.

Operation Iraqi Freedom

Similar to OEF, after major combat operations were ended, the 'small war' phase of the campaign began with stability operations. New tactics, techniques and procedures (TTPs) were developed to address time sensitive and dynamic targets with unprecedented effectiveness.[14] After major combat operations ended, air power continued to provide responsive, concentrated, overwhelming and accurate firepower against insurgents and terrorist groups. The results were truly impressive.

Meticulous and always available CAS backed up soldiers and marines who faced Iraqi ground attacks.

Key Observations for OEF and OIF

Even though these campaigns do not fit into the template of small wars as elucidated earlier, air power was a key feature in these two operations that have many similarities with the characteristics of a small war and remain a significant contributor for ongoing stability operations. The concepts mainly relate to a struggle for legitimacy over a fragmented local populace. Key concepts of air power emerging in these campaigns include applications of precision bombing, application of network-centric warfare, deployment of UAVs and intelligence, surveillance, rconnaissance (ISR) assets, jointness and collaboration with SOF units, redefinition of strategic air power and overall integration of air and space power with all aspects of planning, training, and equipping. However, Iraq and Afghanistan continue to be trouble spots as Coalitions strive to stabilise the two countries. It is clear that, in spite of all the high technology of air power that was witnessed in these campaigns, total dependence on air power alone to provide a complete solution is insufficient. Collateral damage caused by air strikes has repeatedly been used against the Coalition. Insurgents and terrorists are able to blend with the population, rendering aircraft overhead incapable of conducting strikes. Even with longer loiter times and better ISR assets, Coalition forces cannot see everywhere, much less be everywhere that they need to be at once. Additionally, air power is completely unable to communicate on a personal level with individual Iraqis. Thus, conventional applications of air power, even with the capabilities and tactics displayed in OEF and OIF, were severely limited whenever small war situations arose. In OEF and OIF, there were many time sensitive targets (TSTs) which included leadership, terrorists and suspected weapons of mass destruction (WMDs). Another category of targets were called "dynamic targets" which were defined as those which were highly mobile and otherwise important. The optimum technique for striking both types was to divert air-borne strike aircraft in real-time. Striking TSTs was made possible due to the large amount of intelligence which was made available due to the ISR assets. The ISR assets searched for targets for both the air and land component commanders and immediately fed back images for bomb damage assessment. Several types of high-tech electronic and computer programme models based on mathematical theories were used to estimate collateral damage and keep it to a minimum with the help of PGMs. However, as time has progressed in these campaigns, it has become clear that the forces must be even more aware, responsive and precise to effectively prosecute small wars. The largely uninhabited deserts of Afghanistan and Iraq lent themselves well to air operations, where target identification was easier and collateral damage minimal. However, urban operations, particularly in Iraq, have posed immense challenges for target identification, target isolation and collateral damage.[15] Aerial reconnaissance is still incapable of identifying a target in a crowd of people or inside a building. In many cases, air power has simply been inappropriate as an application of force, due to the risks of collateral damage. Many new concepts such as searching for targets in deep caves in desert areas and flushing out terrorists from urban areas were evolved in these campaigns. But the challenges posed by terrain will continue to be relevant in future small wars, more so as the world's population increasingly moves to the cities.

Network-Centric Warfare

Compared to the earlier campaigns, OEF and OIF were far more sophisticated operations, with the forces being heavily networked and focussed. The tremendous precision attack of Coalition forces was the obvious standout characteristic. It marked a dramatic advance over the Gulf War a dozen years earlier. Space and air forces were more closely integrated than ever before. Defence support programme satellites monitored infrared flashes and provided early warning of Iraqi missile attacks. Global positioning system (GPS) satellites formed the web of precision that enabled 5,500 GPS guided joint direct attack munitions (JDAMs) to find and hit their targets. Whenever ISR platforms reeled in hot intelligence, strike aircraft could attack new targets. Most fighters and bombers in these campaigns had some type of data link. The Link-16 and the joint tactical information display system (JTIDS) was the gold standard. Thus, the integrated network-centric warfare reduced the observe, orient, direct, act (OODA) loop tremendously and acted as a real force multiplier.[16] This was just as relevant, if not more so, in the 'small war' stabilisation phases of these campaigns as during major combat operations. Networking of all actors in the battle space has proven essential to responding effectively to bolster the legitimacy of the new governments. Unfortunately, it has been difficult to integrate military and infant civilian agencies to the degree necessary to deal best with small wars. This challenge is perhaps one of the greatest and most essential to overcome to achieve optimal employment of air power in small wars.

Part II

> Israel hoped that air power would avoid the need for a ground war against Hizbollah. It was not the first to be beguiled by bombs.
>
> – *The Economist*

The Lebanon Conflict

The war in southern Lebanon began in 1985 and continues till today as a guerrilla war conducted by the Hizbollah against the state of Israel. The Hizbollah is a conglomeration of terrorist groups with significant sponsorship from Iran, Syria and several other Middle Eastern states. The Hizbollah's stated objective is to create an Islamic nation on the ashes of the state of Israel.[17] Its strategy to achieve this is to incrementally conquer Israel, starting in the security zone that Israel established in southern Lebanon in 1985. On the other hand, Israel's goal is to resist the Hizbollah until a peace agreement can be reached with Syria, after which, presumably, the Hizbollah will curtail operations. Israel's strategy to achieve this can generally be described as a combination of active and passive defence, with strong border security and strike operations against the identified Hizbollah targets in Lebanon. The Hizbollah relies mostly on mortars, rocket launchers and small arms. However, to defend against Israeli armour and aircraft, it has procured AT-3/4 missiles and Strella SAMs, probably from Syria or Iran. The Hizbollah also has considerable explosive expertise, aided and supported by Iran. Furthermore, it has taken full advantage of available technology, including night vision, advanced mines, electronic fuses and late generation communications. Israel employs a broad range of the latest advanced technology, including the Merkava battle tank, the Apache attack helicopter, the F-16 fighter aircraft and UAVs, as well as smart munitions such as laser bombs and TOW guided missiles. Israel also uses the latest early warning, surveillance and target-acquisition systems. From the beginning, Israel has been able to inflict heavy losses on the Hizbollah. However, the Hizbollah has persisted in the struggle, driven by staunch ideology, and resourced by oil rich Arab states. It has largely abandoned fixed facilities and does not attempt to hold ground against the

Israeli forces. Instead, it stays mobile, moves away from Israeli assaults, and reoccupies positions after the Israeli forces depart. In the process, however, much of the Lebanese population has turned against Israel, and many Israeli citizens are beginning to doubt the legitimacy of maintaining the security zone in southern Lebanon. There appears to be no end in sight, as each side continues to adapt new strategies to attack the other.

Small War Fit

The war in south Lebanon fits the definition used here for a small war. Israel, a recognised state, is fighting a non-state organisation, the Hizbollah, which is attempting to destabilise and replace the state of Israel. This conflict is interesting, however, in that the Hizbollah is only attempting to improve its own legitimacy through control, with the intent of destroying Israel. Of the other three elements, the Hizbollah is trying to undermine the security and economic legitimacy of Israel. The Hizbollah also works hard at legitimacy in the international arena, as a way of applying international pressure on Israel. Israel, on the other hand, focusses primarily on legitimacy through control and security, while attempting to interdict the Hizbollah's feeders – through negotiations with Syria.

Israel's strategy in dealing with the Hizbollah is to resist, and mitigate its attacks, while pursuing a peace agreement with Syria. The maintenance of the security zone in southern Lebanon has almost certainly reduced casualties to the civil population. But the Israeli Defence Force has paid a high price in equipment and personnel. The border is lined with an extensive array of fences, sensors, weapons and security forces. Israeli forces conduct aggressive reconnaissance using aircraft, ground sensors and patrols, and engage Hizbollah forces with on-call helicopters, fixed wing aircraft and surface weapons. Additionally, Israel plans and conducts offensive operations against Hizbollah infrastructure deep in Lebanon, and even in Syria. Tactically and operationally, most of Israel's operations have been successful; however, strategically, they do not appear to be reducing the Hizbollah's effectiveness or will. The Hizbollah operations may be interrupted for a short term by Israeli strikes, during which time they shift focus to international Israeli targets. But they eventually return with adapted tactics to reduce Israeli effectiveness. Israel has also been ineffective at undermining the legitimacy of Hizbollah, either in Lebanon or internationally, hampered by the media bias toward the guerrillas. As the conflict drags on, there has been decreasing sympathy, and even animosity in Europe and other parts of the world against Israel and its aggressive tactics to stop terrorist attacks on Israeli military and civilians. Israeli civilians and politicians are beginning to doubt the effectiveness of a security zone in southern Lebanon, and the Lebanese population is largely anti-Israel. In summary, it is reasonable to assess that strategically Israel is losing ground, even though it is tactically successful most of the time.

Application of Air Power

Israel employs air power along conventional lines of operation. Reconnaissance platforms with advanced sensors search for guerrilla activity along the border and deeper into Lebanon. Advanced communications systems relay target data to command posts and strike platforms. Standby aircraft, F-16s or Apache helicopters, engage targets assigned to them, using laser guided or TV guided missiles or guns. When significant intelligence is gained on Hizballah nodes or leadership, Israeli fighters conduct deeper offensive strikes with precision weapons. While Israel successfully strikes its intended targets most of the times, the targets are, at times, imbedded with civilian infrastructure, leading to civilian casualties and collateral damage. This single factor has caused the greatest damage to Israel's legitimacy, both at home and abroad. In summary, aircraft employment by Israel is highly effective at destroying designated physical targets. However, it has been unsuccessful at preventing collateral damage, deterring the Hizbollah from conducting attacks, or stopping the flow of personnel and supplies to the Hizbollah.[18] Air power weaknesses evident in south Lebanon were as follows:

- In an urban environment the operative capability of air power is greatly reduced as the guerrilla fighters easily assimilate into the population, and the fear of hitting civilians who are not linked to the guerrillas, creates severe difficulties for air operations.

- The proximity of friendly forces constitutes another limitation, since air attacks can hit these forces. This problem exists with regard to all types of air warfare against ground forces, and is not unique to counter-guerrilla warfare.
- Lack of precise and updated intelligence on human and highly mobile targets hampers the effectiveness of air power.

As pointed out, advanced sensors, weapons and communications technology have made Israeli air power tactically effective. For strategic success, Israel needs deep reconnaissance platforms that are able to loiter or dwell for long periods with the ability to focus on small areas with high resolution, and able to network with other sensors. Israel also needs weapons with a small radius of destruction, but accurate enough to strike single individuals when necessary. A weapons platform able to loiter over an area without being vulnerable to the Hizbollah SAMs, and able to sustain accurate fire for hours at a time would be a valuable asset. Finally, an effective missile defence technology able to engage the Katyusha rockets, or capable of locating them before they are fired, would be of immeasurable worth to the Israelis. The small war in south Lebanon illustrates that even the most modern aircraft, weapons, sensors and communications do not guarantee strategic success in a small war though they can cause critical and weakening attrition on the morale and physical capability of the non-state actor.[19]

Chechnya Campaign Summary

Chechnya is a small republic located in the southwest corner of the Russian Federation between the Caspian and Black Seas (the Caucasus region of the country). Chechnya broke away from Russia on August 21, 1991, two days after the August coup in Moscow, and declared its independence from Russia on September 6, 1991. Dzhokhar Dudayev, a former general in the Soviet Air Force, was made president. However, the Russians and Russia's fifth Congress of People's Deputies declared Dudayev's regime unconstitutional and considered his presidency illegitimate. In the latter half of 1993, a rebellion developed against Dudayev's government that evolved into a small-scale guerrilla war. In the spring of 1994, the Dudayev opposition called upon Russia to support it and help establish constitutional order. In November 1994, the Dudayev opposition force, supported by the Russian security services, led an attack to unseat Dudayev. The operation failed dismally, and Russia decided to intervene militarily. Russian forces were successful in capturing Chechnya. However, as a result of heavy casualties and several hostages being taken, as well as the recapture of cities such as Grozny by the Chechens, the Russians were forced to sign a truce. Defeated, the last Russian forces left Chechnya in December 1996. Under international law, Chechnya was arguably a constitutional entity of the Russian Federation. Therefore, according to Article 3.1 of the second Additional Protocol of the Geneva Conventions (1949), Russia was entitled to reestablish law and order in the republic. As the conflict was between the Russian Federation (state actors) and the Chechen rebel forces (non-state actors), it can be termed as a small war by the definition used here. The interesting thing about this case is that, realistically, Chechnya had an established government, at least in terms of local legitimacy. The Russian government intervened on behalf of the "non-state actors" who were opposed to Dudayev. Russia succeeded initially based on the element of control, but failed miserably in the other three elements of security, economy and identification, which eventually caused it to lose control as well. The Russian Air Force operated over Chechnya freely after quickly destroying the limited Chechen aircraft inventory. Chechen air defence weapons consisted of Zu-23-2 mobile anti-aircraft launchers and machine guns mounted on Cherokee Jeeps and Toyota off-road vehicles. They also had Shilka ZSu-23/4 anti-aircraft guns and Strela-3, Igla-1 and Stinger SAM systems. The Chechens also used RPG-7 anti-tank grenade launchers against low flying aircraft and helicopters. The Russian Air Force consisted of 140 combat planes (Su-25, Su-22M, and Su-24), 55 helicopters (Mi-24, Mi-8 and Mi-6) and military transport aircraft (An-12, An-22, An-124 and IL-76) and 12 Mi-8MT helicopters. The Russian Air Force used A-50 airborne warning and control system (AWACs) aircraft. They used two to six MiG-31 and Su-27 aircraft at a time in combat air patrols.[20] This was to prevent Dudayev from constructing an air bridge with countries like Turkey. Chechnya's terrain is mountainous to the south and on the eastern and western borders, and plains throughout the centre of the country. This combined with difficult weather conditions contributed to the military's poor performance, especially along the edges of the country.

Use of Air Power

The Russians used the air force to destroy Chechen air assets on runways, ensuring air dominance. Subsequently, the air force conducted CAS, air interdiction missions, and some strategic bombing against smaller Chechen cities. They also bombed the city of Grozny in support of the ground forces.

Rotary Wing Aircraft

At the start of the conflict, Russia had 55 helicopters. This number increased to 105 by March 1995, including 52 Mi-24s. One flight of Mi-9 C2 ships was also reported present. These helicopters were primarily used to transport troops and evacuate the sick and wounded at the start of the conflict. They also supported the movement of columns and acted as communication relays. Army helicopters also operated alone in a mode known as "target of opportunity rovering," and against marked targets or on request from ground troops. In addition to supporting advancing units in the central and southern parts of Chechnya, helicopters also assisted in searching out Dudayev's sabotage/terrorist detachments that had penetrated the Russian troops' rear areas. By the start of August 1995, the Russians had conducted more than 16,547 flights over Chechnya. Nearly 36 per cent of these were fire mission sorties, 44 per cent were transport assault, 8 per cent were reconnaissance flights and 12 per cent were for special missions such as search and rescue, propaganda or radio relay.[21] Initially only the most experienced pilots participated. Pilot tactics included flying at extremely low altitudes and at very high speed to the targets, thereby limiting Chechen visual detection and response time.

They also approached targets from different directions, making hard manoeuvres before the approach to the target. They departed targets at low altitudes, providing mutual covering fire and using EW (electronic warfare) equipment (as well as decoy flares and other devices). Coordination with ground forces was often difficult. This was aggravated by the absence of timely and accurate reconnaissance information. Missions were difficult to perform due to lack of portable radio sets, night vision devices, silencers for weapons and binoculars which are key elements for reconnaissance personnel. Thus, missions to detect enemy fire positions, which made up the defensive system of Chechen rebels in villages, were difficult to perform. The Mi-24, Mi-8 and Mi-6 helicopters were technically obsolete and had limited deployment capabilities in terms of time of day and weather conditions.

Fixed-Wing Aircraft

The workhorse of the Russian aviation effort in Chechnya was the Su 25 (NATO "Frogfoot," Russian "Rook"). The Su 25 is a small, subsonic, reliable and manoeuvrable aircraft of simple design with a good view from the pilot cockpit. It was designed for and used to support ground troops and for ground attack operations. Its powerful armament, reliable navigation and targeting avionics and armour protection were added assets. It could operate from airstrips with artificial surface as well as dirt airstrips. Missions for the aircraft in Chechnya included CAS of troops against small targets in the mountains or on the plains. The Su-25 could attack in mountain gorges due to its special aerodynamics configuration in combination with a high thrust-to-weight ratio. Moreover, it could stay over the battlefield for a long time, making several passes at targets in one sortie. The Russians also utilised long range aircraft. The Tu-22 M3 Backfire was used to drop night flares and propaganda leaflets. By December 1995, Russian pilots had flown more than 9,000 sorties, with more than 5,300 devoted to the conduct of bombing / ground-attack missions, and nearly 700 to aerial reconnaissance (nearly 8 per cent). Principal weapons included S-5, S-8, and S-24B rockets and FAB-250 and FAB-5000 high explosive bombs. When weather permitted, the Russians employed Kh-25ML guided missiles, KAB-500L and KAB-500KR smart bombs and KAB01500L bombs.[22]

Small wars offer the same opportunities for the use of information warfare as any large scale conflict. The Chechens were able to conduct the most powerful information operations through the mass media, mobilising local opinion while demoralising the Russian population. Dudayev's personnel also made good use of communications and intelligence from covert agents. The Chechens controlled mobile air defence weapons via radio, constantly changing system positions. The Chechens also tried to integrate and synchronise the employment of weapons by attempting to engage targets simultaneously with small arms, heavy calibre machine-guns, cannons and grenade launchers. They tried to pin down a helicopter once it entered a zone of effective fire by massing fire from several points. Five helicopters (two Mi-8s and three Mi-24s) were lost to hostile fire in the first three months of the conflict. One of the primary Chechen targets for information intelligence were the forward air controllers (FACs). The Chechens were able to pinpoint the place where the FACs were going with direction finding equipment. The Russians also employed information warfare techniques, most notably in the way they eventually eliminated Dudayev. In April, while talking on a cellular phone, an A-50 tracked Dudayev that relayed the information to Su-25 ground attack aircraft that used laser and TV guided bombs for the kill.[23]

Strengths and Limitations of Air Power in Small Wars

From the case studies reviewed, several strengths and limitations of air power in small wars are evident. First, the speed, reach, and firepower of aircraft are essential to massing air and/or ground forces when and where needed in the battle space. Second, ISR from the air is critical toward better situational awareness. Third, the flexibility of air power is a tremendous asset when dealing with the fluid environment of a small war; it can support a wide variety of actions, including combat, combat support, and civil-military operations. Air power resources must be effectively networked with intelligence sources, command and control elements and other parallel lines of operations, both military and civilian, to respond rapidly or precisely enough to make a difference. Air power is not a global panacea for small wars. ISR capabilities are not yet able to identify individuals on the ground, especially in an urban environment, a critical input to effectively prosecute a small war from the air. Thus, air power is heavily reliant on other sources of intelligence operating on the ground. Current weapon accuracy and radii of destruction limit use of air power in the combat role in dense environments, where targets blend with the civil population. The cost of platforms and weapons are asymmetrically high and must be employed judiciously in a small war, taking into account the relative benefit gained. Air power is only truly beneficial if properly integrated with all parallel lines of operation addressing all elements of legitimacy. Air power is offensive in nature. Use of air power against civilians would not be acceptable in a democratic society and could be counter-productive if not handled properly. Even when air strikes are deemed appropriate, airmen must proactively engage the media to ensure that facts are accurately represented to the public. Airmen handling the media need to be well-trained and knowledgeable about employment of air power. If proper management of the media is not undertaken, it could result in losing popular support, defeating the original purpose of strike operations. Better handling of the media, on the other hand, could have a dramatic effect on the overall effect of strike operations and the morale of the adversary.

Technology in Small Wars

No study of the application of air power in small wars would be complete without considering the impact of emerging technology in the areas of intelligence, sensors, precision weapons, advanced aircraft design and electromagnetic dominance. Small wars are generally characterised by difficulty in finding, identifying and isolating targets, whether operating in mountains, caves, forests or jungle canopy. Intelligence sensors can be broadly classified as wide area surveillance assets and close target reconnaissance assets. Wide area surveillance assets provide information about the overall picture of the target and also help in identifying the locations within the target area that require more intensive investigations.

The following technologies are affecting wide area surveillance capabilities in the context of small wars:

- **Foliage Penetration Synthetic Aperture Radar (SAR) and Moving Target Indicators (MTI).** A severe limitation exists among most present imagery sensors in their inability to see through heavy foliage. Recent developments in foliage penetrating SAR and MTI are making it increasingly possible to conduct wide area surveillance even in regions of heavy foliage. Although these capabilities are still in the early stages of development, they will eventually have the potential to significantly enhance the quality of intelligence gathering, thereby, improving the effectiveness of air operations.[24]
- **Multispectral and Hyperspectral Sensors.** Single waveband sensors have less fidelity than multispectral and hyperspectral sensors. Advances in sensors and processing algorithms using a broader range of frequencies of electromagnetic energy are making possible remote examination of objects with greater fidelity than ever before. [25]
- **Chemical Sniffers.** Miniaturisation technology has made it possible to build small, mobile chemical analysis laboratories that are able to 'sniff' or detect traces of certain chemicals in the atmosphere. Low flying aircraft or ground vehicles equipped with these devices will potentially be able to highlight places where bomb factories, arms caches or potential suicide bombers might be operating. Miniature UAVs carrying spectrometers can be deployed over areas of concern to collect samples or 'chemical signatures' for further processing.[26]
- **Microelectromechanical (MEM) Devices.** MEMs are microscopic devices in which sensors, transmitters, receivers or actuators have been miniaturised to the size of a transistor. These devices are being constructed to detect a variety of visual, thermal, acoustic and biochemical phenomenon. These can be effectively used in a small war scenario, thereby, affect the quality of intelligence collection.[27]

Close target reconnaissance assets provide detailed information about a specific target. New close target sensor technologies with a potential impact on air power are as follows:

- **See Through Walls.** Conventional cameras cannot see through the walls of a building. If the occupants are cautious and it is not possible to plant the device inside the building, there has been no way to collect information on them. But new radars having the capability to see through the walls of a building can determine with modest resolution whether the building is occupied or not. This information can be an important input for planning an attack.[28]
- **Facial Recognition System.** This is an emerging technology developed to identify individuals in a crowd. Complex algorithms scan images for a signature set of features that match a targeted individual. If cameras are placed in areas where terrorists or other key individuals are likely to pass, then the images collected from these cameras can be compared against a database of facial images and other physical features, with an amazing degree of accuracy. This has the potential to revolutionise the way targets are located, monitored and attacked.[29]

Command and Control

Small wars invariably involve potential targets like terrorists who mingle freely with the civil population. Engagement of these potential targets requires a flexible and responsive command and control system to link the "finders" with the "controllers" and the "shooters." New developments under the name of "dynamic engagement control" link shooters with control centres to provide a comprehensive picture of the battle space. Tactical controllers can be incorporated as necessary for proper weapon controlling. Although not new, GPS can greatly enhance the ability of controllers and air crew to locate targets quickly and with great precision. New developments in geo-location systems are refining accuracy and speed. Secure and effective data link communication between the controller and shooter continues to advance, facilitating efficient attack operations by eliminating several potential sources of delay. The JTIDS (joint tactical information distribution system) allows secure digital exchange between aircraft and control centres on relative positions, target locations, weapon availability, fuel status, and other information, thereby, reducing the need for intra-flight voice communication and increasing overall situational awareness. Other systems like data fusion software, interlinked but physically dispersed databases, and large scale communication nets also enable precise application of a network of sensors and weapon systems for swift and effective target engagement.[30]

Precision Weapons

Weapons development on two fronts is particularly relevant to the utilisation of air power in small wars. Firstly, aerospace weapons are becoming increasingly accurate. Secondly, as accuracy improves, weapon developers are able to decrease the lethal radius of weapons, reducing collateral damage and refining weapons effects. Laser guided bombs (LGBs) are old news now, but the systems are increasingly accurate and capable. Current circular error probable (CEP) achievable by LGBs is approaching to within several metres. JDAMs exploit GPS and bomb guidance units to enable bomb accuracies of a few tens of metres in any weather condition against targets beyond visual range, with accuracies continuing to improve. Small diameter bombs take advantage of increased accuracy to reduce the amount of high energy (HE) explosive by half or more, enabling precise targeting with reduced collateral damage. Several concepts and variants are in development. Smaller bombs also mean that conventional airframes can carry more weapons and small airframes such as UAVs can be used to more lethal effect.[31] Several new weapons concepts are being tested for application against small targets in densely populated areas.[32] Amongst them are kinetic energy weapons, which are small, dense, high-velocity projectiles with little or no explosive material, laser guided grenades capable of homing on laser energy and non-lethal directed energy weapons (acoustic, laser, microwave) that disable without killing. Small UAVs specially designed to carry weapons are also being developed for the small and urban war. Nano-energetics is a field of nanotechnology that is being developed with applications toward building smaller but more lethal weapons such as "cave buster" bombs that have several times the detonation force per pound munition than that of a conventional bomb. Over the long term, this will allow small UAVs to carry large numbers of highly effective weapons.[33]

Over and above conventional recce platforms, aerostat systems provide cost-effective wide area surveillance and detection with a fraction of the manpower required by other methods performing the same mission. Such systems make it possible to monitor activities along a border or around a critical node for long periods of time, denying adversaries the freedom to operate in that area. In the final analysis, technological advances have increased the utility of aerospace power in small wars. But, at the same time, they have placed much greater capability in the hands of potential adversaries.

Air Power, Small Wars and India

Legitimacy in India

The contest for legitimacy in India involves the same four general elements as elsewhere – control, security, economy and identification. But, as in every case, the specific nature of each of these elements is unique to India. India is a large country, heavily populated, and interspersed with widely diverse terrain. Many segments of the country are isolated due to lack of roads, limited communications infrastructure, restrictive terrain and limited government presence. Dense populations make it easy for insurgents to blend in, plan and conduct operations without being identified. In order to exercise control, the Indian government must have a strong civil government network, firmly grounded in the rule of law, enabled by effective roads, rail, mass communication and telecommunication infrastructures. Additionally, the government must be able to focus on specific areas to gain intelligence on terrorist/insurgent activities and be able to rapidly apply force where necessary to counter their operations and reduce their level of control. The challenges for security are the same as for control. India must have a baseline civil police infrastructure, and the ability to provide additional force when and where necessary. This will require a robust communications infrastructure integrating civil and military command centres to provide rapid warning when certain elements of the population are threatened. Additionally, forces must be organised and equipped to effectively respond to any threat. In India's case, rapid and long range mobility will be essential to make this possible. Many segments of the Indian population suffer from extreme poverty, with little hope of improvement in the near term. Areas where poverty has reached crisis levels are susceptible to manipulation by terrorist/insurgent organisations. The Indian government must be aware of such areas and able to provide assistance in a responsive manner, while economic development efforts continue. Once again, rapid, responsive, long range mobility will be essential. The cultural, religious and language diversity of India is staggering. It is easy for smaller sects to feel culturally or ideologically isolated from the government. Terrorist/insurgent organisations frequently take advantage of this to widen divisions and sponsor internal conflict. Additionally, in most cases, the non-state actors in India are Indian citizens – not foreigners. Therefore, they identify better with the civil population and derive greater legitimacy. Here again, robust lines of communication between the centre of the Indian government and each community are essential, along with a well developed education system.

Adversary Feeders in India

Non-state actors require the basic feeders of people, material supplies and information to sustain operations for legitimacy. In India, these feeders translate to several specific centres of gravity.

- **Leadership.** Terrorist and insurgent leaders in India are generally selfishly motivated. They are well integrated with the local population and identify well with them, giving them considerable legitimacy. As a result, they are difficult to find, and, once found, they are difficult to target without significant collateral damage. Overt attacks on leadership are likely to cause a backlash among the surrounding civil population. Therefore, targeting of leadership may not always be a viable option in the Indian scenario.

- **Motivation/Morale.** Terrorists/insurgents are highly motivated, with firmly entrenched ideology. They are generally less educated and could have been systematically indoctrinated since childhood. As a result, it is difficult to change their ideology and motivation in any time less than a generation. Hence, only a sustained political effort can address this problem. However, air power can be applied to facilitate this political effort and provide the stability required for it to continue.
- **Popular Support.** As mentioned, the leadership generally enjoys local popular support due to the high degree of identification they have with the people. Even though the people may not be directly involved in the operations, they provide material and moral support as well as security for the terrorists/insurgents. Military strike operations would only decrease the legitimacy of the government with these people. However, air power still has a role in improving the awareness and presence of the government within these populations. This, in turn, enables the government to connect with the population and build its relative legitimacy over time.
- **External Aid.** Indian terrorist/insurgent organisations are highly dependent on external aid. This feeder is dependent on their capability to communicate and move money, technology, weapons, manpower and other items into, and out of, India. Air power can play a number of roles in stemming this flow, in terms of reconnaissance, interdiction and the movement and coordination of security and police forces.

Analysis of the above centres of gravity yields several critical vulnerabilities and associated targets. Air power is one of many elements that must be applied together against these vulnerabilities.

- Terrorist/insurgent leadership – their legitimacy, physical security and freedom of movement.
- Isolation of civil population who are providing recruits and support, in terms of information, physical movement and economic sustenance.
- Terrorist/insurgent training camps and operating bases.
- Terrorist/insurgent lines of communication.

Air Power Roles in Small Wars in India

Air power can play several specific roles in bolstering government legitimacy, while interdicting terrorist/insurgent feeders. It is important to emphasise here that in such cases, air power can and must be used in more than the traditional combat roles to attack these vulnerabilities. Flexibility of thought is a prerequisite for exploiting the flexibility of air power in small wars. *Aerial reconnaissance* will play a key role in tracking terrorist/insurgent activities and identifying operating bases, training camps and supply nodes. Visual, photo, satellite, and UAV reconnaissance will be significant in this effort. Dense vegetation and mountainous terrain complicate aerial reconnaissance. However, advances in systems and techniques will make air power more effective in this role. Key capabilities for effective aerial reconnaissance will be increased loiter time with good survivability, day-night capability; high resolution sensors that can be cued by search platforms; near real-time data link to other sensors, command centres and weapons platforms; and advanced multispectral systems with corresponding processing algorithms. Air power can provide critical intelligence and electronic attack (EA) capabilities in support of feeder interdiction. Electronic support measures (ESM) can be used to identify terrorist/insurgent lines of communication and operating bases, as well as locate key leaders, even across international borders. Intelligence gained from adversary communications can be used to direct operations against them. Additionally, incriminating terrorist/insurgent communications can be publicised to undermine their legitimacy. EA can be employed to disrupt adversary communications and cause confusion. It can also be used to interdict insurgent communications to civil populations where appropriate. EA will also be important to ensure security of friendly force operations. Key capabilities will be flexible collection platforms with direction finding capability and long loiter times; advanced signal analysis and correlation systems; advanced signal decryption systems; rapid communications intelligence processing capabilities; near real-time data link to other sensors, command centres and weapons platforms. The *mobility and responsiveness* of air power are perhaps the most significant contributions that air power can bring to a small war. Air mobility gives the government a 'virtual presence' capability, in which a small reaction force can effectively respond to a large geographic area. With air transport, ground security forces can be rapidly concentrated when and where needed, in many types of terrain. Military air power can also be used to transport police and other civil security elements in response to a crisis. Furthermore, it greatly enhances the speed and reach of humanitarian relief and civil support operations, all of which support government legitimacy and reduce adversary influence. Key capabilities will include flexible transport platforms with sufficient range and the ability to operate from small landing strips or zones; fully developed communications infrastructure allowing rapid coordination within the military as well as with key civilian agencies; integrated civil–military command and control processes; and a systematically developed nation-wide infrastructure of landing strips/zones and maintenance facilities.

Attack helicopters will be just as relevant, and just as vulnerable, in future small wars as they have been since their introduction. They provide a significant reconnaissance and on-call fire support capability that can be a tremendous force multiplier. Such platforms can be used in support of civil security forces, quick reaction forces or larger operations. They can also be used as an escort platform for military or civil ground movements, including humanitarian relief convoys. Low speed, low altitude and smaller munitions mean that attack helicopters can be employed for strike operations with reduced risk of collateral damage. Key capabilities will include enhanced self-defence systems to increase survivability; improved day-night capabilities; advanced target acquisition systems; smaller, more precise weapons; near real-time data link for passing and receiving target data; and flexible command and control systems and structures that incorporate civilian agencies for integrated civil-military operations.

Though punitive strikes by multi-role combat aircraft may not be a very viable option in the Indian context, it is important that the IAF has to be prepared for this role, should the political leadership need it any time. Targets for punitive strike would mainly be training camps or the leadership. Fighters would be the best platforms for executing this mission across the border, and attack helicopters would be best suited for attacking leadership nodes. The importance of real-time intelligence cannot be understated, as these targets are not static. In order to avoid collateral damage in such attacks, precision attack capability would also be required.

Though casualty evacuation is one of the non-combatant roles of air power, it is going to play an important role in small wars. Tolerance for loss of human life in a small war is typically lower than in a full-scale conventional war. Rapid medical evacuation will greatly increase the survival rate of combat injuries. It can also be used to move doctors, civilian or military, around the region, and get civilians to medical care. This again contributes to government legitimacy, but presently does not seem to be a key result area even in our existing conflicts. Air power can also be employed in many ways not traditionally considered in conventional wars. The dynamic environment of small wars demands imaginative use of all resources to achieve the greatest legitimacy and interdict non-state actor feeders. An example of the creative use of air power is in the field of information operations. Frequently, terrorists and insurgents place great emphasis on getting their version of the 'truth' into the media before the government, undermining government credibility. In some situations, it is appropriate for the government to establish a quick launch Press corps with a military security element that could be sent on short notice to the scene of significant events and allow the real truth to be published before the adversary broadcasts a twisted version. Military, civil agencies and the secular Press would have to closely coordinate to make this possible.

Such an organisation would break the mould of current military doctrine, but could be tremendously effective in the real small war struggle for legitimacy. Military aircraft could also be used to transport supplies for an NGO into a remote location, provide genuine assistance to the population and enhance popular support for the government. Alternatively, the military could provide a sortie periodically to allow civilians to sell products outside the local area, enhancing their economic status and aiding in building connections with the central authorities.

Conventional minds will view such non-standard uses of military aircraft as a waste of government resources, but the benefit can have a significant impact in the contest for legitimacy – and save military resources in the long term. *The current air power doctrine of the IAF governs the force structure and deals primarily with conventional wars against well defined adversaries. It does not sufficiently address small wars. Doctrine, structure and procedures should be refined to cater for small war situations with specific mechanisms to allow for effective integration with civilian efforts and parallel lines of operation.*

Summary

Small wars will continue to plague the world in the foreseeable future. These wars will be fought on battlefields that transcend geographical boundaries, and against enemies who would be increasingly protected by a shrinking and multi-cultural world. What is also uncertain is how established states will deal with each conflict and exploit the emerging capabilities of aerospace power. This article has attempted to identify precisely *what can be changed* and what measures can be taken to optimise the application of air power in small wars, particularly in India. It has also tried to identify that small wars are not just about military might, but also about governmental legitimacy. This means that air power must be applied within a broader strategy of mutually supporting parallel efforts (or lines of operation) to achieve greatest possible legitimacy, while interdicting feeders that sustain terrorist/insurgent operations. This, in turn, demands a more holistic and flexible view of how aircraft can be employed to support all parallel efforts, not just combat operations. Force distribution, organisation and command structures must facilitate rapid application of air power to support precision strike as well as civil support. Doctrine must allow flexible use of aircraft beyond the traditional roles of reconnaissance, strike, and military transport. Technology must be leveraged to increase levels of awareness in the battle space; increase speed of response; increase precision of attack; decrease collateral damage; and network both civilian and military elements for a fully synchronised effort. Maximum effectiveness in fighting a small war depends on developing a network-centric force that is also capable of networking with civil counterparts in a small war. All of these initiatives will take time and courage to implement and perfect. Wisdom dictates that each responsible government undertake them before it finds itself in a contest for the greatest relative legitimacy – a small war.

Notes

1. John F. Kennedy, remarks to West Point graduating class, June 6, 1962.
2. USMC, *The Small Wars Manual*, p. 1. "…small wars are operations undertaken under executive authority, wherein military force is combined with diplomatic pressure in the internal or external affairs of another state whose government is unstable, inadequate, or unsatisfactory for the preservation of life and of such interests as are determined by the foreign policy of our nation."
3. Indian MoD, *Joint Services Glossary of Military Terms*, p. 119.
4. CJCS. "An organized movement aimed at the overthrow of a constituted government through use of subversion and armed conflict."
5. Indian MoD, n.3, p. 70.
6. Indian MoD, Ibid., p. 80.
7. The model presented in Fig. 1 was developed by Major Merz (USAF) specifically for this paper. Although it does not come directly from any particular source, many of the concepts reflected by the model come from Dr. Gordon McCormick (Naval Postgraduate School, Monterey, CA, 2000) and from Dr. John Arquilla (Naval Postgraduate School, Monterey, CA and RAND, 2000).
8. Peter Chiarelli and Patrick Michaelis, "Winning the Peace: The Requirement for Full Spectrum Operations," *Military Review*, July-August 2005, pp. 4-17.
9. Indian MoD, IAP 2000, n.3, pp 15-16.
10. Leites and Wolfe, *Rebellion and Authority: An Analysis Essay on Insurgent Conflicts* (RAND Corp, 1970), pp. 1-5.
11. Wikipedia. "Vietnam War," at http://en.wikepedia.org/wiki/Vietnam
12. S.S. Deshpande, "Employment of Offensive Air Power Against Insurgencies," *Trishul*, Autumn 2004, pp19-27.
13. Deshpande, Ibid.
14. Anthony Cordesman, *The Iraq War-Strategy Tactics and Military Lessons*, (CSIS, 2003).
15. Cordesman, Ibid.
16. Cordesman, Ibid.

17. *Ha'aretz,* October 29, 1997, p. B2.
18. Ibid.
19. "An Enduring Illusion-A Special Report on Airpower," *The Economist*, August 26, 2006.
20. Mercel De Haas, "The Use of Russian Air Power in the Second Chechen War," Conflict Studies Research Centre 2003.
21. De Haas, Ibid.
22. De Haas, Ibid.
23. Timothy L. Thoma, "Air Operations in Low Intensity Conflict: The Case of Chechnya," *Air Power Journal*, Winter 1997, pp, 51-59.
24. David Ochmanek, *Military Operations Against Terrorist Groups Abroad: Implications for the USAF* (RAND Corp., 2003).
25. Ochmanek, Ibid.
26. Ochmanek, Ibid.
27. Rudman-Hart Commission, *Technology and the Future of Warfare* (US Government Publication, 1999).
28. Ochmanek. n.24, p. 24.
29. Ochmanek. Ibid., p. 24.
30. Benjamin Lambeth, "Technology and Air War," *Airforce Magazine*, vol. 79, no. 11, November 1996.
31. "Defense Update Small Diameter Bomb" at http:// www.defenseupdate.com/ products/s/sdb.htm
32. Ibid.
33. John Gartner, "Military Re-Loads with Nanotech," *Technology Review*, January 21, 2005, pp. 1-3.

9

Military Space Organisations of the USA: Lessons for India?

K.K. Nair

The profound impact of air and space power in furthering national influence and effects is well established in the new millennium as also the fact that the US is the world's leading air and space power. While most air forces are yet to complete the transition from second to third generation fighter aircraft, the US is set to transit to third generation space systems for enabling military competencies to its war-fighter. The critical lynchpin enabling the evolution and sustenance of such outstanding competencies and capabilities are its military institutions and organisational edifice; in particular, the US Air Force (USAF) and its Air Force Space Command (AFSPC) which have spearheaded and actually enabled the acquisition of such unparalleled and hitherto unheard of military capabilities. The role of these institutions in utilising, integrating and operationalising space to provide solutions to national objectives has been truly consistent and exceptional. Their seminal role in promoting US national military space competencies has been so widely recognised that a variety of nations with disparate doctrinal inclinations, capabilities and interests, ranging from the Chinese to the Israelis, earnestly attempt acquisition of similar capabilities by replicating the US model. It is in the above context that a balanced examination of the evolution of the US' national military space institutes and organisations is attempted to comprehend the evolutionary, doctrinal and organisational challenges, the challenges to operational integration and a host of other factors. Looking back retrospectively and attempting to draw inferences from the evolutionary experiences of others makes eminent sense, especially so in a costly and technologically challenging endeavour like space. The same has been attempted in this paper.

Examining how the US Organises its Overall Military Space Effort

The USAF possesses the world's most powerful military space apparatus and its capabilities dwarf those of most nations. Even amongst US military organisations charged with the military utilisation of space, the USAF has persistently dwarfed the other Services not only in terms of sheer size, responsibility and custody of resources but also in the seminal role it has historically played in the research, build-up, acquisition and operational utilisation of US national space capabilities.

During the initial experimentation stages of the 1960s-1970s, it was the USAF which led the evolution of US national military space competencies. In thc 1980s, the need for operationally responsive space systems led to the creation of an Air Force Space Command. Other space commands like a joint US Space Command (USSPC) for consummation of the Strategic Defence Initiative (SDI) as well as a Navy Space Command (NAVSPC) and Army Space Command (ARSPC) also followed later to fulfil the organic needs of the navy and army. Nevertheless, while the AFSPC grew and expanded rapidly in the following years, its contemporaries like the joint USSPC, the NAVSPC as well as the ARSPC were either disbanded, stagnated or were merged with other institutions. Even later ventures of the new millennium like the prevailing joint US Strategic Command (USSTRATCOM) are yet too nascent to match the AFSPC in terms of resources or responsibilities.

Many changes have been taking place in the last over four decades since space came into the reckoning. In the above atmosphere of change, the only consistent feature has been the persistent organisation of national military space efforts by the air force. A permanent feature of the evolution of the US' capabilities has been air force stewardship of national military space activities which began around four decades ago and continues till date, as apparent from the prevailing distribution of space resources. Distribution of national resources in terms of personnel and budgetary allocations provides an indication of the agency spearheading national effort and the same has been examined below.

Fig. 1: Distribution of US Space Resources Among Different Commands, FY 05

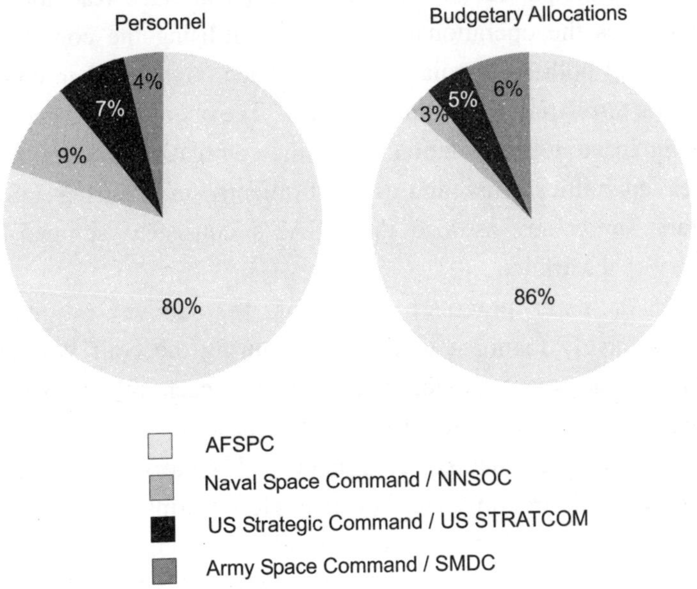

Nevertheless, the transition to national and international stewardship of military space affairs was not an entirely smooth and unencumbered process. Parochial inter-Service and political considerations, immature employment doctrines as well as technologies ensured sub-optimal military utilisation of space for quite some time since the first American foray into space with an Explorer-1 launch on January 31, 1958. The USAF had to undergo numerous evolutionary changes and revolutionary transformations to arrive at the present levels of military space competencies and maintain its lead. The changes generally corresponded to increasing comprehension of the military utility of space as also a maturing of the military employment doctrines and technologies related to space. As employment doctrines evolved from the high-ground to aerospace, the quantum of air force resources and responsibility in steering the national military space effort correspondingly increased. These corresponded to the US' increasing involvement in projecting influence and power well beyond the homeland as also the need to protect the US homeland from air-and space-borne threats. Looking back, the principal factor that sustained its military lead through the decades was the operational rationale of utilising the complementary attributes of both the media of air and space (aerospace) in concert for obtaining terrestrial war-winning effects.[1] The operational compulsion of utilising space not in isolation but as the cumulative product of air and space capabilities was (and is) instrumental in ensuring US global military supremacy as also the USAF's consistent seminal role in military space affairs.

The eminent practical logic of the above rationale was demonstratively manifest to the world during the Gulf War of 1991, when air and space power complemented each other operationally through detection and acquisition of targets by air-and space-borne systems, satellite enabled command and control of air missions, navigation and targeting, etc. For example, information fed by sensors and radars on air-borne platforms like unmanned aerial vehicles (UAVs), air-borne warning and control system (AWACS), etc as well as space-borne platforms like satellites enabled continuous surveillance of enemy force movements. This integrated air and space picture enabled hitherto unknown levels of battlefield situational awareness and manoeuvre. Communication satellites enabled transmission of this information to the most suitable platforms and navigation satellites enabled precise navigation of aircraft as well as delivery of munitions onto the targets, finally enabling the ground troops a complete walkover. The military utility of navigation satellites came to the fore during the Gulf War when these enabled location, navigation and targeting information to all three military forces. Nevertheless, the maximum benefits and operational utilisation accrued to the air force. Bombing inaccuracies were the bane of air strikes on account of the exceptionally high speeds and tempo of air operations. High speeds automatically implied reduced scope for correcting targeting inaccuracies unlike in the case of the surface forces wherein the comparatively lesser speed and tempo of operations allowed much greater scope for correction of targeting inaccuracies. Navigation satellites changed all that and made air operations more effective. They enabled automatic target updates of even time-sensitive targets, and real-time navigation dispensed the need of obtaining position fixes, updating aircraft navigational systems, etc, thereby, providing air crew more time and means to make air strikes more accurate and safer. As a matter of fact, precise targeting and delivery of platforms and munitions multiplied the efficiency of military operations in general and air operations in particular as never before.

Ever since the cumulative potential of air and space systems in enabling decisive military success became demonstratively apparent, most nations covet and pursue military capabilities akin to the US. Nations across the globe attempt to modernise their military apparatuses by building their air and space capabilities and fulfil national aspirations by emulating institutional models like those of the US. The above emulatory trend is evident across the globe, considering that the Israeli Air Force established a Space Branch in 2003, changed its nomenclature to Israeli Air and Space Force in 2004 and followed it up with a Military Space Command in 2005,[2] South Korea announced the creation of an Air Force Space Command[3] and India also aspires for one. Similarly, Britain's RAF (Royal Air Force) Strike Command, the United Arab Emirates' (UAE's) Air Force, China's People's Liberation Army Air Force (PLAAF), the Chilean Air Force and numerous other national air forces comprehend and pursue the acquisition of national military space capabilities by emulating the US model. Nevertheless, most nations trail the US in terms of military space capabilities by at least two decades or more.

Most nations, including ours, are where the US was around four decades ago. Their historical rather than existing challenges would have greater lessons to draw upon. Hence, to comprehensively assess the challenges to the evolution and integration of space capabilities into military operations, it would be essential to explore how the US historically organised its national space efforts and the same is dwelt upon as below.

Historical Perspective on Organising National Space Efforts

Pre-Sputnik

The military need to foray beyond the atmosphere into space was a direct result of the extraordinary emphasis placed by military doctrines on acquisition of the 'high ground' for successful prosecution of military operations. As a natural corollary of the same, the need to deliver ordnance higher and better, through the higher reaches of air and space with aircraft and missiles, as also the need to survey and observe higher and safer to protect the US from surprise attacks by high level Soviet aircraft and inter-continental ballistic missiles (ICBMs) led to the pursuit of space-based capabilities for performing military tasks better.

The air force operated in the higher reaches of the environment and, hence, it apparently was the natural candidate to better exploit the high ground for the pursuance of military objectives. As in the case of air, the initial military utility of space was also perceived to be for high level observation and ordnance delivery. Observation was deemed to be fulfilled by high level reconnaissance satellites and ordnance delivery by missiles. Thus, the primary role then was professed as being an extension of strategic air power, which, in turn, was a core competency of the US Air Force.

US air power in those times was in its primacy considering that even in early 1946, the air force was yet to evolve beyond an army air force (AAF).[4] The AAF then had three major combat commands: the Strategic Air Command (SAC), the Tactical Air Command (TAC), and the Air Defence Command (ADC). Post-World War II, the US' accent on strategic deterrence increased in view of the advent of nuclear weapons, the Soviet threat (especially after it acquired nuclear weapons) and, hence, long range strategic delivery by missiles and bomber forces, was accorded highest priority. Strategic delivery of military ordnance by bomber aircraft was the mainstay of the SAC. The US, hence, began supplementing the great armada of bombers of the SAC with ballistic missiles (BMs) also. This led to inter-Service disputes, with the army and navy also demanding their share of BM assets. The disputes were settled by handing over responsibility of strategic missiles to the air force, tactical missiles to the army, and submarine launched missiles to the navy. The air force, thus, had two elements of the "triad" of strategic weapons (bombers and land-based missiles) while the navy had the third (submarine launched missiles).[5]

With regards to satellites, their potential utilities were explored and envisioned long before the first Sputnik launch of October 4, 1957. During the 1940s, the USAF had conducted a series of studies to establish the technological feasibility, cost-effectiveness and military utility of satellites. The air force's RAND Corporation spearheaded these studies. For example, the RAND Corporation had proposed a military satellite system as far back as in 1946. Technological feasibility and military utility of space-based communications and reconnaissance, etc were also established early on[6]. The air force, thus, had the doctrinal groundwork in place (no matter how rudimentary) for establishing military competencies in space and Sputnik only proved to be the catalyst enabling the consummation of the air force's military aspirations in space.

Nevertheless, in the pre-Sputnik era, missiles and satellites were initially perceived as competitors for scarce national resources until comprehension dawned that their complementary capabilities demanded centralised control.[7] Centralised control, in turn, devolved onto the air force which embarked upon the aforesaid space missions. In pursuance of the same, the US Air Force Research and Development Command established the Western Development Division (WDD) in 1954 for developing space capabilities (operational ICBMs and military reconnaissance satellites) which would be the basis of all their later space and missile capabilities.[8] As a direct consequence of the same, launch vehicles like the Atlas and space systems like the WS-117L reconnaissance satellites were accorded top priority and space capabilities were built around these missions. Thus, the early perceptions on the use of space as an extension of strategic air power paved the way for the USAF's preeminence in launch vehicle and space systems as well as its development of the same into future core competencies.

Post-Sputnik

All said and done, in the pre-Sputnik period, the overall national space efforts were sporadic, characterised by inter-Service clashes and also limited by the then prevailing political compulsions of "peaceful use of outer space" until the "*Sputnik shock*" galvanised the US into action. With Sputnik, not only did the Soviets display greater technological prowess, they also demonstrated greater military prowess in that they now had the powerful troika of nuclear weapons, ICBMs and satellite launchers. The Soviets now had the nuclear ordnance as well as the means of delivering weapons from space. Within the US, domestic concerns escalated as never before and fear soon gave way to national panic. The immediate reaction to Sputnik was a thorough reexamination and reorganisation of national space efforts in the US to address both security and technological concerns. Action to create a national spacc programme was initiated. Its focus was centred first on organisational reform and revision, followed by policy formulation. This led to the reorganisation of its national space programme into civil and military branches. In July 1958, the US government passed the National Aeronautics and Space Act which officially divided the civilian and military sectors, creating the National Aeronautics and Space Administration (NASA). With the above Act, the US formally established a dual space programme comprising separate civilian scientific and military application projects. Both were officially directed at scientific, and "peaceful", defensive, non-aggressive use of space. The creation of NASA was a deliberate step by President Eisenhower to separate military and civilian space activities. Among other things, he wanted to publicly stress that the US was interested in the peaceful uses of space, but at the same time, continue the pursuit of space-based capabilities for military applications. The primary goal of Eisenhower's space policy was to examine and exploit the potential of space to open up the closed Soviet state by using satellite reconnaissance and the second major goal was to investigate space for scientific purposes. The 1958 National Aeronautics and Space Act, which specified that military space activities be conducted by the Department of Defence (DoD), enabled fulfilment of the primary goal and the less pressing requirement of science was fulfilled by the creation of NASA. Following the above legislation and consequent distribution of civil and military responsibilities, the military went into an overdrive and a number of satellites were placed into orbit, with the air force launching the majority, followed in lesser measure by the navy and the army. The period ranging from late 1957 to 1961 comprised the watershed years of the US national space programme and forged the air force's preeminent place in it.

Apart from the above, the period also witnessed the activation of the North American Air Defence Command (NORAD)[9] in 1957 since US policy-makers perceived a direct Soviet military threat of nuclear ICBMs coming undetected and uncontested through the realm of space. By 1959, systems aimed at tracking space objects as well as incoming Soviet missiles were in place and NORAD's mission expanded to operational control of all space defence responsibilities with the formation of the Space Detection and Tracking System (SPADATS).

Additionally, in keeping with the intelligence requirements, the political limitations of the times as well as a preponderance of the sanctuary doctrine,[10] satellite reconnaissance programmes and organisations like the highly classified National Reconnaissance Organisation (NRO) also came into being by August 1960,[11] though its existence was not publicly revealed until 1992.[12] The NRO primarily fulfilled intelligence requirements and was headed by an air force official, who, nevertheless, reported to the secretary of defence and director of the Central Intelligence Agency (CIA), not the secretary of the air force or the air staff leadership.[13] Thus, within the next three years following Sputnik, a powerful troika of three security organisations and one civil organisation were overtly and covertly pursuing the development of American military competencies in space.[14]

Central Agency for Organising Military Space Efforts

Overall, it was perceived that while enormous effort was put in, it was largely uncoordinated and haphazard. Thus, there was a need to bestow national military space responsibility on a single Service which would coordinate and streamline national efforts. Consequently, every Service put forth its rationale to the government for acquiring the responsibility of national military space activity. The most convincing (though hotly contested) rationale was that of '*aerospace*' which evolved as a natural corollary of the '*high ground*' approach.

The USAF operated in the higher reaches of the environment with conventional aircraft; in the higher reaches of the atmosphere, it operated with aircraft like the SR-71; and beyond the earth's atmosphere, it operated with ICBMs and other ballistic missiles. It, thus, operated in the entire vertical dimension of air and space. By then, the Soviet strategic threat (nuclear and conventional) had evolved to include strikes by bomber aircraft and increasingly, ICBMs. Matters related to defence of the US from both air and space assumed priority. The US responded by increasing ICBM detection capabilities with ballistic missile early warning (BMEW) systems, by handing over responsibility and resources for both air and space defence to the air force[15] and also building up the strike elements of the air force with both bombers and ICBMs. Hence, apart from operating in the vertical dimensions of air and space, the USAF was also responsible for countering threats from the entire vertical dimension of air and space or aerospace. Therefore, relying on the 'aerospace' rationale, the air force represented that it was the logical Service to head a unified Defence Department oriented national space programme that would serve both military and civil requirements.

The air force's contention and increasing involvement in space did not go uncontested and unnoticed by the army and the navy. Their aspirations for a greater say in the affairs led to proposals for a unified space command[16] as also accusations of non-cooperation against the air force. The air force, in turn, went public with lengthy rebuttals.[17] The above disputes served little purpose apart from reinforcing the already critical views of national legislators on inter-Service rivalries.

In April 1959, Chief of Naval Operations, Admiral Arleigh Burke, made "a bold bid for a major share" of the space mission by proposing a unified space command. In effect, he advocated a unified command for space, based on the "very indivisibility of space" and the interests in space of all three Services. The Army Chief of Staff Gen Maxwell D. Taylor also endorsed the same, arguing that space activities transcended the particular interests of any one Service.[18] However, the Air Force Chief of Staff Gen Thomas D. White opposed the proposal on the grounds that it violated the practice of treating space systems on a functional basis. He argued that space systems represent only a better means of performing existing missions and, hence, should be assigned to the appropriate unified or specified command.[19] Secondly, he asserted that the air force was capable of providing effective leadership for the nation's space programme and of being responsive to the needs of the other Services also.[20] From the foregoing it is apparent that Gen White evidently was not against joint exploitation of space assets with a unified command but was a strong advocate of the aerospace rationale that space assets enabled better exploitation of the entire vertical dimension of air and space in support of terrestrial military operations. Hence, it was essential that space capabilities be nurtured and evolved within a parent organisation like the air force.

Finally, in 1959, subsequent to Congressional hearings which afforded equal opportunities to all three Services to present their case, the secretary of defence agreed to the air force stand and the major share of military space programmes was handed over to the air force. Between a unified and a specific organisational structure, the choice fell on the air force. The claims of the army and the navy were not found to be substantial enough except in some specific cases like satellite-based communications which were addressed by joint ventures like the defence communications agency. The air force emerged from the post-Sputnik inter-Service struggles over space with the major share of responsibility and authority on the grounds of the operational functionality of space.

Nevertheless, the navy was not entirely convinced and the following year (May 1960), Admiral Burke again challenged the air force position on space operations. He reiterated the need for a joint military space command on the grounds that several space systems had reached "operational threshold" and that NASA projects needed substantial inter-Service support, etc. The proposal was again rejected on the same grounds as the previous one and the secretary of defence reaffirmed the decision his predecessor had taken in 1959.

USAF as Central Military Space Agency

In March 1961, Secretary of Defence Robert McNamara rejected Admiral Burke's proposal for a joint military space command and designated the air force as the military Service for space research and development (R&D), thereby relieving the army and navy of any significant space responsibilities and leaving only the air force as the central military agency in space. This also diminished the prospects of disruptive inter-Service rivalry. Following the decision, the US, by 1962, increased the air force's space funding by a factor of almost 120, from \$2.2 million to \$249.7 million.[21] In response, the air force reorganised its R&D elements to provide a stronger focus on space issues. The air force, in the final analysis, had staked its claim to space through the logic of aerospace and it had been accepted.

National Implications

By 1962, the air force had responsibility for 90 per cent of the military space effort and its dominant role in space was acknowledged. The implications of the above move are apparent when considering the US' national performance pre-and post-1961. National military space development and capabilities sky-rocketed post-1961 in both literal and figurative terms; the military space programme forged ahead as never before; launch success rates registered a dramatic upswing; the number and variety of payloads in orbit for military purposes increased dramatically; and by 1967, almost the entire range of space capabilities essential for military force enhancement were in place. The period up to 1967 was the only historical instance when American launches and payloads in orbit far exceeded those of their rivals, the Soviets. With a singular agency spearheading the national effort, space activities continued to grow considering that throughout the 1960s and 1970s, the army, navy and primarily the air force continued to advance and expand space-based capabilities in the areas of communication, meteorology, geodesy, navigation and reconnaissance, etc. Gen White's commitment to the US of the air force providing a balanced leadership of military space activities to the mutual benefit of all the Services had stood the test of time as evidenced by over two decades of successful, responsible management of military space affairs for the benefit of all the Services.

Reorganisation for Operational Focus

The air force by then had already launched, and was operating, the majority of space systems; it performed most military space missions and programmes; it had also been formally designated by the DoD as the central agency for all space system development and, hence, over a period of time stewardship of national military space activity automatically devolved onto it. By the 1970s, space systems demonstrated important operational utilities during the Vietnam War. The primitive satellite communication links initially established by the air force demonstrated the potent applicability of space systems to operational and tactical needs. Weather satellites followed communications and were utilised to furnish tactical weather information for planning close air support, enabling air-to-air refuelling, air-borne support and other tactical missions. Soon, satellite communications provided regional links between commanders within Vietnam as also transcontinental links from Southeast Asia to the US. The critical role of weather and imagery satellites in the lengthy effort to destroy the Than-Hoa Bridge as well as the Son-Tay raid to rescue American prisoners, etc established the operational value of space systems. Thus, it was perceived that space applications needed to be extended beyond strategic to operational and tactical missions. It was perceived that an operational focus, in addition to the prevailing strategic focus, was essential to optimally exploit space for military purposes and, hence, the air force began studying ways and means to improve its organisational structure for prosecuting space operations. In view of the increasing importance of space for operational commanders, the need for an operational space command was acutely felt.

Secondly, over a period of time, space system functions had become internally distributed to various agencies and, hence, the overall effort was distributed and discordant. For example, the Air Force Systems Command retained control of communication satellites whereas the Strategic Air Command managed meteorological satellites; space surveillance networks rested with the Air Defence Command, whereas testing and development of air launched anti-satellites (ASATs) was under the purview of the Tactical Air Command, etc. Thus, operational efficiency suffered and, hence, the need to consolidate operational efforts was acutely felt across the air force.

Air Force Space Command for Operational Focus

A series of studies in the late 1970s and early 1980s also led to the conclusion that the time had come for a more comprehensive and operational focus on air force space programmes. This reinforced the belief that an operational space command was required for the nation and particularly the air force, to expand its potential in space. As a consequence, to manage its affairs better, a series of internal reorganisation, adjustments and transfers were undertaken in the air force.[22] In many cases, these adjustments responded to a growth in responsibilities for space operations and space mission management. For example, while the Weapons Development Division (WDD) sufficed to serve the launch and application missions of the1950s, by the 1960s, to meet the R&D requirements of developing space systems, the Air Force Research and Development Command was created, followed later by an Air Force Systems Command to fulfil the requirements of a DoD defence directive assigning the air force responsibility for development and acquisition of all future US military space systems.[23] The Air Force Space Command also came about on similar lines to fulfil operational military requirements. It came about to enable greater exploitation of the inherent characteristics of air power like range, perspective, elevation, etc and also to enable prosecution of decisive military operations in places far removed from homeland support bases.

In late 1981, Gen James V. Hartinger, commander-in-chief of the Aerospace Defence Command, along with Gen Robert T. Marsh, commander of the Air Force Systems Command raised the issue of how the air force should organise for space operations. Gen Hartinger developed a plan which showed how the air force might immediately create a major command for operational management of space resources on par with the Strategic Air Command, Tactical Air Command, and Military Airlift Command. Following some more deliberation and discussion, on June 21, 1982, Air Force Chief of Staff Gen Lew Allen, Jr., announced the impending formation of a single Air Force Space Command (AFSPC) that would coordinate and consolidate all air force space assets and activities effective September 1, 1982. Thus, following three years of restructuring its units and forces, the air force combined space operations into one command when it activated the space command on September 1, 1982.

Thus, overall responsibility for 'operationalising' space and integrating space capabilities into the US' conventional military apparatus was handed over to the AFSPC. Hence, activities essential to operational integration like military space capability acquisition and development, launches, space systems manufacture and operations, space surveillance, space telemetry tracking and control, offensive space operations, etc were placed under the purview of the AFSPC, whereas the R&D function was continued with the Air Force Systems Command (AFSC). Apart from the above, it also included a transfer of personnel: for example, it brought together both operators from the SAC as well as technicians from the AFSC under the aegis of a single agency, the AFSPC.[24] Authority and responsibility for operational space matters was, thus, consolidated under a single agency and a single commander. Secondly, it also enabled development of an operational focus that facilitated creation of operationally capable space systems which would fulfill the needs of the war-fighter.

Creation of a Naval Space Command

By the Seventies, in keeping with the policies of Admiral Sergei Gorshkov, the Soviet Navy was undergoing rapid expansion. It had evolved beyond coastal defence and ground support and was expanding its capabilities as a worldwide naval power. In doing so, the Soviets had changed their naval strategy from a basically defensive one to a more assertive offensive strategy of forward deployment aimed at global influence. Thus, beginning from the Baltic, Northern, and Black Sea Fleets, the Soviets progressively extended their spheres of influence out of their traditional deployment areas. The Black Sea Fleet began deploying into the eastern Mediterranean while the Northern Fleet journeyed into the mid-Atlantic. By the early 1970s, the Soviets were deploying to the Cuban and South African areas and into the Indian Ocean, and by the late 1970s, Soviet naval influence had expanded across the globe. Its expansion was supported and enabled by space-based navigation and communication capabilities.

In keeping with their domineering global posture, the Soviets began fielding space systems that were aimed not only at the US homeland, but also against the US Navy across the globe. The US Navy was apparently threatened and sought to counter the Soviet threat with matching capabilities. As a result, it desperately sought space support systems typical to naval needs in order to counter and contain the Soviet threat.[25] It, hence, came up with a three-pronged strategy of initially using USAF satellites to fulfill emergent requirements and gain experience in orbital surveillance, followed by the launch of electronic intelligence (ELINT) satellites and later dedicated satellites for ocean surveillance. Nevertheless, the above were not enough for observation and containment of the surface and sub-surface fleets of the Soviet Navy widely dispersed across the globe; hence, dedicated efforts to support the specific global requirements of the navy were essential. Systems to support specific maritime needs were distinctly different from other applications and, hence, demanded dedicated efforts for development as well as operation.[26] The need for global maritime observation as also the need to enable naval navigation and communications necessitated a separate agency for operating and maintaining naval space systems.

The USAF which had the sole responsibility for acquiring US military space systems was focussed largely on meeting the national intelligence, strategic defence and strategic nuclear deterrence priorities of the Cold War and it could do little to address the tactical requirements of the navy.

The focus was primarily on obtaining and maintaining the US' strategic advantage over the Soviets with missile launch warning satellites, intelligence satellites, survivable strategic communication systems, etc and for fulfilling the overall military needs of the nation. The USAF had neither the expertise nor the resources to fulfil distinct naval needs or operate and maintain naval systems and, hence, the navy sought a separate organisation for developing, operating and maintaining capabilities typical to its needs and requirements. The air force on its part did not contest the navy's claims. There was no major conflict of principle, structure or management here.

The navy, hence, sought a revision of the earlier DoD directive assigning all acquisition and development of space systems to the air force. The DoD directive was consequently revised to enable all the Services to develop their own space systems under broad DoD purview. The revision enabled the other Services to come up with their own space organisations to operate and manage capabilities specific to their needs and roles. Thus, in October 1983, a Naval Space Command was also formed with the declared mission of operating its space systems rather than development or acquisition of new systems.[27]

Creation of a Joint US Space Command

While the concept of a unified command was propounded as early as the 1950s, serious efforts toward forming a joint space command were not forthcoming until the 1980s. The intense focus of President Reagen's SDI or "Star-Wars" programme was the main driver for a joint USSPC[28]. Secondly, it was also perceived by some quarters that control and management of space forces would improve further if the air force consolidated the residual space resources of its Air Defence Command, Air Force Space Command, and the US portion of NORAD into a single organisation.[29] This unified command would integrate operational space systems, surveillance systems, missile defences and ASATS, etc into the national command structure and help ensure control and management of space forces for directing war-fighting needs on earth and in space. It was largely aimed at consummation of the "Star Wars" vision of the SDI.

Hence, the air force formulated a concept for a joint US Space Command, headed by a commander-in-chief (C-in-C). It was reasoned that if space was to become a theatre of conflict, an operational command for space operations was a logical evolution. Nevertheless, the Canadian government had serious reservations about the SDI and associated issues and, hence, NORAD continued as a separate entity.

Notwithstanding the above, the Joint Chiefs of Staff (JCS) took specific steps toward the formation of a unified space command. After studying a proposal made by the chief of staff of the air force, the JCS recommended establishment of such a command. Secretary of Defence Casper Weinberger recommended to the National Security Council (NSC) that the president approve such a proposal. With President Reagan's approval on September 23, 1985, a unified US Space Command staffed by personnel from the army, marine corps, navy and air force was activated to consolidate all military space efforts under the direction of one C-in-C. The C-in-C was directly responsible to the president through the secretary of defence and chairman, Joint Chiefs of Staff.

Creation of an Army Space Command

The US Army's role in the US' military space affairs has been relatively miniscule. It has traditionally been confined to the area of ballistic missile defence (BMD) and providing specific-to-Service needs of the army. It did pioneer the development of BMs and launch vehicles in the 1940-1950s; nonetheless, since it had a limited mission and role in space, its role diminished progressively. Therefore, it attempted to cling tenaciously to its residual space launch programmes by coming up with extraordinary proposals like the 1959 "man very high" proposal which envisaged firing a man riding in a Jupiter reentry vehicle on a ballistic trajectory 150 miles downrange. The proposal was rejected by the secretary of defence and ridiculed as having "about the same technical value as the circus stunt of shooting a young lady from a cannon."[30] The 1972 Anti-Ballistic Missile (ABM) Treaty further restricted the scope for development of the BMD agenda.

In brief, the US Army had limited operational military applications for space and, hence, an extremely limited role for over three decades until the arrival of the SDI concept. After a long hiatus, for a brief spell, the US Army's role was rejuvenated by the SDI which urged an active BMD concept comprising ASAT systems with ground-based lasers, neutral particle beams, ground-based kinetic energy interceptors, etc. Thus, in April 1988, the US Army also came about with an Army Space Command (ARSPC) for developing the above systems in fulfilment of its SDI role as well as for missile defence.

Implications of Multiple Military Space Agencies

Thus, towards the end of the 1980s, in keeping with its strategic and operational requirements as also the SDI vision, a total of up to six agencies[31] drove the pursuit of military space competencies and capabilities in a variety of directions. The entire national effort affair was no longer a concerted drive under a single agency; rather it was a multi-directional overdrive under "broad DoD purview." The multiplicity of military space agencies automatically implied enormous monetary investments[32] with no reciprocal guarantee of optimal utilisation or exceptional military space support. To make matters worse, by the end of the 1980s, the technological and economical challenges of the SDI became more apparent and the SDI programme itself was shelved. Thus, the US was in a piquant situation with an organisational edifice for SDI already in place minus the original SDI agenda. Under the DoD's broad purview, centralised direction and focus were lacking, mutual coordination was found wanting and national policy on space was also unclear. This led to considerable disarray and duplication. The situation was ripe for organisational turbulence and, hence, inter-organisational as well as inter-Service tensions and rivalries resurfaced. Internal squabbling amongst and within the Services for greater resource allocation and stewardship of national space activities began afresh. The air force's stewardship of national space activities was contested, and it was accused of ambivalence, non-cooperation, etc. The tension was not confined to the Services only and extended even within the Services with the Air Force Systems Command also contesting the AFSPC's claim over principal responsibility for air force space activities.[33] Comparatively speaking, the chaotic late-Eighties were a dismal period for American space activities, with US performance being nowhere close to their rivals, the Soviets, who clearly outraced them in terms of numbers and performance.

The Soviet military space organisation was fairly simple with the Strategic Rocket Forces (SRF) responsible for ballistic missiles and space launches (strategic offence mission), the Air and Space Defence Forces (PVO/PKO) looking after ballistic missile defence and the Soviet Air Force (VVS) responsible for space systems, cosmonaut training, vehicle recovery, etc. The navy and ground forces had no apparent major responsibility apart from participation in certain satellite programmes.[34]

Reverting to the Air Force Space Command

Following the dismal state of affairs briefly outlined above, a number of reviews on the efficacy of national military space capabilities and the organisations driving the same were carried out. The consequent consensus veered back to assigning central responsibility to the AFSPC for operationalising and "normalising" national military space efforts.[35]As a matter of fact, the most important report of the times, *The Blue Ribbon Panel Report* commissioned to address the full spectrum of military space concerns, reiterated the principal role of the air force as the DoD's agent for military space activities and with regard to ownership and control of national military space assets, it was unambiguous on recommending responsibility and authority on the AFSPC.[36] The recommendations of the report were also codified into the US' national, DoD and air force space policy documents, paving the way for clear future direction in military space affairs.

As a consequence, by 1990, operational control of space launch missions was withdrawn from the R&D community of the Air Force Systems Command and handed over to the AFSPC. Responsibility for associated launch facilities and downrange tracking sites was also conferred on it. By 1993, AFSPC had also taken over control of

American ICBM forces. It, hence, exercised almost complete control over launches, ICBMs, satellite tracking as well as most application satellites for military use ranging from communications, surveillance, navigation, etc. The above was in keeping with the US' expanding global interests and influence as well as requirements of strategic and long range strike (power projection) rapidly across the globe. The above is a mission typical to the USAF and was demonstratively manifest even recently during the close air support missions in Afghanistan.Thus, after another round of internal squabbling, review and reform, the consensus veered back to the AFSPC having the overwhelming responsibility and resources for conducting military space operations, providing services, and for promoting American military competencies and capabilities in space.

The Rumsfield Commission Recommendations

The above status, nevertheless, did not continue unchallenged for long, and towards the end of the 1990s, mounting concerns in some quarters that the USAF was not exercising proper stewardship of the national military space effort led to the establishment by the US Congress of a "Space Commission" to assess the adequacy of existing military space arrangements. The primary recommendations of the commission, released in the new millennium, were:[37]

- That space should be placed among the nation's highest security priorities. It deserves the attention of the highest levels of national leadership, from the president downwards. The president should consider declaring and treating space as a US national security priority, without which, drift and a lack of focus and due funding support were bound to persist.
- With regards to military space stewardship, the commission unanimously concluded that the air force was doing well at managing the nation's military space effort and, hence, there was no immediate need to establish an independent US space service. The commission further recommended amending Title X of the US Code to assign the air force formal statutory authority to organise, train, and equip for

offensive and defensive space operations. They also recommended that the secretary of defence formally designate the air force as the executive agent for space within the DoD.

- As for the technical competence and organisational efficiency issues, the commission recommended giving the Air Force Space Command full responsibility for providing resources to execute space R&D, acquisition and operations.
- With regards to financial support for military space activities, they recommended that a separate DoD budget category for space be created to ensure greater transparency of space spending by all the Services, and that a serious effort be pursued in the realm of space control to ensure protection of the nation's increasingly vital space capabilities.

Dissolution of Joint USSPC and Merger of Army and Naval Space Commands

In promulgating the organisational recommendations of the Space Commission, as of 2002, the US Space Command (USSPC) formed in 1985, was disbanded and merged into the US Strategic Command (USSTRATCOM). The Army Space Command created under the auspices of the SDI concept faced an uncertain future following the demise of the SDI vision. Neither did it have much operational utility for space nor a coherent employability doctrine. Hence, it was initially merged into the Army Strategic Command in the early Nineties and later into the rechristened Army Space and Missile Defence Command (SMDC). The Naval Space Command likewise was merged into the Naval Network Warfare Command and evolved into the Naval Network and Space Operations Command (NNSOC). By contrast, air force missions and role in space grew exponentially. The AFSPC, hence, experienced no disbandment or merger; it actually burgeoned further following implementation of the Space Commission recommendations. As a matter of fact, even the earlier command and control arrangement of a single C-in-C being responsible for the AFSPC, USSPC and NORAD has now been done away with. As of 2002, AFSPC has been elevated to the position of a separate air force command with the designation of the AFSPC commander as a four-star position distinct from the commanders of the USSPC (or present USSTRATCOM) and NORAD.[38]

Thus, while the rest of the space commands continued performing their original missions or stagnated as in case of the NRO and NORAD, or were subordinated to other commands as in case of the Army and Naval Space Commands or altogether eliminated as in case of the joint USSPC, the AFSPC kept expanding in terms of resources and responsibilities. Unlike the other Services which have experienced nascent growth in national military space issues and have largely been devoted to providing customised services to their parent military organisation, the AFSPC has displayed enormous growth and sustained stewardship of the US' military space capabilities over the decades as evidenced from Table 1 below.

Table 1

Distribution of Space Resources

Command	Personnel	FY 05 Budget[39]
US STRATCOM	3,738	$ 497 million
Air Force Space Command (AFSPC)	40,000[40]	$ 9,400 million
Naval Space Command/ (NNSOC)	4,834	$ 273 million
Army Space Command / (SMDC)	1,832	$ 678.5 million

Evolutionary changes have been rampant in the last over four decades since the US' foray into space. The needs during the Cold War and post-Cold War were significantly different. The Cold War emphasised the strategic utility of space for military gains largely as an addendum to strategic air power missions. Post-Cold War, episodic experimentation led to increasing awareness of the operational gains enabled by information from mutually supporting air and space platforms for precise strikes over targets, operational manoeuvre, coordination and deployment of forces, etc. The 1991 Gulf War brought to fore the increasing lethality of air and space systems in prosecuting precision warfare at extended ranges in all-weather conditions. It also demonstrated the ability of space assets to enable a global perspective, precision and flexibility in the use of air power for supporting terrestrial operations. With every successive war-time experience, ranging from the Balkans to Afghanistan, the US' ability to exploit the potential of air and space systems progressively increases. The combination becomes increasingly lethal and instrumental in fulfilling their national objectives. Time is critical to air operations and advancing air and space technologies have progressively reduced their critical process to detect, identify and hit targets with every conflict. For example, during the 1991 Gulf War, the process took about a day; in Afghanistan, it averaged about 45 minutes; in Iraq the average was about 11 minutes; and the USAF now aspires to a goal of one minute.[41]

Post 9/11, the focus has expanded to include counter-terrorism also. Advances in air- and space-based sensor technologies, extended communications, precise acquisition and targeting capabilities as well as extended ranges of aircraft, etc have enabled expansion of the role across the spectrum of conflict. The only consistent factor in the above environment of change and expansion of requirements has been the ever expanding role of the USAF in stewarding the US' national military capabilities. Ever since US military capabilities in space evolved in the 1950s, successive rounds of review and reform have only served to add greater roles, responsibilities and resources onto the USAF until the present wherein almost the entire national effort is under the purview of the USAF.

Inferences and Lessons

The US has evolved to the present levels of military space competencies and capabilities over the past five decades or so. Its evolutionary history is a mixed saga of remarkable successes as well as failures. Its operational military experiences bear testimony to the fact that apart from playing a crucial role in sustaining credible nuclear deterrence, space capabilities have enormous potential to be applied for conventional military operations also. Tremendous military advantage accrues to the side that effectively employs space capabilities.

As in the case of any new endeavour, duplication, disappointment and blunder were encountered in the evolution of space capabilities for military purposes. The USAF, after the initial tentative steps, has demonstrated remarkable tenacity in stewarding the US' military space efforts and delivering results in spite of inter-Service turf battles, political pressures, slashed budgets and a variety of other factors inimical to harmonious evolution of capabilities. The US' evolutionary history with regards to military space activities is replete with inferences and lessons for nations with nascent capabilities like ours which are yet to lay the institutional foundations for developing space capabilities enabling military support. In view of the same, the inferences drawn are recounted as below.

- After extensive experimentation and turf battles, the USAF continues to prevail and has been accepted as the lead agency as well as the primary user of space for strategic and operational efficiency. The above is because of the simple fact that combat power is greatest and most effective when the inherent characteristics of both the media of air and space are closely integrated to obtain solutions to military objectives. For example, information obtained from a combination of sensors and radars on both satellites and aerial platforms like AWACS, UAVs, high altitude aircraft, etc would have greater operational advantage than isolated inputs from air- or space-based platforms. Similarly, it would be essential to integrate the two media to obtain solutions for defending the homeland against strikes from air and space.
- The US' national space resources and responsibilities have always rested with the USAF. The USAF Space Command is allocated 80 per cent of the budget and 86 per cent of the manpower of the total national military investment in space. The missions and roles of air power are based upon its typical characteristics of speed, range, elevation and three-dimensional perspective which are similar to those of space and yet fundamentally different from those of land and sea. These characteristics provide distinct military advantages, especially the capability to enable rapid deployment and power projection at extended ranges for a swift response. US history is replete with numerous instances when space and air power (whether land- or sea-based) provided a near-instantaneous response and solutions in places

far removed from the homeland. The US' primary repository of air power is the USAF and, hence, it experiences maximum operational involvement in space, unlike the army or the navy.

- The US Army and Navy maintain their own space commands for fulfilling their specific-to-Service needs while relying on the USAF Space Command for building and employing overall capabilities.
- The bulk of the role of the space commands pertains to:
  - Early warning of strategic strike.
  - Aerospace defence to secure the homeland against strikes from air and space as well as protection of space assets.
  - Providing the wherewithal for future missile and nuclear missile defence capabilities. During the Gulf War, satellites designed for BMEW played a crucial part in providing pre-launch information on tactical ballistic missiles. The combination of the USAF's Defence Support Programme (DSP) satellites, its E-3 AWACS and FPS-79 detected and passed pre-launch indications to air force bases which, in turn, designated the launchers and missiles to the closest aircraft or missile battery for interception and destruction. The above concept is being worked upon to make it more effective for interception of tactical ballistic missiles also.
  - Enhancing counter-air and counter-space operations. Counter-air operations are an essential precursor to prosecuting successful surface operations; by extension, counter-space operations are perceived as an essential precursor to successful prosecution of air and surface operations, thus, enormous efforts are being put into this mission area.
  - Enabling greater perspective and target acquisition by covering wide swathes of areas and very large geographical territories with sustained space-based intelligence, surveillance, reconnaissance.
  - Enabling rapid communications and data transfers to optimally utilise aircraft air-borne for comparatively short periods of time.
  - Providing accurate navigation and positioning in the three-dimensional environment for air and space operations.

These roles (and more) are not really the primary functions of land and naval forces. Their major requirements are comparatively much less though not in any way less important. Their requirements primarily deal with obtaining space-based communications, navigation and position location.

- Space capabilities also impact all the three military Services of air, land and sea in varying degrees. The empirical evidence of the military exploitation of space in the US since the last five decades clearly points to the fact that the operational function rather than any parochial or other consideration ensures a greater role for air power and by extension, air forces, in space. Unlike the space commands of the other two Services, whose involvement was largely restricted to providing customised services to their parent Service, the air force, and in particular the AFSPC, was engaged in developing national military space competencies in addition to addressing the needs of the three Services. It had (and continues to have) a seminal role in the development of strategic as well as operational space capabilities as also in the integration of space capabilities into the national security apparatus.

Conclusion

In view of the above, it can be inferred that the consistent role of the USAF in shaping the military space destiny of the US is attributed to the greater utility of space to fulfill national strategic objectives typical to air force operations rather than tactical army or marine functions. The large numbers of military satellites of the US like the Defence Support Programme satellites, etc which have been in orbit for decades with nil use for the army or navy bear stark testimony to the above fact. Political support and other factors could at best provide temporary spells of national leadership in military space affairs; what enabled consistent stewardship for the entire five decades of its evolution could only be solid operational logic and military functionality. The point is, national air forces are most suited for strategic exploitation and operational integration of space systems due to the commonality of operational functions. Most national air forces mentioned previously are in the process of building military space competencies on the same operational logic. The logic in our unique context would be no different, especially considering that most strategic missions here also would be performed by the air force.

Notes

1. The US' erstwhile rivals, the Soviets, also alluded to the above rationale. As a matter of fact, the Soviets regarded space as an extension of the medium of air for all operational military purposes. For details, see Squadron Leader K.K. Nair, *Space: The Frontiers of Modern Defence* (New Delhi: Knowledge World Publishers, 2006), Chapter 4, pp.66-69.
2. For details, see Martin Sieff, "Israel Expands Space Effort, EU Ties," Washington DC (UPI) July 1, 2005 at http://cndyorks.gn.apc.org/yspace/articles/israel_eu_ties.htm and *Space Security Index,* pp. 22 of 222 at www.spacesecurity.org
3. Certain reports indicate that South Korea announced the creation of an Air Force Space Command. See Noah Shachtman, "Space Race Going Global" at http://www.defensetech.org/archives/001599.html and Space Security Index, pp.22 of 222 at www.spacesecurity.org
4. The Department of the Air Force was created when President Harry S. Truman signed the National Security Act of 1947. It became effective on September 18, 1947, when Chief Justice Fred M. Vinson administered the oath of office to the first Secretary of the Air Force, W. Stuart Symington, a position filled by presidential appointment.
5. By 1950, the air force was given official responsibility for developing both long range strategic missiles as well as short range tactical missiles. For details, see David N. Spires, "Beyond Horizons," Air Force Space Command in association with Air University Press, Washington DC, pp.41, 42, 43.
6. For example, the feasibility reports issued by the RAND Corporation on artificial satellites led to the important "Project Feedback" report of the 1950s which laid the ground work for future military capability development in space.
7. This led to the evolution of the school of thought that centralised management of all military satellites and missile programmes would minimise the problems of competition for scarce resources and avoid schedule delays. Central management under the WDD was considered the best alternative. Hence, operational control of missiles and satellites devolved onto the air force, which, in turn, developed the same into a core competency.
8. The WDD developed the US' ICBM programme, the Corona/Discoverer satellite-imagery programme, and also its launch programmes. The division was the home for communications, weather, and navigation satellites as well as for

MIDAS, the first missile-detection programme.

9. NORAD became operational on September 12, 1957, to detect and report on any ICBM attacks. It was responsible for the air defence of both the US and Canada. Commanded by a USAF four-star general, with a Canadian Air Force three-star general, NORAD provides missile warning and aerospace surveillance, plus the capability to defend against air attack. In 1981, NORAD underwent a name change, substituting the word "Aerospace" for "Air" to reflect the growing importance of space defence and missile warning.

10. The Sanctuary Doctrine emphasised the military value of space forces for observation, treaty verification and promotion of nuclear stability.

11. In those times, US military space policy emphasised the observation potential of satellites for arms limitation treaty verification. President Eisenhower emphasised the idea of open skies as a means of ensuring a verification capability. This observation bias led the US to embark upon satellite reconnaissance programmes. Concealment of the programmes was primarily aimed at protecting their political vulnerabilities.

12. The existence of the NRO was declassified by the deputy secretary of defence, as recommended by the director of the Central Intelligence Agency on September 18, 1992. For details, see Jeffrey T. Richelson, "The NRO Declassified." *Electronic Briefing Book* No.35, US National Security Archives at http://www.gwu.edu/ ~nsarchiv/NSAEBB/NSAEBB35/index.html

13. Power point presentation, slide number 31 of the "US Military and Intelligence Space Program" based on Dr Eligar Sadeh's *Space Policy Course* at www.space.edu/spst200/milnintel.ppt.

14. Apart from the US militaries (primarily the air force), NORAD and NRO, NASA also evidently aided and abetted the military programmes as evidenced by the US Congress' creation of the "Civilian-Military Liaison Committee" to coordinate NASA and DoD activities as also the National Aeronautic and Space Council (chaired by the president as commander-in-chief of the US military to create a national space policy).

15. Nevertheless, the army was allowed to retain control of its anti-aircraft artillery and develop capabilities for point defence. Refer to Walker J. Boyes, "The Rise of Air Defense," *Air Force Magazine* on line, vol.82, no.12, December 1999.

16. In April 1959, Chief of Naval Operations, Admiral Arleigh Burke, proposed a unified space command. For details, see Spires, n.5, p.76, and also Paul B. Stares, *The Militarization of Space: US Policy: 1945-1984* (Ithaca NY: Cornell University Press, 1985) p.43.

17. In the same year, Gen Medaris accused the air force of a long history of non-cooperation with the army ballistic missile agency to Senator Symington's committee. USAF Gen Schreiver, in turn, provided a lengthy detailed rebuttal to the charges. Spires, n.5, p.76.

18. Quoting from Spires, Ibid., p.76.

19. Spires, Ibid., p.76.

20. Spires, Ibid., p.172.

21. Benjamin S. Lambeth, "Mastering the Ultimate High Ground," (RAND Publications, 2003, MR-1649), p.36.

22. For example, in 1979, administrative control of space surveillance and missile warning assets was transferred from the Air Force's Air Defence Command to the Strategic Air Command. By 1981, based on a study by the Scientific Advisory Board, the air staff also created a Directorate of Space Operations under the deputy chief of staff for operations, plans and readiness.

23. To largely fulfil responsibilities assigned by the DoD Defence Directive No.5160.32, the Air Force Systems Command was created on April 1, 1961. For details, see F. Futrell, *Ideas, Concepts, Doctrine: A History of Basic Thinking in the US Air Force* (Maxwell AFB, Alabama: Air University Publications, pp.385-386.

24. See AFSPC History in *Air Force Space Command Almanac*, 2004-2005, Chapter 1, p.4.

25. For details, see "From the Sea to the Stars," *Naval Historical Home Page*, Chapter 3.

26. For example, the type of sensors required for maritime intelligence, surveillance and reconnaissance (ISR) were distinctly different from those employed for earth observation.

27. When Commodore Richard H. Truly became the first commander of the Naval Space Command, he stated that the command's mission was to operate space systems, not develop nor acquire new systems. See USSPACECOM from the original USSOUTHCOM Asymmetrix Toolbook archive at the Air Force Air University, http://tuvok.au.af.mil/au/database/research/ay1995/acsc/95-002.htm

28. Adam L. Mortensen and Simon P. Warden, "Military Ground Control Centres, US," in *Encyclopedia of Space Science and Technology* (A John Wiley & Sons, Inc., Publication), vol.2, p.79.

29. n. 25, Chapter 4.

30. See reaction of the secretary defence and remarks of Dr Hugh Dryden, director NASA, in Spires, n.5, p.75.

31. The six agencies mentioned include the joint USSPC, the three Service Commands of the air force, navy and army, the NORAD as well as the NRO.

32. To cite a case in point, US space funding for defence touched an all time historic high of $ 22,943 million in 1989; similarly, budgetary allocations devoted to defence space funding also were the highest ever in the periods ranging from 1986-1990. For precise budgetary allocations, see Jeffrey Mason,

"Space:Battleground or Frontier of the 21st Century," Centre for Defence Information at www.cdi.org/ issues/bmd/21stcent.html

33. Lambeth, n. 21, RAND Publications, 2003, MR-1649, Chapter 2, p.31.

34. For details, see Nicholas L. Johnson, *Soviet Military Strategy in Space* (London: Jane's Publishing Company, 1987), Chapter 2, p.48.

35. Spires, n.5, Chapter 6, p. 210.

36. For details, see Lambeth, n.21, Chapter 2, p.33.

37. Recommendations sourced from the Report of the "Commission to Assess US National Security Space Management and Organisation," available at www.defenselink.mil/pubs/space20010111.pdf

38. n.24.

39. Budget figures sourced from Tamar A.Mehuron, "2004 Space Almanac," *Air Force Magazine*, August 2004.

40. The number of personnel of the AFSPC as of 2006 include 28,300 active duty military and civilian personnel as well as 11,700 contractor employees. Figures sourced from home site of the USAF and speech of Gen Lance W. Lord, commander AFSPC, as well as speech of Vice Cdr AFSPC, Lt Gen Frank Klotz, at a meeting of the Air Force Association, Orlando, Florida, March 2, 2006.

41. Rich Tuttle, "New Tactics," *Aviation Week and Space Technology*, June 9, 2003, p.51.